STAGE MANAGEMENT

READINGS IN THEATRE PRACTICE

Series Editor: Simon Shepherd

Voice
Jane Boston
978-1-1373-0194-9

Sound
Ross Brown
978-0-2305-5188-6

Clown
Jon Davison
978-0-2303-0015-6

Puppetry
Penny Francis
978-0-2302-3273-0

Costume
Alison Maclaurin and Aoife Monks
978-1-1370-2948-5

Props
Eleanor Margolies
978-1-1374-1335-2

Light
Scott Palmer
978-0-2305-5190-9

Direction
Simon Shepherd
978-0-2302-7622-2

Forthcoming:

Acting: A Guide to Concepts and Practices
John Matthews
978-1-3503-8722-5

Training Actors: A Guide to Concepts and Practices
John Matthews
978-1-3503-9039-3

Magic: The Performance Practices of Conjuring Illusion
Nik Taylor
978-1-3503-7896-4

STAGE MANAGEMENT

COMMUNICATION DESIGN AS SCENOGRAPHY

Michael Smalley

methuen | drama
LONDON • NEW YORK • OXFORD • NEW DELHI • SYDNEY

METHUEN DRAMA
Bloomsbury Publishing Plc
50 Bedford Square, London, WC1B 3DP, UK
1385 Broadway, New York, NY 10018, USA
29 Earlsfort Terrace, Dublin 2, Ireland

BLOOMSBURY, METHUEN DRAMA and the Methuen Drama logo are trademarks of Bloomsbury Publishing Plc

First published in Great Britain 2024

Copyright © Michael Smalley, 2024

Michael Smalley has asserted his right under the Copyright, Designs and Patents Act, 1988, to be identified as author of this work.

For legal purposes the Acknowledgements on p. xii constitute an extension of this copyright page.

Series design: Ben Anslow
Cover image: *The Phantom of the Opera* calling script on the prompt desk of the Majestic Theatre, Broadway. (© Greg Livoti)

All rights reserved. No part of this publication may be reproduced or transmitted in any form or by any means, electronic or mechanical, including photocopying, recording, or any information storage or retrieval system, without prior permission in writing from the publishers.

Bloomsbury Publishing Plc does not have any control over, or responsibility for, any third-party websites referred to or in this book. All internet addresses given in this book were correct at the time of going to press. The author and publisher regret any inconvenience caused if addresses have changed or sites have ceased to exist, but can accept no responsibility for any such changes.

A catalogue record for this book is available from the British Library.

Library of Congress Cataloging-in-Publication Data

Names: Smalley, Michael (College teacher), author.
Title: Stage management: communication design as scenography / Michael Smalley.
Description: London; New York: Methuen Drama, 2024. | Series: Readings in theatre practice | Includes bibliographical references and index.
Identifiers: LCCN 2023019135 (print) | LCCN 2023019136 (ebook) | ISBN 9781137607683 (hardback) | ISBN 9781350360549 (paperback) | ISBN 9781137607706 (pdf) | ISBN 9781137607690 (ebook)
Subjects: LCSH: Stage management.
Classification: LCC PN2085 .S63 2024 (print) | LCC PN2085 (ebook) | DDC 792.02/3–dc23/eng/20230721
LC record available at https://lccn.loc.gov/2023019135
LC ebook record available at https://lccn.loc.gov/2023019136

ISBN: HB: 978-1-1376-0768-3
PB: 978-1-3503-6054-9
ePDF: 978-1-1376-0770-6
eBook: 978-1-1376-0769-0

Series: Readings in Theatre Practice

Typeset by Deanta Global Publishing Services, Chennai, India

To find out more about our authors and books visit www.bloomsbury.com and sign up for our newsletters.

For Bianca and Rose who continue to teach me the coordinates, ensuring I don't get too lost.

CONTENTS

List of Figures	ix
Series preface	x
Acknowledgements	xii

Introductions		**1**
	Assumptions	3
	Synopsis	5
	Interviews	6

Part One Various stage management approaches   13

1	**Developments over time**	**15**
2	**Cultural differences**	**20**
	Different stage management approaches in the UK, North America and Australia	21
	Intercultural stage management	28
	Cultural diversity and stage management	31
	Conclusions	36
3	**Content-driven differences**	**37**
	Genre	38
	Different scales of production	46
	Conclusions	59
4	**Recent developments**	**61**
	Communication technology	61
	Performance technology	68
	New approaches to maintaining productions	70
	Developments in health and safety management	74
	Conclusions	76
5	**Three models of stage management practice**	**77**
	The administrative model	77
	Features	79
	Limitations	83

Contents

The managerial model	90
The artistic model	96
Artistry	96
Communication design	100
Audience experience	102
Conclusions	107

Part Two Scenographic stage management — 109

6 Scenographic stage management — 111
- Other technical theatre disciplines — 113
- Scenography — 116
- Analysing scenography — 120
- The coordinates model of scenography — 125
- Conclusions — 134

7 Objectives of stage management — 135
- Selective information flow — 135
- Targeted information flow — 137
- Distributed cognition — 141
- Controlling the mood and atmosphere — 145
- Translation — 150
- Conclusions — 153

8 The properties of communication — 154
- Message — 157
- Mode — 158
- Distribution — 162
- Updates — 163
- Conclusions — 164

9 Rationales, implications and conclusions — 166
- Rationales — 166
- Implications — 173
- Conclusions — 185

Notes — 191
Bibliography — 198
Index — 201

FIGURES

1	Lighting design: medium, properties and objectives (after Pilbrow)	114
2	The three coordinates of scenographic possibility	126
3	Stage management: medium, properties and objectives	165
4	Reflexive production process	187

SERIES PREFACE

This series aims to gather together both key historical texts and contemporary ways of thinking about the material crafts and practices of theatre.

These crafts work with the physical materials of theatre – sound, objects, light, paint, fabric and – yes – physical bodies. Out of these materials the theatre event is created.

In gathering the key texts of a craft it becomes very obvious that the craft is not simply a handling of materials, however skilful. It is also a way of thinking about both the materials and their processes of handling. Work with sound and objects, for example, involves – always, at some level – concepts of what sound is and does, what an object is and does . . . what a body is.

For many areas of theatre practice there are the sorts of 'how to do it' books that have been published for at least a century. These range widely in quality and interest but next to none of them is able to, or wants to, position the doing in relation to the thinking about doing or the thinking about the material being used.

This series of books aims to promote both thinking about doing and thinking about materials. Its authors are specialists in their field of practice and they are charged to reflect on their specialism and its history in order, often for the first time, to model concepts and provide the tools not just for the doing but for thinking about theatre practice.

The series title 'Readings in Theatre Practice' uses the word 'reading' in the sense both of a simple understanding or interpretation and of an authoritative explication, an exegesis as it were. Thus, the books first gather together people's opinions about, their understanding of, what they think they are making. These opinions are then framed within a broader narrative which offers an explanatory overview of the practice under investigation.

So, although the books comprise many different voices, there is a dominant authorial voice organizing the material and articulating overarching arguments. By way of promoting a further level of critique and reflection, however, authors are asked to include a few lengthy sections, in the form of interviews or essays or both, in order to make space for other voices to develop their own overviews. These may sit in tension, or indeed in harmony, with the dominant narratives.

Authors are encouraged to be sceptical about normative assumptions and canonical orthodoxy. They are asked not to ignore practices and thinking that might question dominant views; they are invited to speculate as to how canons and norms come into being and what effects they have.

We hope the shape provides a dynamic tension in which the different activities of 'reading' both assist and resist each other. The details of the lived practices refuse to fit tidily into the straitjacket of a general argument, but the dominant overview also refuses to allow itself to fragment into local prejudice and anecdote. And it's that restless play between assistance and resistance that mirrors the character of the practices themselves.

At the heart of each craft is a tense relationship. On the one hand there is the basic raw material that is worked – the wood, the light, the paint, the musculature. These have their own given identity – their weight, mechanical logics, smell, particle formation, feel. In short, the texture of the stuff. And on the other hand there is theatre, wanting its effects and illusions, its distortions and impossibilities. The raw material resists the theatre as much as yields to it, the theatre both develops the material and learns from it. The stuff and the magic. This relationship is perhaps what defines the very activity of theatre itself.

It is this relationship, the thing which defines the practice of theatre, which lies at the heart of each book in this series.

Simon Shepherd

ACKNOWLEDGEMENTS

This book would not have been possible without support from others. First and foremost, it owes a great deal to those stage managers who were willing to let me observe their practice and to discuss stage management with me. Thank you for those inspiring and insightful experiences, and I hope I have managed to capture some of that here.

Academically, I am grateful to have received the steady guidance and encouragement of Dr Rebecca Scollen and Professor Andrew Hickey who helped ensure this book passes academic muster. I am also indebted to Emeritus Professor Simon Shepherd who convinced me to write a book when I actually wanted to read one and who has patiently provided support, encouragement and references along the way. Thanks to all my colleagues and students in universities who have taught me as much about scenography as I taught them. In this regard, a special mention must go to Dr Darryl Chalk and Professor Laurie Johnson for introducing me to the field of distributed cognition.

On the publishing side, I have benefitted greatly from the services of Mark Dudgeon as senior publisher and Ella Wilson, assistant editor for Theatre and Shakespeare Studies at Methuen Drama. Of course, the support of Simon Shepherd as the series editor for *Readings in Theatre Practice* has been invaluable here as well. I am also indebted to Eduardo Canalejo for turning my scribbles into the diagrams found in this book.

Those deserving of the most thanks are Bianca and Rose, my wife and daughter. Both of them have taught me a lot about theatre, stage management and communication design. They have both also endured me dragging them around the world so that I can 'talk shop' with other stage managers. They have given their unconditional support and love throughout this long journey, sharing the joys and frustrations along the way, and provided the practical support necessary for anyone who loses themselves to their projects so completely as a theatre-maker and researcher.

INTRODUCTIONS

The field of stage management encompasses a diverse set of practices. This diversity stems from different approaches to stage management historically, geographically, according to differing performance genres and individually. Despite this vibrancy, stage management literature seems to still consist largely of practicing stage managers recording their personal approaches and documenting their process, often in the absence of a critical framework. This remains the dominant paradigm even after Schneider noted this 'instruction manual' approach as an issue in 1997.[1] Similarly, accounts of stage management practice have not, to date, attracted sustained attention from theatre scholars or researchers (let alone those from broader social science fields). Scholarly explorations of contemporary stage management practice may allow for a more thorough understanding of this diversity. Through seeking out common threads, it may be possible to develop conceptualizations of stage management which can place the field within a theoretical framework. This may enhance theatre practice and situate stage management as a focus for further research. This is my attempt to do just that.

This book, then, is not a *how-to* of stage management. As already mentioned, many such books already exist and can be found in the references at the end of this book. This book is more of a *why-to* for stage management. By reviewing stage management literature, and through over twenty interviews with an array of English-speaking stage managers in Australia, the United Kingdom, and the United States, both the variety of approaches inherent in and the common rationales for contemporary stage management practice are explored.

This process has uncovered at least three conceptualizations of stage management practice. The first, predominant in the extant literature, is what I will term *stage management as administration*. This conceptualization judges stage management chiefly on its ability to ensure a project's activities adhere to relevant processes and procedures. To the extent that stage management's role is understood at all by people outside the field, it is in this sense. When people talk of an event being 'well stage-managed' they generally mean that everything has gone according to plan, if they are speaking generously. They may also mean that any opportunity for spontaneity, creativity or allowance for a genuine interaction with the audience has been diminished, especially when they speak of an event being 'tightly stage-managed'. It is not surprising that this conceptualization is predominant in the literature because it lends itself well to the individually written instruction manual approach.

The thematic analysis of the interview material presented in this book, informed as it is by critical and theoretical approaches applied to other technical theatre disciplines, seeks to broaden the thinking about stage management. The aim of considering the multiple perspectives of many interviewees is to offer balance to the predominantly idiosyncratic existing literature. Placing the analysis within relevant critical frameworks seeks to consider stage management more theoretically rather than procedurally. The results suggest at least two other conceptualizations of stage management can be seen in operation in contemporary stage management practice. One of these prioritizes the management functions of stage management. This I will term *stage management as management*. This view regards stage management as a particular instance of managing organizations with stage management fulfilling many of the same responsibilities as managers of other organizations. This is especially true with regards to human resource management. As such, stage managers wishing to develop their understanding of this aspect of their role have the whole field of management theory from which they can draw. The other conceptualization of stage management emphasizes the artistry involved.

The artistry of stage management can be thought of as designing communication in order to influence the project with the audience's experience in mind. That communication is central to stage management is a viewpoint shared with both other conceptualizations of stage management. However, rather than this design orientation of artistic stage management, from a managerial perspective communication is vital in order to ensure that the organization as a whole has a shared vision and that the morale of the company is enhanced. Meanwhile, administrative stage management values the efficiency and the accuracy of this communication's dissemination and archival, with the implied goal being that all information should be shared completely, impartially, as soon as possible, in predictable, inflexible formats. Even if such a goal was attainable, the artistic approach contends that it would not be desirable. Stage management has much agency over what is communicated; when, and how, that communication occurs; and whether, and how, that communication is recorded. In this sense we can say that the communication is designed by stage management. This allows stage management to be considered in much the same way that other elements of a performance are designed.

An artistic conception of stage management centres this agency over communication and proposes that stage managers enact this agency, like designers, in the hope that they will have a positive influence on the performance event. To be clear, employing communication strategies to enhance the morale of the company, or to achieve the efficiency and accuracy valued by the administrative model, usually does exert a positive influence on the performance event and, therefore, the practices of administrative, managerial and artistic stage management may often appear identical. However, the *goal* for administrative stage management is to be accurate and efficient. The *goal* for managerial stage management is to enhance the organization's well-being. The *goal* for artistic stage management is to control the influence they have on a production.

Within the paradigm of stage management for live performance this influence is likely to involve the 'manipulation and orchestration of the performance environment' which is McKinney and Butterworth's definition of scenography.[2] Contemporary theatrical stage management can therefore be conceptualized as a scenographic pursuit. I will therefore term this conceptualization *stage management as scenography* (as a more precise synonym to artistic stage management). The conception of stage management as scenography has not been widely accepted historically, by stage managers, scenographers or theatre researchers, but this book aims to demonstrate scenography as a central rationale of much contemporary stage management practice in order to offer a vocabulary which enables further critical exploration of stage management processes for theatre researchers and practitioners.

It is hoped that presenting these conceptions of stage management will prove useful in at least three ways. Firstly, by enabling stage management practitioners to better articulate and manage their artistic contribution to their projects. This could be achieved either through applying the scenographic stage management model presented here if it is helpful to them or by encouraging them to develop their own conception of stage management. Secondly, if stage managers and those they collaborate with understand the role of stage management in artistic terms and that they share responsibility for the scenography of their projects, then collaboration between theatre-makers may be enhanced. Thirdly, by enabling theatre (and other social science) researchers to gain a better understanding of stage management's role within theatrical production and its place within their critical frameworks. Any further research may, in turn, reflexively enhance both stage management practice and the broader fields from which such research emanates.

The remainder of this introductory chapter will outline some of the other assumptions that inform the rest of the book. Then it will provide a synopsis of the following chapters. Finally, it will provide an overview of how these conceptions of stage management were developed through the conducting and analysis of interviews.

Assumptions

In order to concentrate on formulating broad conceptions of contemporary stage management practice this book makes several assumptions. Firstly, in this book when the term *stage manager* is referred to, it is assumed to be equally applicable to any member of the stage management team.

There are multiple ways of dividing up the labour between different-sized teams and different titles for similar roles around the English-speaking world. These divisions change between different regions and in different genres of theatrical performance. The distinctions between what is normal practice of a Broadway Production Stage Manager and, for example, an Assistant Stage Manager in a performing arts educational institution in Australia are many, varied and would be vitally important for a book that concentrates on the *what* or *how* to do of stage management. Some of these distinctions, and their implications, are discussed in Part 1 of this book. However, unless specifically discussing these regional or industrial differentiations, I have considered anyone whose primary contribution to a production is concerned with the coordination or management of a performance's elements to be a stage manager. For clarification purposes, when discussing the specific variations, capitalization of the role will be used. Hence, a Stage Manager is a specific position in a specific geographical and industrial context, while a stage manager may have any number of actual job titles.

Stage Management

This definition seeks to distinguish stage management from those whose primary concern is the actual composition of one or more of those elements of a performance (e.g. directors, actors and designers), on the one hand, and those whose primary concern lies outside of the performance itself (e.g. general managers and marketing staff), on the other. Given my personal experience as a stage manager in Australia, the UK and Canada, and the fact that the interviewees for this book have worked in many places around the world in a wide variety of capacities and on a wide variety of productions, I am comfortable in making this assumption. Outside of the English-speaking world, I am aware that approaches to stage management are even more disparate and I make no assumption that the conceptions of stage management presented here are applicable there. I am aware, and have deliberately chosen, that this definition of stage management may capture Company, Technical, or Production Managers (and variations of those titles) whose role may primarily regard managing venues, people, other resources or – most likely – a combination of these focal points, rather than specifically coordinating a performance's elements. It is also important to note that the distinction between a Director's role in composing the performance's elements and the stage manager's in coordinating them is particularly fuzzy. This suggests if not considerable overlap, then, at the very least, the need to work very closely together with a shared understanding. I hope that all these professionals find much of this book directly relevant to them or at least helpful in their close dealings with those more clearly in the stage management team.

The second assumption I have made for the purposes of this book is that stage management is a singular set of practices which has an influence over any performance environment, despite the vast difference in daily practices that stage managers working on the wide variety of genres of live performance may exhibit. I have deliberately chosen not to consider the stage management of commercial (industrial) and other events where stage management is often crucial but where the goal is not necessarily an artistic experience for an audience. This is because the influence a stage manager wishes to exert on the event might have different goals from their artistic contribution. However, many of the stage managers interviewed have also stage managed such events, so some of the conclusions here may also be relevant to that field. This assumption, like the one about precisely who is a stage manager before it, enables the consideration of stage management broadly. Of course, there are distinctions in stage management practices which are specific to the genre of performance and some of these are considered in Chapter 3 of this book. However, the analysis of the interviews from stage managers from a wide variety of performance genres suggests that they have much in common. I hope, therefore, that these conceptions of stage management are useful to those who are interested in the worlds of theatre, musicals, operas, dance and circus, for example. Because of my own bias as a stage management practitioner who has mainly worked in theatres and in the interest of brevity, I have often used the term theatrical or variations thereof, as a generic term to include all these different genres of performance events.

Another important assumption that informs this book is that multiple perspectives are possible and, usually, preferable. One of the reasons for including material from over twenty interviews in this book is to address my concern that much published about stage management represents a particular individual's approach to the topic. While this book outlines three conceptions of stage management and primarily discusses the conception of the stage manager as scenographic artist, it is assumed that other conceptions of stage management are possible. Indeed, one of the aims of this book is to encourage others to develop their own conception of stage management. This book will be far more worthwhile if it encourages stage managers, and others, to think more deeply about what stage management is or could be, then if it simply replaces one conception of stage management with another. To this end, no effort has been made in the coming sections of this book to hide departures from the scenographic stage management model. On the contrary, they are often highlighted and explored as potential sites for other conceptions of stage management.

Synopsis

The remainder of this book is divided into two parts and a conclusion. Part 1 examines various approaches to stage management. Part 2 explores the conceptualization of stage management as scenography in detail. The concluding chapter examines some of the implications of broadening the thinking about approaches to stage management practice.

Part 1 examines what the major differences in stage management are as a result of changing times, geographies, scales or genres of performance. In Chapter 1 a brief overview of how stage management has changed over time will be outlined. This history partially explains the different approaches to stage management seen geographically. This is explored in greater detail in Chapter 2 which considers the different approaches to stage management arising from the different typical divisions of labour in contemporary Australian, UK and US stage management. This chapter also briefly considers issues of cultural difference as they relate to stage management. Chapter 3 examines the impact different types of performances have on stage management. Consideration is given to both the genre and scale of a performance. Chapter 4 looks at recent developments in the field of stage management. Chapter 5 suggests that while approaches to stage management on a granular level may be individual, common rationales in these approaches can be determined which lead to distinctive models of stage management. The key differences between three of these models (namely administrative, managerial and scenographic stage management) are outlined.

Part 2 discusses scenographic stage management in more detail. This is because it is the least acknowledged of the three models in the current literature and practice of stage managers. Chapter 6 introduces the field of scenography and suggests that stage management belongs within this field via comparing key definitions and analytical approaches of scenography with the comments made by the stage managers in the interviews. Chapter 7 examines the objectives of stage management from a scenographic perspective. Chapter 8 outlines how stage managers manipulate the properties of communication to achieve these objectives. This approach consciously mirrors how other technical theatre arts demonstrate their artistry and contribution to scenography.

Stage Management

This will help to connect stage management thinking with other theatrical practices and to establish the relationship between stage management practice and a range of theoretical disciplines. The concluding chapter, Chapter 9, explores the implications of establishing this relationship in terms of the practice, research and pedagogy of stage management and the fields in which it can be situated.

Interviews

This book is a direct result of conducting reflexive research through observations of stage management practice and interviews with practicing stage managers. While borrowing concepts from Davies's reflexive ethnography[3] and Stake's multiple case study analysis,[4] the primary dataset was induced via 'semi-structured life world interviews'[5] with field notes observing stage management practice providing additional context. This methodology was chosen as it seeks to celebrate reflexivity and a social construction of knowledge wherever possible. By socially constructing knowledge about stage management as it is currently employed, and through employing academic research methodologies, I hope this book can extend the published material about stage management by representing multiple voices about the importance of, and what is important to, stage management.

The sites for the data gathering were selected to get a sense of current stage management practice in the English-speaking theatre world. I immersed myself in stage management cultures in New York, Sydney and London for periods of about six weeks each. Stage management practices observed ranged from student stage management teams and their professional mentors at the National Institute of Dramatic Art in Sydney, Australia, with many in the stage management team undertaking their roles for the first time, to observing seasoned professionals run performances of the longest-running Broadway production ever (*The Phantom of the Opera*). I also conducted interviews with stage managers outside of these centres to get a taste of how stage management may differ in other parts of their respective countries. I am indebted to all who gave up their time to allow me to watch them work or to 'talk shop' with me.

In the end the direct observations I captured of stage management practices, while useful to the book in many ways, do not appear in the following pages. They were useful in the proof they provided to me that stage management practice is recognizable regardless of the location or the scale of the work. They also proved useful as reference points within the interviews. Direct reportage of the practice of stage management, however, was not useful. This is because, as already mentioned, whether a stage manager is functioning as an administrator, manager or scenographer the appearance of their actions is often identical to an outside observer.

In contrast, the words of my stage management colleagues will feature directly throughout the following pages. They are, in effect, co-authors of this book. Because of this, I thought a few words of introduction to each of them may serve as a minimal acknowledgement of their contribution. The introductions may also provide useful colour and context to their comments. These notes are deliberately kept very brief and

Introductions

in no way do justice to the range of expertise any of those interviewed hold. Where the present tense is used, it refers to the time of the interview. Obviously, such statements may be outdated by the time they are read.

Marybeth Abel is a Broadway Production Stage Manager. She is currently, and has been for some time, the Production Stage Manager for *Wicked*. She is also an Adjunct Professor at Columbia University where she specializes in teaching stage managers about long runs.

Jo Alexander is a freelance London-based stage manager. Her professional credits span the gamut of theatre and opera from fringe to leading repertory companies, touring and the West End. Companies she has worked for include Birmingham Repertory Theatre, The Hall Company and English National Opera.

Jim Athens is a Broadway stage manager. He is part of the stage management team on *The Phantom of the Opera*. Other Broadway credits include *Evita* and *Les Misérables*.

Mel Dyer is the Head of Stage Management at NIDA in Australia. She has experience in a wide variety of theatrical forms including drama, physical theatre, dance and devised work. She has worked for leading Australian theatre companies, such as Belvoir and Sydney Theatre Company, and has toured shows regionally, nationally and internationally.

Ian Evans is the Head of Stage Management at the Royal Welsh College of Music and Drama. He was the Technical Director for World Stage Design in 2013 and is an official delegate (and previous chair) of the Education Commission of OISTAT (International Organization of Scenographers Theatre Architects and Technicians).

Andy Fenton is a Broadway stage manager who is the Production Stage Manager for *The Phantom of the Opera*. Previous Broadway credits include *Mama Mia!* and *Seussical*.

Jo Franklin is the Head of Technical Theatre Arts at the Guildford School of Acting within the University of Surrey. She has worked as a stage manager in a wide variety of contexts including with leading repertory theatres, on tour, in the West End and with the Royal Shakespeare Company.

Chris Freeburg is a Production Stage Manager at Steppenwolf Theatre Company. Before Steppenwolf, her career has spanned from storefront (fringe) theatres to leading theatre companies including Weston Playhouse and Lookingglass Theatre.

Susan May Hawley is the Lecturer in Stage Management at the Royal Conservatoire of Scotland. Her varied career in stage management includes experience with dance, theatre, musical theatre, events, site-specific work, with many leading companies including as the Head of Stage Management for Scottish Ballet. She has extensive experience with touring shows of all scales across the UK and Ireland as well as throughout Europe, America and China.

Sharon Hobden is a freelance London-based stage manager. Since establishing herself as a touring stage manager and working for repertory theatre companies across the UK, she has become a specialist Deputy Stage Manager for new West End musical theatre productions.

Peter Lawrence is a Broadway Production Stage Manager. He has been a production stage manager for more than thirty years on Broadway, with highlights including working on many productions directed by Mike Nicholls, written by Neil Simon or produced by Cameron Mackintosh. He is the only stage manager to win a Tony Award and is the author of *Production Stage Management for Broadway: From Ideas to Opening Night and Beyond*.

Adam Legah is the Subject Leader in Stage and Events Management at Rose Bruford College, London. Before his academic career, he was a freelance London-based stage manager working with leading companies including the Royal Court Theatre, the Millennium Dome and the National Theatre.

Greg Livoti is a Broadway stage manager. At the time of interview, he was on leave from his role as the Production Stage Manager at *The Phantom of the Opera*. His other credits include working with Williamstown Theatre Festival, the Manhattan Theatre Club and Roundabout Theatre Company.

Pip Loth is a freelance stage manager based in Brisbane, Australia. Her varied career has included stage managing regional, national and international tours of many productions and serving as the resident Production Coordinator at Queensland Theatre.

Peter Maccoy is the Course Leader in Stage Management at the Royal Central School of Speech and Drama in London. His career has included technical roles as a scenic carpenter and fly operator, as well as the full gamut of stage management positions from fringe theatres to working at the National Theatre, and touring productions across the world. He is also the author of *Essentials of Stage Management*.

Natasha Marich is a freelance stage manager based in Melbourne, Australia. Before training as a stage manager, she studied music and the visual arts. She has worked with leading Australian performing arts companies on genres as diverse as dance, comedy, puppetry, drama and opera. Companies she has worked for include Red Stitch Actors Theatre, Chunky Move, Opera Australia and Bell Shakespeare. She is also the founder and administrator of the Facebook group Stage Managers of Colour (SMOC) Australia.

Abigail McMillan is the Technical Theatre Skills Officer at the Scottish Drama Training Network (SDTN). Before working for the SDTN, she had a freelance career as a stage manager and theatre technician working with such companies as Stellar Quines Theatre Company and then was resident for ten years as the Arts Production Manager at the internationally renowned Arches Theatre in Glasgow.

Ira Mont is a Broadway Production Stage Manager and the third vice president of Actor's Equity Association. His credits include *Jagged Little Pill*, the revival of *Cats*, *The Producers* and *Young Frankenstein*. He is also a member and past chair of the Stage Managers' Association, has lectured on stage management at many leading US universities and is also the first vice president of Broadway Cares/Equity Fights AIDS.

Jillian Oliver is a Broadway stage manager where she is currently a member of the stage management team on *The Phantom of the Opera*. Other Broadway credits include *Chinglish* and *Race*. She has also worked for other leading performing arts companies such as Williamstown Theatre Festival and Boston Ballet.

Michael Passaro is the Associate Professor and Head of Stage Management at Columbia University. He is also a Broadway Production Stage Manager whose recent credits include *Moulin Rouge! The Musical* and *The Cher Show*. His Broadway career spans back to being a part of the team for the original productions of *Starlight Express* and *Angels in America*, for example.

Joanna Rawlinson is a London-based freelance stage and production manager. She has worked for many theatre companies including Nottingham Playhouse, Soho Theatre Company and Greenwich Young People's Theatre. She is also the Creative Producer for Invisible Flash and a lecturer at Rose Bruford College.

Justin Scribner is a Broadway Production Stage Manager. His Broadway credits include *Once on This Island, God of Carnage, RENT* and *Skittles Commercial: The Broadway Musical*. He has also stage managed for such companies as the Manhattan Theatre Club, Atlantic Theatre Company and the Kennedy Center Sondheim Festival. He has also taught stage management at leading higher education institutions around the United States.

Mark Simpson is the Academic Program Manager at Rose Bruford College in London. He has worked extensively across genres as diverse as opera, ballet, theatre, music, and other events. His career has included serving as a Stage Manager and a Company Manager for many leading performing arts companies in the UK, including the Royal Opera House and Cheek by Jowl.

Dr Sue Fenty Studham is the Head of Stage Management at DePaul University in Chicago. She has stage managed theatre, dance and large-scale performance events in thirteen countries. In addition to working with many leading mainstage companies in Australia and the United States, she is an expert in stage managing intercultural theatre.

Her research interests include regional identity and theatrical processes which respect cultural variation.

Abbie Trott has worked as a stage and production manager in Australia for over twenty years with companies including version 1.0, Vulcana Women's Circus, Belvoir and Kooemba Jdarra Performing Arts Company.

With the goals of the social construction of knowledge and reflexively developing conceptualizations of stage management in mind, I personally conducted all the interviews. This allowed me to readily share my thoughts about stage management and those of the other interviewees to see where consensus (or controversies) lay. In effect this meant the interviews were planned, conducted and analysed according to academic standards[6] which allowed them to be conversational. Consequently, the extracts included here often contain as much from me as the interviewees. Because of this, I thought I should introduce myself in the same way.

Dr Michael Smalley is a theatre-maker and researcher and is a Senior Lecturer in Production at the Guildford School of Acting. His professional practice has mainly involved stage managing many productions through the UK, Australia and Canada. Highlights include getting stuck between two horses while ASMing at the Blyth Festival. He has also lectured in stage management, technical theatre and scenography at universities and presented his research at many academic conferences including the Prague Quadrennial.

These brief introductions may serve to give a sense of the focus that each of the interviewees gave to certain aspects of stage management and their connections with specific genres or geographies. Understanding that such biases are influential and inevitable was encouraged. All those interviewed only spoke from their personal experiences and expressed their individual opinions. Any claims to their statements being applicable more broadly are mine. Where I make such claims, one of the reasons I am confident in them is because they are corroborated by other interview material. In most places where I have chosen an interview extract to demonstrate a point, I was spoilt for choice and restricted myself to the clearest examples in order to continue moving the argument forward, rather than getting bogged down demonstrating the amount of corroboration. This process was supported by the accompanying data analysis.

The data generated underwent a thematic analysis. This analysis informed both the content and the structure of this book. This, too, was a reflexive process. Identifying broad categories in common in the earlier interviews challenged my pre-existing notions about current stage management practice and enhanced the structure for later interviews. Themes emerging within these categories that resonated with many interviewees provided the focus of chapters. This suggested links to other critical material that could be shared with later interviewees and inform the analysis of the transcripts. Earlier material was re-read and re-categorized according to the concepts emerging from the data. Excerpts from the interviews are used throughout this book as both evidence of and to provide context for the argument. This contextual material may support the argument and provide greater clarity or concrete examples of how the aspect of stage management under discussion is deployed in the field. At other times this material may be contradictory and provide an alternative viewpoint. A common theme throughout many of the interviews has been that there is no one right way to stage manage or to think about stage management. This theme provides a frame of reference for Part 1 which considers various stage management approaches.

PART ONE
VARIOUS STAGE MANAGEMENT APPROACHES

Stage management, according to the broad definition used in this book, is primarily concerned with the coordination and management of a performance's elements. With such a broad definition, it is not surprising to find that there are a wide variety of approaches to this task.

This section of the book details some of this variety and explores its causes. Firstly, Chapter 1 briefly outlines the evolution of the role of stage management over time. Chapter 2 explores some of the different approaches to stage management geographically. Specifically, some of the differences between stage management in the United States, the United Kingdom and Australia are considered. Also considered are issues of cultural difference as they relate to stage management. Chapter 3 examines some of the differing approaches stage managers adopt due to the type of performance they are working on. This is explored both in terms of the genre of the performance and its scale. Chapter 4 looks at recent changes to the field – those that the interviewees identified as taking place during their careers. Thus, this section of the book demonstrates some of the causes, and celebrates the richness, of contemporary stage management practice's diversity.

Despite this diversity, a number of themes recur throughout the discussion. Some of these themes coalesce into what I term models of stage management. Three of these are outlined in Chapter 5. The first prioritizes its administrative function. This is the most prevalent way of conceptualizing stage management currently. The second regards stage management as a specific instance of business management. This conception emphasizes the organizational management function of the role and suggests stage managers could look to the field of business management for furthering their development. Finally, the third emergent theme suggests an alternative model of stage management which celebrates the practice's craft, art and creativity may be possible. This artistic model of stage management demonstrates that the practice is a scenographic artform.

Each of these different models is useful to contemporary stage managers and those who work with them. Stage managers working today must be proficient with the administration of production processes; be capable managers of organizations, especially with regards to human resource management; and be in control of their artistic contribution to the projects on which they work. Part 2 of the book will concentrate on the artistic model because, to date, it is the least well understood. In the end, it is believed that the best stage management teams excel in each of these areas, and that they are all interrelated.

CHAPTER 1
DEVELOPMENTS OVER TIME

Stage management has evolved over time. This chapter briefly investigates what might be considered the origin of stage management and its evolution until the middle of the twentieth century when stage management teams took the forms which are largely still in use today. This investigation establishes two of the recurring themes throughout this book. Firstly, the assumption that effective stage management should remain invisible is interrogated and problematized. The second recurring theme is that stage management has always changed in response to the needs of, and the technological means available to, the production. The fact that this chapter doesn't consider changes to stage management after this period is not meant to suggest that developments in the practice of stage management have stagnated. On the contrary, stage management continues to evolve and these more recent changes are considered in Chapter 4.

Given the broad definition of stage management used here and the fact that this definition is not dependent on actual job titles, defining the beginning of what might constitute stage management becomes problematic. This is partly because there is a dearth of published material on the history of stage management, and my own expertise is as a stage manager and not a historian. However, in recalling the words of Aristotle's Poetics, 'For the power of Tragedy, we may be sure, is felt even apart from representation and actors. Besides, the production of spectacular effects depends more on the art of the stage machinist than on that of the poet,'[1] perhaps it is not too much of a stretch to suggest that coordinating the elements of a performance is as old as performance itself. When Aristotle dismisses this production of spectacular effects with the comment 'of all the parts, it is the least artistic'[2] we also have the first evidence of people assuming that stage management's function offers little to the artistry of performance.

With regards to the practice of stage management's development in the English-speaking world in more recent times more extensive scholarship is available. Cattell[3] gives a detailed account of how the field of stage management evolved in Britain, mapping the development of *the book* (in some places and times better known as *the prompt copy* or *the bible*) for a production as the chief stage management tool and the cueing of a show as stage management's primary function from Miracle Plays of the late sixteenth century to the middle of the twentieth century. It is telling that this work which, in my view, is one of the most authoritative accounts of stage management's history is an unpublished thesis. This fact perhaps reinforces Cattell's argument of the invisibility of stage management both within the theatre profession and the academy.[4] This notion of the invisibility of stage management will be a recurring theme throughout this book as it, ironically, can be viewed from many angles. For now, suffice to say that this book and Cattell's thesis share the goals of making stage management's relevance within the theatre profession and academy *more* visible. The other theme from Cattell's thesis that resonates through this book is that stage management evolves in response to the needs of the productions which they manage.

For Cattell the development of *the book* and hence something akin to stage management as we know it today begins with the role of Ordinary in Miracle Plays.[5] This term, Cattell argues convincingly, is not used in the sense of a *normal* person as opposed to an *actor* in the performance but, rather, someone who is concerned with imposing *order* which at this stage in history largely meant keeping the performers *on book*. As the elements of the performance grew in terms of their number, technological complexity and artistic significance, this role continued to evolve both in terms of the job description and its name.

By the time of the early modern playhouses, the role was given a variety of names, but one of the most common was Book Keeper.[6] The Book Keeper's duties included maintaining the official licensed copies of the play texts, including making the annotations necessary for the running of a performance, and the creation of a *plot* for hanging in the tiring house as a ready reference for performers and others in order to navigate each performance, and according to Cattell 'held ultimate responsibility for many of the theatre company's administrative tasks'.[7]

Tribble outlines that, relatively speaking, for documents associated with the rich scholarship of the Elizabethan stage, these plots have 'received little sustained attention'.[8] This is partly 'because of the difficulty in interpreting them. They are contradictory and inconsistent and the individual information they display varies considerably.'[9] According to Tribble, 'many scholars have declared themselves to be flummoxed about the precise function of the plots'[10] and those who have attempted to interpret them have come to wildly divergent conclusions. For example, Greg argues that they were 'prepared for the guidance of actors and others in the playhouse',[11] but Bradley concludes their inconsistency and incompleteness would not suit this purpose, commenting that none of them display 'evidence of a fully settled and regular way of registering whatever information it is they are intended to register'.[12]

Stern describes the general form and contents of these documents.[13] I am not an early modern scholar, nor have I seen these documents first-hand, but upon reading Stern's description I was not flummoxed. I am sure that other practicing stage managers would recognize the utility of a document which was sturdy enough for heavy and repeated use; prepared with great care for legibility at a distance; dividing the whole play into clearly divided units at a glance; sometimes scrawled with additional annotations; concerned with readying actors and effects backstage; and designed for display backstage. I immediately recognized an antecedent to the contemporary running lists, scene character breakdowns and shift plot charts of current stage management paperwork. Of course, the specificity of such documents is anachronistic to early modern playhouses, but the function of these plots seemed to be obviously related to the coordination of a performance's elements.

This is a clear example of the invisibility of stage management practices and its function in academia. As Tribble points out these documents 'were not meant to solve problems for scholars four hundred years hence, but to help a company put on a play'.[14] Even Tribble and Stern who acknowledge their function as backstage documents take issue with their lacunae calling them 'maddeningly incomplete'[15] and 'lackadaisical',[16] respectively. While these scholars may be right and are certainly better placed to judge than I am, I am sure that scholars looking for completeness of information in any of my stage management paperwork today would reach similar conclusions. Especially if they had no knowledge of how that paperwork was to be used during a performance. Tribble rhetorically asks, 'what sort of "skilled vision" might be required to read the plots?'[17] Even though it's rhetorical and Tribble provides an excellent answer, I would contend that a stage manager's skilled vision would be a good place to start. Of course, there is no reason why theatre scholars should intuitively understand how stage management functions; it is up to stage management to show that it has much to offer theatre scholarship.

To be fair, Tribble recognizes that these documents are one part of a system and therefore 'necessarily incomplete'.[18] I am very glad that Tribble did not look to contemporary stage management practices to understand how and why the information 'missing' from the plots may be seen as a strength rather than a weakness. In turning instead to the field of distributed cognition for an explanation, Tribble introduced me to terminology and theory that has been helpful for me to be more precise in my description of this objective of stage management. Theatre scholarship has a lot to offer stage management. Distributed cognition is discussed in more detail in Chapter 7.

This evolution of stage management continued from the Restoration theatre and throughout the eighteenth century into a role, usually given the job title of Prompter, which Cattel describes as having an 'essential, authoritative, and co-ordinatory function'.[19] By the end of this period, the Prompter's responsibilities included 'the setting and handling of props and furniture, the correct dressing of the actors, the performance of offstage sounds, the changing of the scenes, the playing of music, and, later in the century, the cueing of lighting'.[20]

With the increasing technological demands and professionalization of the theatre throughout the nineteenth century the term 'Stage Manager' emerges. The increased resources required to mount productions, especially the larger number of people involved, resulted in a need for increased supervision, coordination and delegation. This is what has remained constant about what it means to manage a stage ever since. From this, the origin of the conception of stage management as management is apparent.

The other conceptions of stage management explored in this book are also recognizable by this time. The promptbooks that were celebrated at this time bore a rigorous attention to detail, enabling highly regulated staging and precise cueing.[21] This suggests that stage management was becoming valued as an administrative undertaking. Equally, throughout this period it was increasingly common to split the labour of the stage management team between the aesthetic and the mechanical aspects of coordinating a performance's elements. Originally a Stage Manager was in control of the artistic side of this split and supervised Prompters to implement the mechanical (see e.g. the relationship between Wilton and Pitt at the Britannia from the 1860s).[22] This suggests that at the emergence of the term Stage Manager it was partially conceived as an artistic role.

This earliest iteration of a Stage Manager shares much in common with what would now be termed a 'Director'. The term itself evolved from the actor-managers of theatres who are often seen as some of the UK's first Directors as they are now called. However, it is interesting to note that 'influential actor-managers and playwrights of the period, such as W. S. Gilbert, Tom Robertson, and Henry Irving, were recognised, or described themselves, as "stage managers" in the directorial sense as it was understood in the latter half of the nineteenth century'.[23]

This confusion between the functions and, indeed, terms of Stage Manager and Director was not quickly resolved. Bourdon[24] valorized the stage manager as the source of English staging's superiority over the French in 1902, citing both their more efficient management of more elaborate stages and their greater facility for artistic interpretations of the plays than their French counterparts. The former aspect we would associate with stage management today, but the latter would fall to the remit of what is now called a Director. In 1905 Edward Gordon Craig used the terms Stage-Manager and Stage-Director interchangeably in calling for an artist who can interpret the plays of the dramatist and design sets, lighting and arrange the bodies of the performers on the stage.[25]

Throughout the first half of the twentieth century, in the UK, as the demands for staging continued to grow, the role of Stage Manager split again. During this time, the demands of physically changing scenery and other aspects of staging were growing quickly and, in addition, the number of theatres that had the capacity to cue electric lighting effects and recorded sound effects was growing rapidly. As the staging effects required more preparation and coordination the head of the team became the Stage Director. The Stage Director's team included the Stage Manager whose responsibilities involved cueing other departments.[26] During this period, theatrical styles were also experiencing rapid developments and change, as the influence of such leading theatrical practitioners as Stanislavski, Brecht, Meyerhold, Grotowski and Artaud was felt. This necessitated more *direction*, especially of the acting company.

This produced yet another split in those involved with the coordination of performances, again along aesthetic and operational lines. According to Howe,[27] in the UK, the Producer or Director was the new term for those in control of the 'spirit' of a production, while the Stage Manager is 'competent to deal with the letter'. At this time, in the UK the word Producer was the most common term for the role which is currently known as the Director.[28] Presumably, this is partly because the term Stage-Director was in use as the head of what we would now call the stage management team. This split represents the beginning of the separation of stage management from members of what would be termed the creative team. The relationship between what is now classed as direction and stage management goes deeper than the slipperiness of the terminology. The overlap between the functions remains particularly palpable in the current stage management practice of the United States. There is less overlap between directorial and stage management functions in the UK system partly due to the evolution of the role now called the Deputy Stage Manager.

In the UK, this evolution and standardization of job roles to their current practice happened because of increasing professionalization, specifically the negotiation of the first union stage management contract.[29] This process saw what was called the Stage-Director change to Company and Stage Manager (or in theatres that had a dedicated Company Manager already, simply Stage Manager). This was adopted partly so as not to cause confusion with the term Director which was being increasingly adopted for the person with the overall aesthetic vision. It also meant the position that had been called the Stage Manager, who had the closest connection with the acting company and undertook the increasingly important role of cueing the show, was called the Deputy Stage Manager. Remaining members of the team were Assistant Stage Managers. These changes were solidified by the time Baker's[30] influential handbook of stage management was published in 1968. Baker's descriptions of the roles and the book's widespread usage within theatre companies and as a textbook for the emerging formalized training programs of stage management further entrenched this system. This codified the Deputy Stage Manager position's place and role in the hierarchy which is the source of much of the difference between stage management approaches in the UK and North America today. These regional differences, and their implications, are explored more fully in the next chapter.

This chapter demonstrates that stage management practices have evolved in line with the available resources and demands of the performances they seek to coordinate. This is a reflexive process. As the expectations of performance-makers and audiences change, the resources needed to meet those expectations also change. Further, as technical innovation means different resources are utilized on the stage, the expectations of performance-makers and audiences evolve. This process has administrative, managerial and artistic implications for stage managers. While this chapter concludes its exploration around the middle of the twentieth century, it is important to note that this process is ongoing. More recent developments and their implications for stage management approaches are considered in Chapter 4. Part of this evolutionary process has resulted in different approaches to stage management in different regions. This is partly due to the cultural differences between them. This is explored in the next chapter.

CHAPTER 2
CULTURAL DIFFERENCES

This chapter explores some of the implications of the varying approaches to stage management that arise from cultural differences. Firstly, the differences in typical approaches to stage management teams in three different English-speaking regions (Australia, the UK and North America) are discussed. Then some of the considerations stage managers must make when they are working on a production outside of their own culture are examined. Then other issues regarding cultural diversity and stage management are briefly examined.

Choosing to nominate such considerations under the heading cultural differences implies some definition of what culture may be. As stage management is a practice that always involves communicating with a diverse group of people who have their own disciplinary cultures[1] (designers, technicians, directors, performers, etc.), I believe the fields of stage management and cultural studies have a lot to offer each other. Indeed, one motivation for this book is to introduce stage management and various concepts of social sciences to each other.

While a fulsome treatment of how cultural studies and stage management overlap or, indeed, the notion of 'culture' itself is outside the scope of this book, I encourage others to do further research in this area and stage managers to learn about the field of cultural studies. The introductory treatment here is limited by space and the limitations of my own experience and my choice in interviewing Anglophone stage managers who practice predominantly in Western developed countries. For the purposes of this book, I will simply acknowledge that terms such as 'culture', 'intercultural' and 'intersectional' are contested and dynamic and refer to where I have adopted my definitions from. Baldwin et al. provide an overview of the competing definitions of the word 'culture' and their origins and state these competing views 'suggest that any single definition of culture will probably represent only certain research and theoretical perspectives'.[2] My preference is to use Samovar and Porter's definition of culture as 'the deposit of knowledge, experiences, beliefs, values, attitudes, meanings, hierarchies, religion, notions of time, roles, spatial relations, concepts of the universe, and material objects and possessions acquired by a group of people in the course of generations through individual and group striving'.[3] This is because this definition enumerates the diversity of issues which the stage managers interviewed identified as factors influencing their approach to their practice.

The key distinctions between the UK and the North American system are the use of a Deputy Stage Manager (DSM) in the UK and a stronger demarcation between stage management and the remaining members of the technical crew in North America. The Australian system, in general, operates without the position of a DSM like North America but has the more relaxed attitude towards demarcation present in the UK. These distinctions, and the implications they have on production practices, suggest that (again, in general and relatively speaking) stage management is more likely to be perceived as a technical role in the UK, as a creative role in North America and as a profession in Australia.

There are different considerations for stage managers when they find themselves working outside their own culture. Miscommunication is more likely to happen when dealing with culturally and linguistically diverse collaborators. Preparation, demonstrating respect, questioning assumptions and striving for clarity in communication become even more important in such environments. Especially when working with different cultural groups within the same geography, stage managers must acknowledge and sensitively navigate notions of belonging, power, security and comfort with collaborators and audiences.

While the interviews uncovered these significant differences in approaches to stage management, the interviewees were usually at pains to point out that most of these distinctions have both positive and negative implications, and that one approach is not necessarily better than another. The other general finding was that despite the variety of approaches needed to navigate these cultural issues, the core goals of stage management remained the same. That is to say, the cultural backgrounds of all the collaborators on a production, including the audience, are one of the many aspects of a production a stage manager must consider when working out their approach. The overarching goal of stage management is to respond to the needs of each production.

Different stage management approaches in the UK, North America and Australia

Having worked in, and interviewed members of, stage management teams in the UK, North America and Australia, I can attest that the English-speaking world of stage management is – to mangle a phrase – many countries divided by a common language. In terms of stage management practice, the major practical differences are in the specifics of job titles and the assumed responsibilities of those roles.

While there are many variations to the way labour is divided and to the size of a stage management team, it is possible to make some generalizations. Maccoy[4] provides a useful summary of the distinctions between the UK and the North American system. As I outlined in the previous chapter, the UK developed a three-person team: a Stage Manager (SM), Deputy Stage Manager (DSM) and one or more Assistant Stage Managers (ASMs). The SM is concerned with overall coordination of the production elements, the welfare of the performing company of cast and crew and ensuring that performances flow smoothly by managing backstage functions. The DSM is the member of the team who is in rehearsals, keeps the prompt copy and calls the show. ASMs are intimately involved with acquisition and maintenance of the show's needs, especially with regards to props, and in the running of the performance, to assist the stage manager in managing backstage functions.

In North America, the job title of DSM is virtually non-existent, and so on smaller shows there is often a two-person team. The SM is the member of the team who is most likely to be found in the rehearsal room, fulfilling the functions listed earlier of the DSM. They are also concerned with overall coordination and the welfare of the performing company. In this system, the ASM is more responsible for the management of backstage functions, rather than the procurement or maintenance of the elements required for the production.

In Australia, like in many fields of endeavour, they use elements of both the UK and the North American systems. For two-member teams, they are likely to use the North American system but with the added expectation that ASMs will have a more hands-on role in procuring the elements required, especially props. For larger teams, Australian productions sometimes have an SM and multiple ASMs, or they may adopt the UK approach with a dedicated DSM.

I hope this brief introduction to the distinctions between the practical differences in stage management teams in these three regions provides enough context for the far more interesting and nuanced observations about these differences that the stage managers interviewed for this book shared. The distinctions which seem to matter most to those interviewed were the presence of the DSM in the UK system and the fact that stage management in the UK system was much more likely to be involved with the sourcing of production elements and their manipulation during the actual performance. The main implication of the first point is that the head of the stage management team in the UK does not have as close a relationship with the director and the cast as in the North American system. This is because they are often not present in the rehearsal room. This partially explains why, in North America, the responsibility for stage management to maintain the artistic integrity of the show is done much more directly and why a 'British actor would not be responsive to taking [acting] notes from a stage manager'.[5] The main implication from the second point is that the stage management team is much more strongly identified as part of the technical team in the UK, rather than managers of it, which has ramifications for how communication flows between departments. Comments made in interview by Ian Evans and Michael Passaro attest to these distinctions in approach:

> Evans: If you go into the bigger scale theatre ... [especially] if you go to America, you can't touch anything if you haven't got a union card to let you do it. Within the UK, [especially] within smaller theatre, everybody tends to muck in, which I love and that's great.
>
> Passaro: It's interesting because I have spent a lot of time with stage managers in England and London ... But stage managers in London are viewed more as part of the crew. Which isn't a negative, it's just very different from the US.
> To that point, on the London West End shows that I observed, among other duties, the ASMs are exclusively responsible for props ... So it's very different in that regard. The day-to-day company leadership is left to a company stage manager; only one stage manager [the DSM] calls the show, the job descriptions

are far more stratified and don't seem to come under any kind of unifying theme. They don't have the same kind of rotation that we have here in New York in terms of coverage between deck tracks, calling, and especially artistic maintenance.

These comments may appear contradictory as Evans talks about everyone tending to 'muck in', but Passaro suggests the job roles are more stratified. This is because Evans is talking about stage management's relationship with the rest of the crew, while Passaro is referring to within the stage management team itself. On Broadway at least, the stage management team members rotate through all the various stage management positions. All members call shows, manage wings and run office administration. Importantly, in terms of artistic maintenance, this means a member of the team is often available to watch performances. Even for smaller-scale (or shorter-duration) North American productions where it is not possible to provide for rotation amongst the stage management team, the head of the stage management team is the one who has spent the most time with the director and cast in the rehearsal room and is the one who calls the show. This leads to different levels of respect for the stage management teams' creative input as Peter Maccoy and Jo Franklin point out:

> Maccoy: From talking to American stage managers, I kind of get the feeling they have more authority and are more respected in a different way . . . Not that stage managers aren't respected in the UK, but the respect is slightly different . . .
> I think stage managers in the UK generally don't see themselves as creative, which I fight against because I think they are. And I think increasingly a new generation of directors and stage managers are actually seeing a more creative aspect to it . . .
> There is still though an element of thinking of stage managers as almost a glorified secretary and the communicator and the facilitator rather than a creative contributor I think.

Franklin believes that the respect for, and appreciation of, the creativity inherent in stage management is increasing in the UK and suspects that this may be a result of an increasing number of shows travelling between the United States and the United Kingdom.

> Franklin: There is more of a respect now, there's more of an understanding, (and I've seen this in the more American model of stage management) that stage management is creative . . . I've increasingly seen the influence of American stage management in the West End over the last few years, as shows come over with an American creative team and American ways of working. Obviously, British stage management tend not to think that. But some of that knowledge and understanding, and concepts of how stage management work, is rubbing off on British stage management who deal with that sort of project . . .
> I think we've started to see the nice influence of that. I'm not saying everything is brilliant in Broadway, because we all know there are many issues with unionization, and other things. But I think stage management being respected as

a creative collaborator has been a positive motivator in the UK, certainly in the West End over the last few years.

As discussed, a major component of this distinction is the fact that in the British system the DSM always calls the show. This doesn't allow for the rotation and the ability for the SM team to watch the show seen on Broadway. It also means that the position responsible for what is arguably stage management's greatest artistic contribution to the performance is not the head of the stage management team. The hierarchy also means that even DSMs are likely to see their role as part of the technical team and identify as part of the crew, rather than as part of the creative team. All these factors influence the different approach to artistic maintenance adopted in the UK. Maccoy discusses some of these issues and focuses on this role of the DSM in the British system.

> Maccoy: I would say that the DSM here is probably in a slightly different situation. . . . Certainly, the DSM would be seen as part of the creative aspect in many shows because of understanding the calling aspect of it and being in the rehearsal room and being able to understand where the director is coming from and the designers.
>
> Michael: I got a sense that . . . in North America there was a different approach in terms of the role of stage management with regards to maintaining a show.
>
> Maccoy: Well here, certainly, a big West End show would have an Associate Director who is in charge of the understudy rehearsals and adding new cast and maintaining the integrity of it definitely. It used to be the job of the Company Manager or Company and Stage Manager who would be responsible for running those understudy rehearsals and for monitoring the show and for holding rehearsals if you need to. . . . British actors don't like being given notes by Stage Management to do with the acting. . . . There's an element of resentment, I think, which from my perception of stage management in the States, there's no resentment and it is expected that the Stage Manager will give acting notes and so on. So that's a difference and I think that's still prevalent.
>
> Michael: In my head, that has a lot to do with the fact that in the different hierarchies, the head of stage management, *the* Stage Manager, if you like, isn't in the rehearsal room.
>
> Maccoy: Yeah.
>
> Michael: So I don't know if a British actor is more attuned to taking line notes or whatever from a DSM?
>
> Maccoy: Yes they would be. . . . Even working with Associate Directors, the DSM is usually backstage running it because they know the show; they know where the cues are, they've got the blocking; it makes more sense for them to feed into that. And where I've worked with Associate Directors, they've been looking more at helping the understudies particularly find their characters . . . which isn't something that a British stage manager would feel comfortable with. But I think probably a Stage Manager in the UK would spend less time in the rehearsal room.

> Michael: The few years that I worked in the UK, I was never comfortable with the terminology of Deputy Stage Manager.
>
> Maccoy: I'm not comfortable with the term Stage Manager. It doesn't really describe what Stage Managers do. And no, I'm not comfortable with the term Deputy Stage Manager. In a way the American system is clearer because actually they're the linchpin to a production, they're key to it.
>
> I don't like the hierarchies; it slightly devalues what a DSM does in terms of them understanding the show and being . . . like another member of the cast. They're a member of the creative team . . . In a musical, they are another member of the band in a way because they're having to coordinate all of that and that's a real skill. So deputy is the wrong word.

Sharon Hobden embodies Maccoy's comments about the problems with the hierarchy of the SM and the DSM in Britain in that she has become a career 'show caller'. She prefers working with a resident or associate director in terms of maintaining the artistic integrity of the performances. Many Production Stage Managers working on Broadway I talked with were not enamoured with the importation of the role of an Associate Director from Britain. This is discussed further in the section on Broadway in the next chapter. Hobden's comments here portray British stage management's relationship with directors and directing.

> Hobden: I've stage managed one production, but decided that I prefer show calling . . . This is my 28th professional year working, and I've probably spent 24-25 of those being a DSM, which is quite unusual. A lot of people shoot straight through to SM . . .
>
> The thing that's quite different over here there'll always be an associate or resident director. My creative input in terms of the directorial stuff with the actors, is far less than it would be in other environments . . . And it's not the thing about the job that interests me. I find it fascinating in rehearsals. Listening to backstories, why we're doing things, motivation. But I don't then want to be turning the understudies out. I can absolutely help, if the resident wants me to . . . I'm happy to say 'You have to stand here, because the light's here. You have to stand here because this goes past you and then you can move up.' Happy to do all of that, but don't really want to be involved in that directorial side of it.

Hobden's comments refer to the technical notes she feels comfortable giving actors, while eschewing a 'directorial' stance. This positioning of stage management is telling and speaks to traditions in the British system of stage management being regarded as part of the technical team. This is not only due to the hierarchy but also due to their more active involvement in the technical operation of performances. Depending on the production's scale and resources, sourcing props, maintaining costumes, performing scene changes, operating lighting or sound are seen as part of the normal remit of stage management.

In short, stage management teams in North America have been seen as creative managers of a production, whereas in the UK they have been seen as members of the crew. These distinctions seem to be blurring. There also seems to be a growing recognition of the benefits and disadvantages to both approaches. Hopefully, this evolution will result in a best of both worlds approach to stage management appearing.

The Australian landscape, with its hybrid cultural influence of the United Kingdom and the United States, might have already produced this utopian vision. However, having worked extensively in both Australia and the United States (and many other countries besides), Dr Sue Fenty Studham suggests the key difference between stage management approaches in both countries firmly places Australia on the UK side of the divide:

> Studham: In the [United] States you pay attention to acting, give notes on intention and train understudies. This is less common in Australia.

Further, Natasha Marich identifies that in Australia stage managers tend to be seen as glorified secretaries and not creative contributors. This is a vision of stage management that Maccoy and Franklin felt was changing in the UK. It is important to note that stage management in Australia has a similar approach to maintaining the artistic integrity of a show to the UK. That is, generally, Australian stage managers rely on a member of the directing team to give acting notes. This is despite usually adopting the North American model where the Stage Manager is the one in the rehearsal room and calling the cues during performances. Marich also suggests that often stage managers in Australia don't benefit from being regarded as part of the crew and are often seen as an administrative assistant to the production manager. Attempts to 'muck in' as Evans would call it are often unwelcome. Again, this is despite stage managers in Australia often having to work in the 'grey areas' like their UK counterparts.

> Marich: I feel the reason the administrative approach is predominant is because it is measurable. It is easily measurable by way of a tangible document, the rehearsal report. Whereas the other approach [being a creative contributor] remains unseen by your production manager unless they are in the rehearsal room to gauge the benefits of your input and observe how you engage with artists and respond to their needs in the rehearsal process.
> Michael: Does this go back to what you called a lack of respect for the depth and the scope of the position?
> Marich: A director, or the actors, might certainly appreciate your input. Outside of that, you can often be regarded as the biggest nuisance.
>
> I expect this is because there are many companies with production departments who don't expect stage managers to have the ability or interest to be invested in finding creative solutions to staging problems. We're perceived to have a far more diminished purpose which is simply to act as a glorified secretary.
> So, for a stage manager to make any offers – however mindful we are about our

sensitivity to artists and our intent to maintain the integrity of the design – is to risk attracting unnecessary attacks on your understanding of the role.

And I'm flabbergasted at that because I'm simply using the rehearsal report to try to share information, engage personnel outside of the rehearsal room to be part of the solution, to solve a staging issue, to serve the rehearsal process, to support the performers and the performance.

Michael: Why do you need a stage manager if it's not someone to make those kinds of . . .

Marich: Observations?

Michael: Yes! . . . observations in the rehearsal room.

Marich: The only solution . . . is to overtly qualify every question I need to ask as a stage manager and every offer of a potential solution [in such a way] to ensure that the question or solution is perceived to be from the director rather than the stage manager.

To summarize, the major distinctions between the approaches to stage management revolve around job titles, the division of labour and in the relationship stage management teams have with other production team members. This includes their participation in the direction of actors and maintaining the artistic vision of a production.

These distinctions correlate with some broader philosophical differences about stage management approaches geographically. In the North American system, the person leading the team is the team member most often in the rehearsal room, spending the most time with the director and cast and calling the cues in performance. Stage management's operations backstage are usually more concerned with the management of those functions, rather than their actual operation. This is especially the case in unionized houses which are more numerous and stricter in terms of what stage managers can and cannot do. This leads to stage management teams being viewed as responsible for the supervision of backstage activity and having the freedom of more time and space to take oversight of its operation. Unsurprisingly, this results in a greater acceptance of stage management's role in maintaining a director's artistic vision, providing acting notes and, in some senses, making a creative contribution to the productions.

Meanwhile, in the UK system, the person leading the stage management team tends to be more concerned with the technical provision and allocation of the theatre's resources of space and time and managing the traffic backstage. The actors' movements and show calling are tracked and managed by the DSM and are seen as a significant part of the technical system, rather than the driving force of stage management's contribution to the performance. Stage management's operation backstage, in this system, is intimately involved with operational matters, and stage managers are much more likely to take an active role in the running of backstage activities, with distinctions between stage management and other running crew members less clear. Consequently, the technical and operational aspects of stage management are emphasized over the creative contribution.

Stage Management

In the Australian system, the stage management team is usually hired by the Production Manager, and indeed production management is seen as the usual career progression for stage management. In a sense, this system is like the UK's except the UK SM and DSM have been renamed the Production Manager and Stage Manager, respectively. However, an Australian Production Manager has even less contact with the rehearsals, director, performances and the intimate details about the aesthetic needs of the production than a UK Stage Manager does. This means that stage management itself is viewed largely as a function of production management, and the pragmatics of time and budget management are emphasized, with any suggestion that stage management makes a creative contribution to productions being seen as suspicious, especially within productions that already have a large creative team. To make a sweeping generalization, it feels like stage management is regarded as part of the creative management in North America, part of the technical crew in the UK and as part of the administrative aspect of production management in Australia.

Intercultural stage management

The earlier section presupposes monolithic cultures and the methodologies of the largest mainstage theatres in each geography as the source of the cultural practices for all stage managers working there. However, in a globalized world and in one where, hopefully, marginalized voices are heard more often, stage management practice increasingly lies outside these points of cultural hegemony. Some of the stage managers interviewed were very experienced in working on productions generated from outside their culture and shared their thoughts about the differences in approach to stage management that result.

These observations consider what it means to be working in a culture that is foreign from your own in a variety of contexts. While a comprehensive treatment of intercultural theory is outside the scope of this book, some definitions and key resources might help contextualize stage management practice within the field. This may in turn encourage future cross-disciplinary research into intercultural stage management. Given the number of aspects that make up a 'culture' in the definition used here and the variety of ways culture impacts the use of language verbally, non-verbally and rhetorically[6] it is perhaps surprising that intercultural communication is ever effective. For this book, I use Baldwin et al.'s definition for intercultural communication which is 'communication between people of two different cultures in which cultural differences are large enough to impact the production or consumption of messages'.[7]

Studham, who has a wealth of experience working interculturally, spoke about the increased likelihood of miscommunications inherent in this practice. Studham points out that cultural differences are always present in a group of people and that these issues apply to any stage management practice. When the cultural differences are more apparent it is easier to anticipate that you will make incorrect assumptions. These, Studham explains, are a leading cause of miscommunications.

Michael: What tips could you give someone about trying to minimize miscommunication when you are working interculturally?

Studham: So, this applies within your own culture as well, but I suppose it's because I've worked so much interculturally that I pay a considerable amount of attention to nonverbal language. And I keep going back to assumptions that we make because that is where there is a stumbling block.

Working in the same culture, working in the same town, you might have grown up together, but you still might have different cultures. Making assumptions about what a gesture means: you might speak the same language and you might have had a conversation, but you translated that sigh or a nod or a look as something significant when it meant nothing. It had nothing to do with your conversation.

Michael: I'm suddenly very self-conscious about how I'm carrying myself!

Studham: Oh, no, no! But you know it affects communication. So, you change tack because you've interpreted something and without even having said a word, you're adjusting to a miscommunication based on an assumption that you made.

Michael: So checking and testing your assumptions is the key? In some ways understanding that you're making assumptions might be more apparent when you're working interculturally because then you're aware that you're going into a different culture?

Studham: You might not be aware that you're assuming things for your whole career if the right circumstance hasn't come up. I know that it was about 15 years before I really clocked that 'Oh, we don't all do it the same way!' Because I had worked within a specific culture, I'd gone out on tours, but we were the guests so people were adapting to us. And when they weren't adapting to us, I suppose I was making assumptions about why they weren't.

Franklin agrees with Studham that the first step required to work effectively interculturally is to become aware of your own cultural assumptions. Franklin also believes that the skills required to work interculturally are getting more important because stage management is becoming more globally connected.

Franklin: The whole approach to working interculturally, suddenly I've realized with the new MA and having foreign students from overseas . . . the main thing I've learned is how much of the stuff I take for granted is cultural. It's about how I relate to other British people, as a British person within that culture. And every culture has a different way of doing things.

Studham explained that some of the common sources of cultural differences include assumptions about protocols, language, time of day, gender and punctuality. This eclectic list accords with the definition of what constitutes culture from Samovar and Porter discussed earlier.[8] These different cultural assumptions mean that two people can have widely divergent interpretations of the same interaction. Studham advises that being aware of, and celebrating, this cultural diversity through questioning assumptions, demonstrating respect and seeking clarity in communication is key to effective intercultural stage management.

> Studham: In Italy in one of my first tours when I was twenty-one [I was wondering] 'Why won't they listen to me? How come everyone's on break?' . . . Was it the time of day and what that meant in that culture? Was it something that happened within the festival? Was it gender-based? I don't know.
> Michael: But now you're aware of all those things.
> Studham: I'm aware of it now and I wasn't then. . . . In retrospect, now that I've done more cultural study I can work out, 'Oh, that's probably why this happens. Right, that's not what I thought was happening.' So you're actually living different realities in that moment.
> Michael: So of course, miscommunication happens then.
> Studham: And then there are approaches to time.
> Michael: That works very differently across different cultures.
> Studham: It certainly does. And the reason behind it also is different. And what is important in the moment is different. . . . Time is a chapter in my thesis.[9] . . . The reasons why people are late, or incentives to getting people on time don't translate across cultures either. Maybe it will eventually down the line, I don't know. But . . . I hope that that doesn't happen because that means there will be more of a merging of cultures . . .
>
> So how can you be clear on your communication? . . . If you are talking across cultures, then maybe you need a cultural advisor. Maybe you need an interpreter. Maybe you need to think, 'okay, I'm going to be direct about this, but in certain cultures directness is rude'. So you may need to have someone to guide you or interpret what you're saying in a way that is culturally respectful.

Studham and Peter Lawrence explain that to be respectful of different cultures requires adequate preparation and a commitment to adapting behaviour to the norms you observe of how people interact in that culture.

> Studham: Now picture communicating across cultures when you don't know the coding of the body language or the coding of social interactions. And you won't know if you haven't done any research . . . What sort of prep are you actually doing before you go into the different cultures? Is there some basic prep that you could do? Or what about if you don't have the time to do it? . . .
>
> Look at least at the basics of respect and awareness and if you don't know or haven't had time to do any research about the culture that you're about to go into, be aware of that as well and observe how interactions are happening. And proceed with respect really. And know that the way you respect someone, may translate differently. For example, looking someone in the eyes because that is how you were taught to be respectful, but in other cultures it is in fact disrespectful.

Lawrence: I've taught a course in World Stage Management about what the differences are around the world are and what to expect. . . .

These differences are very interesting. For example, when I directed a show in the Philippines, I made a gigantic mistake there. I was so upset because critics were invited when an understudy was on that I assembled the Producer and Press Agent and I yelled at them. It cannot be done in Asia. Especially in the Philippines. Good family feelings are the basis for everything there and you're a barbarian if you raise your voice or criticize overtly. Had I [prepared properly] in advance I would have known that.

I now know it, and I teach it because if you're going to work around the world you have to know what the expectations are in each country.

The advice of Studham and Lawrence outlined here, especially with regards to preparation, accords with Holmes and O'Neill's Prepare Engage Evaluate Reflect model[10] which I recommend as a useful overview for any stage manager wishing to improve their intercultural communication skills. In fact, as stage management routinely deals with people from a variety of what Porter and Alcorn term 'discipline cultures'[11] this model may be helpful to all stage managers.

Cultural diversity and stage management

Working interculturally within your own geography raises slightly different concerns. These revolve around the issues of belonging, power, security and comfort. Of course, navigating such issues sensitively is made easier with the commitments to understanding, respect, questioning of assumptions and clear communication already outlined. Abbie Trott, a non-Indigenous Australian stage manager, discusses what needs to be considered when working with Indigenous performing arts companies. Adam Legah, Joanna Rawlinson and Marich discuss issues they have encountered as stage managers of colour, particularly while working in the UK or, for Marich, in Australia. They contemplate how to increase the diversity of audiences and theatre-makers and some of the barriers which remain for stage managers whose backgrounds are different from the cultural mainstream of the theatre industry in which they work. Despite the variety of approaches and considerations that must be factored in when working sensitively with people from culturally diverse backgrounds, there seems to be a common core that is central to all stage management practice which revolves around communication skills.

Trott discusses some of the nuances involved when working on a production that is made by, and for, marginalized cultures when you are from the dominant culture. Trott suggests that respecting the culture producing the work in this instance requires understanding that to support the show effectively may mean having less creative input as a stage manager, resisting the temptation to impose your own cultural practices and searching for opportunities to make space for opportunities for technical theatre artists from within the marginalized culture.

Trott: I have also done a lot of work as a stage manager in kind of culturally sensitive environments.

And then that adds a whole other layer to the communication. If you're working with an Indigenous company, of course, you need to be aware of Sorry Business and culturally sensitive material et cetera. But also the process is often different. It can be slower or more drawn-out or happen quicker. And I think as a non-Indigenous person working in an Indigenous project I'm always like, 'Well where is the Indigenous stage manager? Why isn't there an Indigenous person doing this job?' How do we find them to mentor them into the process?

I think there's also a cultural thing of being a non-Indigenous person: how much creative agency can I even take in that situation? Hardly any at all.

Rawlinson started work in fringe theatre and with small-scale theatre companies. After having worked in main house theatre she sought out further opportunities within small-scale theatre companies as she had a greater interest in issue-based theatre and Theatre for Young Audiences. Rawlinson makes a convincing argument for funding to make the arts accessible to ensure diversity in employment opportunities and for audiences.

Rawlinson: When I graduated I left college with a provisional Equity card, to get any stage management job you needed to have this card. Theatres generally had one or two full cards to give out a year so getting the first job was quite difficult.

I started work as a dresser in the West End then stage managed a fringe show.

Black Theatre Co-op were doing a show in the same venue and they needed somebody to help the designer. So I was that person, it was being a runner for a designer, but I enjoyed the company and got to know them. Being a person of colour, it was easy to network within Black theatre companies: everyone knows someone.

Through contacts at the same venue I was offered an ASM job with Soho Theatre. But then after that it was still difficult to find stage management jobs. That's when I did a lot of work in Black theatre. But it was so interesting. I was ASM at Talawa and then stage manager for Black Mime and I was touring for a year or so. I worked for them for a couple of years and got that kind of touring experience. Small scale touring and issue-based theatre was something that I realized that I was interested in . . .

I really, really enjoyed it. Made some life-long friends. And then Black Mime collaborated with Nottingham Playhouse on a show and then their stage manager job came up. And I applied for and got that job . . . it's a big regional rep theatre. I did several seasons there, learnt a lot.

And then realized that I missed working on smaller shows. I was interested in working with the people who worked on the other side of the road at Roundabout theatre in education.

Theatre for Young Audiences and Education is still where my focus is . . .

Particularly with the arts now, funding is paid for out of the public purse, art should be for everyone. . . . For many years, the people accessing art (that everybody was paying for) were white middle-class people going to the big theatres in London or the regional reps ... You know, I was very fortunate in my school and because I discovered an interest in the arts early on, that I went to those places. I was able to access that art.

I think what's really important now is that we do a lot of work that anybody can access, and that might be a performance that's an installation outside. It might be a show in a shopping centre, it might be a crazy promenade. It might be a show that centres around a bar. And to enable those shows to happen, to be a part of that team, you have to be on board with the whole creative process.

Legah also talked about how important it is for stage managers to feel connected to the work they are doing. This includes the company they work for, the material they work on and the audiences they connect with.

> Michael: Do you need to be conscious while you're building your career that you're finding the right home, the place that feels like it belongs to you?
>
> Legah: Absolutely. Like it belongs to you, because you have to have that connection. I couldn't get it with the people that I worked with at a large institutional theatre company. I couldn't get it with the audience. And I think that's another thing, the audience has to be with you. At the Royal Court I could go watch a play because it felt relevant to me.
>
> At this institutional company, although there were times when I'd have to go watch a show, because it's part and parcel of my job. I would go to watch the show, and I'd be dressed like this [casually]. Because I'd been working all day, and it wasn't as if I was going to go home and get changed into a suit to go watch a show. But the audience members around me were going, 'What is he wearing?'
>
> Michael: 'How did they let him in?'
>
> Legah: 'Why is he not with anyone?' I'm not saying everyone felt that, but there were clearly moments when you just felt, 'I don't feel welcome here.'

Legah sees notions of elitism in theatre as a large barrier to increasing the number of culturally diverse theatre-makers and building culturally diverse audiences. Breaking down such elitism is harder than occasionally programming material which may be relevant for diverse audiences. It involves always making them feel comfortable in the space which as Sedgman points out involves challenging notions of audience etiquette which our 'institutional frameworks do *in the main* operate to entrench privilege in the privileged, and to further marginalise the marginalised'.[12]

> Legah: When new leadership came in there was a shift around that time. It stopped being just about the subscribers, predominantly the white upper-middle class older people that used to come to watch the shows.
>
> And the programming changed as well. I would have loved to have worked there then to see the changes they were implementing take shape. Because they

also challenged the staff in their creative process. They asked, 'What actually are you doing here? You've become comfortable.' They went, 'Actually, we're going to put a stop to this.'

Michael: And comfortable theatre very quickly becomes elitist theatre, I think.

Legah: Absolutely.

Michael: And then it's not welcoming for-

Legah: For anyone.

Michael: . . . for anyone apart from that group that has grown comfortable with that theatre company, as an audience.

Legah: When I was there, we put on a production of *Jitney* by August Wilson . . . It was an all-black cast that came in from America. I don't know how the phone call came into our office, but it did. I had an irate woman phoning me to go, 'Why were there no black people in the audience in that theatre?' . . . She said, 'There was me, my husband, my two children, and that was it. You've got an audience of around 1,000 people and I looked around and we were the only black faces I could see. Why?'

'Well, what are you asking me for?' And she went, 'You need to do more.' And I said, 'Look, I'm not going to disagree with a member of the audience', but equally I did turn around and say, 'The problem I have with what you just said there is, people don't want to come.' And I said, 'Look, speaking as someone who is of Asian background, they won't come to shows, because they don't see this as a place for them. What more can we do?' She said, 'You should advertise in black newspapers.' And I go, 'But I think the marketing team probably did that.'

We used to have the same kind of attitude here [Rose Bruford College] on the performance courses.

Michael: Do you mean why are we trying to force them to do something they don't want to do?

Legah: Absolutely, absolutely. It doesn't work like that. They say 'But there's no students from the global majority'. And they go, 'What can we do to get these people here? There's not a very diverse mix of people.'

I get really cross about that when we talk about it in these committees. It should be about what are we doing to get these people interested in the theatre, rather than to get them to come here. Because if they don't want to come . . . If the oddballs want to find this place of work, then they will find this place of work. There is nothing we can do.

Michael: Of course, I'm sure that you have stripped out any barriers and would welcome any applicants with open arms, but you can't go out and drag people in off the street and say, 'Here, learn to be a stage manager.'

Legah: Absolutely! And actually what I get cross about is, whilst we are addressing the ethnic diversity of our students, what about working-class kids? I'm a working-class person from a relatively humble background. I didn't have money . . . It doesn't matter what your skin colour is. If you ain't got money, you ain't got money.

What do we do to bring those people in? I think we're improving that with our course . . . We've found out that people see theatre as an elitist thing, but people see events as something that anyone can do. So we made the conscious decision of making this a stage and events course, in order to promote that and get a slightly more diverse mix of people.

When Legah argues against notions of cultural diversity in theatre that concentrate on one aspect of marginalization over another, he is suggesting that increasing diversity in the arts needs to be approached with an intersectional framework. According to Collins and Bilge, 'Intersectionality investigates how intersecting power relations influence social relations across diverse societies as well as individual experiences in everyday life'[13] and suggest that 'intersectionality can be a useful analytic tool for thinking about and developing strategies to achieve campus equity'[14] and, I would contend, equity in access to the arts for arts workers and audiences alike. I would encourage stage managers, and the institutions they work with, when tackling such issues to adopt intersectionality as an 'analytic sensibility' which adopts the stance that 'what makes an analysis intersectional is not its use of the term "intersectionality," nor its being situated in a familiar genealogy, nor its drawing on lists of standard citations' and addresses 'what intersectionality does rather than what intersectionality is'.[15] In these ways we can continue to improve our understanding of the barriers which may prevent some people from participating in the arts fully.

According to Marich, barriers certainly remain for culturally diverse theatre-makers in Australia. These barriers reduce their ability to be heard, which can have both personal and professional impacts.

> Marich: What people think of me, I don't really care about, as long as it's not going to impact the work I need to deliver. That's another branch of issues that we've touched on when I made mention of touring to country New South Wales and the issues I encountered there in communicating. Which was more a socio-political issue, when people don't want to hear you or acknowledge you.
> Michael: People dismissed your very presence because of how you look in this case?
> Marich: Yes.
> Michael: Which is ridiculous in the extreme, but it still happens everywhere.
> Marich: If anything, I'm experiencing it more and more in the capital cities.
> Michael: Really?
> Marich: Absolutely. I think the nature of the shift in [Australia's] political climate and the social politics of the country over the last twenty plus years has given permission for overt and covert expressions of various prejudices that have not been helpful in the arts.
> Michael: They're not helpful anywhere, but especially so in the arts, I would contend.
> Marich: I say that because one does not necessarily expect to encounter it in the arts. I thought if anything, when I was a teenager, I would find refuge from that in the

arts, but that hasn't been the case. I don't know why I thought that. That was my idealistic, naïve self.

Michael: I still hold onto some idealism about the arts being a more liberal, accepting, tolerant industry or sphere of activity than others. But that might just be naivety, and privilege, on my part.

Marich: Well, we are in the business of image making to an extent or we certainly deal with images, so I expect that has something to do with it. In fact, I've actually been informed that I do not fit the image of certain companies – whatever that means!

The common theme amongst all these different perspectives on issues of cultural diversity in stage management is communication. All theatre-makers need to be able to listen to each other effectively; to be given the space to be heard; and to understand how to speak to and listen to their audiences. These issues are complicated by issues of cultural diversity, whether overt or covert, acknowledged or denied. While this applies to all theatre-makers, I believe it is especially applicable for stage managers as their role revolves around effective communication.

Conclusions

This chapter examines cultural diversity in terms of what Porter and Alcorn call geographic culture which is 'the most obvious cultural factor'.[16] But as they point out (in agreement with the first point Studham made in this chapter), stage managers need to account for cultural diversity even when working on productions where all collaborators share a geographically and ethnically based culture. For Porter and Alcorn, there are three other cultural layers: the interior, discipline and production layers.[17] Interior culture refers to an individual's mindset and habits. A discipline culture refers to the norms, language, habits and needs shared by collaborators working in the same area of theatre-making. The production culture refers to the practices shared by the genre of the production which will be discussed in more detail in the next chapter. While the geographic culture may be the most obvious, stage managers need to be able to recognize 'the different facets of each culture, and creat[e] an environment where all viewpoints are recognized, valued, and respected'[18] and to 'constantly navigate and translate the demands inherent to collaboration across multiple cultures'.[19] This translation forms a key part of the objectives of stage management as discussed in Chapter 7.

In this way, responding to the cultural diversity of a production is normal practice for stage managers. Each production will develop a unique culture arising from these layers and how the collaborators manage the interactions of them. Regardless of the cultural differences involved, the stage manager's goal continues to be to respond to the needs of the specific production they are working on. This will be a constant refrain as we look at the other aspects of productions that are likely to demand a different stage management approach. These aspects, and approaches, are simply noteworthy examples of how a stage manager responds to each different production they encounter.

CHAPTER 3
CONTENT-DRIVEN DIFFERENCES

Stage managers not only adapt their approach to changes in the field over time and what is appropriate to the cultural context they are working in but also because of the very nature of the production they are working on. There are two main aspects to what I have termed *content-driven differences*: the genre and the scale of the production.

In terms of genre, analysis of the interviews suggests that stage managers need to be sensitive to both the artform and key aspects of the methodology of a production. It may seem obvious to note that stage managers working in the differing worlds of theatre, opera, musicals, dance, circus and other genres should adapt their approaches depending on the needs of these different artforms. Helpful overviews about some of the key differences for stage management across various genres (both within and without the performing arts) can be found in Vitale's introduction.[1] However, many stage managers interviewed (who were familiar with working across genres) emphasized the similarities, rather than the differences. For example, Susan May Hawley said, 'regardless of the artform you do, I always tell my students here, the nuts and bolts of stage management, the everyday job, doesn't change. You just learn to adapt your nuts and bolts to whichever toolbox they're fitting into'.

The interviewees also pointed out that each of these artforms involves multiple production methodologies that also influence a stage manager's approach to the production. For example, within theatre, whether the production is site-specific, or devised, or even differing styles of a scripted play within an established theatre building may influence a stage manager's approach. These differences may be more influential for stage managers than the artform chosen. For example, Trott suggested the approach to stage managing a devised contemporary dance production may be more similar to that which is needed for a devised play than to that required for a ballet.

The other content-driven factor that has a major influence on the approach to stage managing the production is scale. Each different scale of production makes different demands on stage managers. This is true from the smallest scale where the stage manager is the only technical support to the largest commercial hits on Broadway or productions mounted at the grandest subsidized palaces of 'high' art. The scale of a production is also related to the tone of the producer, and Legah and Chris Freeburg highlight how this influences stage management. The interviews also revealed that mounting a touring production teaches stage managers a lot about the importance of scale. As Pip Loth explains, this is not only due to the demands involved in managing a tour itself, but it also brings into focus the impact that different venues and audiences have on stage management. The issues for stage management which are involved in managing the scale of an open-ended, long-running production on Broadway, in particular, were also discussed. Most of these issues revolve around maintenance of the production as Marybeth Abel emphasizes. In a similar fashion to genre, the differing demands placed on stage management may inform a stage manager's preference for working on productions of a specific scale. The similarities in demands from productions of a similar scale seem to be helpful ways to categorize and generalize certain aspects of stage management's overall concern which is to respond to the needs of the specific project.

Genre

Many of those interviewed had stage managed in a wide variety of genres and discussed how different genres influenced their approach to stage management. Like most of the discussions presented throughout Part 1, many of the stage managers interviewed were keen to point out that while there are key differences, there is a common core to much stage management practice. In addition to Hawley's comment earlier about the nuts and bolts of stage management not changing, Studham and Trott also pointed out that despite the differences between genres, the core of stage management remains the same. This is true precisely because stage management responds to each production's needs, and the considerations of genre are just one aspect of a production's needs.

> Michael: Is stage management different from events to dance to theatre to opera? What changes and what stays the same?
> Studham: I think that the foundational skills that you learn at university are really important. But you should understand that they are foundational and that you will adapt depending on the genre, because there are some very large differences . . . but I think that going back to my core definition of the role, that flow of a performance, being responsible for that. No matter what the genre is, it's still the same role.
> Michael: That's at the heart of it.
> Studham: It's that you need to adjust and adapt to the different genres and the specifics of a show even. It could be two vastly different types of performances in the same genre.

Trott comes to the same conclusion from the opposite direction, starting with the premise that every show is different even within the same genre.

> Trott: Every show is different. No matter what the genre. I think it really depends on the team and the director. You can work on a theatre show with one director and even the same show with a different director and they're two different beasts.
> Michael: I'm interested in that. So, regardless whether the show you're working on is from a different or the same genre than your previous productions, it's like any

> other show, because every show is different? And a stage manager's job is, really, to respond to each show's needs?
>
> Trott: Yes.
>
> Michael: So that doesn't change? . . . You bring a certain set of skills, and you're responding to the show's needs?
>
> Trott: It's doing your job to make sure all the things and the people are in the right place at the right time.

In these extracts, there is a tension between the common core of stage management and the need for a stage manager to adapt their approach due to the differing demands of the genres they encounter. Both Studham and Trott claim this common core remains despite generic differences. However, each expresses what this common core is differently: 'controlling the flow of a performance' and 'ensuring all the things and people are in the right place at the right time'. The resolution of this tension is similar to that of the last chapter about the commonalities and distinctions when working with different cultures. This is hardly surprising, as many of the differences due to genre are a result of what Porter and Alcorn call differing production cultures.[2] That is to say, the demands made by differing genres are just common examples of how a stage manager needs to adjust their approach depending on each production's specific needs. The goal for stage management then becomes understanding the needs that are typically derived from the production's genre and considering whether these are needed in each case. This, of course, begs the question what might be considered the typical demands of each genre.

In terms of the differences, the interviewees suggested stage managers need to understand that each genre has its own focus. Trott suggests that each different genre has a *score* which is based on some aspect of the performance that drives the action. Thus, dance may have a movement-based score or opera may have a musical score. Some genres, or specific productions, have a combination of these different scores. Hawley makes similar distinctions about the relative focus between the artforms of theatre, ballet and opera.

Trott uses the notion of where the *score* is coming from as being a key concern for stage management regardless of the genre. Trott also suggests that what is driving the score also has implications for the scope of stage management's artistic interpretation of the work in the notion of the differing levels of precision required.

> Michael: What's the difference between stage managing for circus and theatre?
>
> Trott: I think there is a lot more resistance to traditional stage management in circus – especially community circus in Australia. Often in circus the stage manager joins really late. It's more of a production manager role. And so I would often struggle because I'd come in and go, 'Well I want to write it down.' And they'd be like, 'Why?' I went, 'So that we remember it.' Because it's devised. I've got a lot of experience working on devised work, where part of my job is to collate the script or the score. So even in circus, or dance, you still have to collate the score. As a devised work, you have to collate the book that the show is coming from. So you

have to notate a physical score in the way you have to notate a physical score for dance or for some physical theatre.

    In some ways it has to be more precise. I guess that's a big difference. It has to be more precise than theatre. I was thinking about this recently: if there's acting there is maybe a little bit more room for - not improvisation, but for – more nuance in your calling in a way. But if you delay that half a second in your circus routine it might be bad.

Michael: It could have tragic consequences.

Trott: Yes. It could have tragic consequences, but I also think if it's a very straight up and down circus performance, each routine is very much its own thing, and it doesn't bleed in to what happens between.

Hawley discusses this issue of the focal point in contrasting stage managing opera, ballet and theatre. When contrasted to theatre, Hawley suggests the need for stage managers to be very comfortable reading music is a key distinction in both opera and ballet. When compared with each other, however, it is the primacy of a movement-based score in ballet as opposed to the primacy of an orchestral score in opera which has implications for stage management practice.

Michael: I'm interested because I've got no experience with stage managing dance at all, let alone ballet. And so is there a major difference in terms of stage management?

Hawley: For ballet, yes. But the main difference is that you need to be able to read music. Now although I could read music to a certain standard, nothing really prepared me for actually cueing shows with a live orchestra, because of course they're not going to stop if you get it wrong and lose your place. So that was quite terrifying the first time. It's like a sort of an initiation which is something you have to go through to feel that gut-wrenching terror, with your stomach sinking to the bottom of your kneecaps. . . .

    The difference between ballet and opera was that with the ballet, the orchestra are actually second place to the dancers, whereas in opera it tends to be the other way around. So, for instance, in opera you get your stage-piano rehearsals and stage-orchestra rehearsals, and when you have the stage-orchestras, the conductor (they call them the maestro) becomes the person that everybody refers to, including stage management. Whereas in ballet that doesn't happen so much. In ballet we have tech rehearsals and dress rehearsals that stage management is still going to start and stop if we need to, and the orchestra and the conductor will go with whatever needs to be done.

    So if you get an opera conductor who comes in to do the ballet for once, sometimes tensions could happen, and it needs to be explained that actually, that's not quite the same way that this is going to be run. That's sometimes a bit awkward, but mostly it was fine.

The common thread to these discussions is understanding what is primarily driving the experience for the audience in that artform. It is likely to be the movement of the performers in dance or circus performances, while in opera or orchestral concerts it is likely to be the music. In theatre it is likely to be the relationships between the characters. In a musical any of these might be the primary focus throughout the production, or at different moments different aspects may be the primary focus. Of course, any particular production may be primarily driven by any of these or something else entirely. This primary focus will influence the methodologies of the practitioners involved and the audience's experience. This requires stage management to form and maintain different kinds of relationships.

Part of understanding the different artforms, and therefore the approach required by stage management, then, is understanding the differing demands they place on the performers and other production team members. Hawley and Jillian Oliver both noted that there is a major distinction between the relationship stage management has with the performers in ballet and in theatre. Studham points out that while the focus between different movement-based artforms are very different, they all share some common elements in stage management approach in terms of looking after the health and safety of the performers.

> Hawley: I think ballet dancers are very different performers. They have their certain things they need to do. Ballet dancers have class every day; temperature is very, very important for them; and first aid is very important for them. They don't necessarily know what stage management do, really, whereas in theatre you're sort of part of the bigger picture and they know what you're doing in the rehearsal room. Ballet dancers tend not to, because it's not something they're used to having through their training. . . . You have to sort of earn your place a bit more when you work in ballet.
>
> And different kinds of performers have different personalities as well. I think you get opera singers, you get musical theatre performers, you get actors, and you get ballet dancers and each of those personalities are very, very different.
>
> And the more that you work with different types of performance, the more you get used to working with different personalities. And so ballet dancers for me, to start with – well I came from actors and musical theatre performers who want to be heard a bit more. Dancers are a little bit more insular because they'll come in and quietly find a corner and stretch and do their exercises, and they won't talk. And so it took a long time for them to actually talk to me, just in general conversation, and that was quite difficult to start with.
>
> I remember having a bit of a crisis of confidence thinking 'Is there something wrong with me?', but it was only that they just take a while to do that. And once you get to know them, they're exactly the same as anybody else.

Here it can be seen that these differences in personality in different types of performers are partially driven by the different demands the genre places on the performer. Actors and singers are well-practiced in using their voices, while dancers aren't as much. Oliver points out that stage management's role in terms of artistic maintenance is also very different in ballet from that of theatre or musicals, and this has an impact on the relationship as well.

> Oliver: I was with Boston Ballet, and I remember needing to visit the dancers' dressing rooms for the first time and being like, 'Oh, wait, where are their dressing rooms?' There's just not the same level of interaction that there is with a company when you're doing a play or a musical. It's a very different relationship – there's merits to both, to be sure . . .
>
> It's also structured very differently. At least at Boston Ballet the stage managers aren't maintaining a show, which is a massive part of the interaction with the company in theatre and musicals. There was always someone called the 'artistic'. It was one of five people. They were the ones that were walking the building and talking to dancers about their performances and what was happening that night. . . . There were just more people in the chain between the dancers and stage management. . . . So there was definitely a distance that way.

Studham argues that while the focuses of different movement-based genres are disparate, they share an increased demand on stage management to monitor the physical well-being of the performers.

> Studham: So even within dance there are very different considerations. I mean they may all be movement-based but look at the differences from classical dance to contemporary dance to physical theatre to circus. Very different focuses. But in all of those you're going to have a heavier focus on safety [than theatre]. I mean safety is a huge part of my focus and I don't know if that is because I started so early with dance. I think that safety is a part of every stage manager's focus, but there are minute details that I will check on because I'm used to working with performers for whom an injury could be the end of their career.

Hawley points out that different genres can also impose a higher level of formality to the relationships, especially for those working in 'high' art genres.

> Michael: And does that translate to different personality types between directors and choreographers then?
>
> Hawley: Yeah I think so. I think in theatre in Scotland in particular is much more family oriented. It's a very small circuit really, and everybody knows everybody else, and therefore it tends to be a bit more sort of, everybody gets on with it together. I think in ballet, and in the opera world as well, in those so called 'high' artforms, you get a lot of conductors and a lot of choreographers who are very, very famous who expect a certain something. And they expect to be talked to in a certain way, treated with a certain reverence.

Understanding how the artform places different demands on the other collaborators and how it relates to the audience are the keys to understanding both the similarities and differences of the variety of approaches stage managers take when working across different artforms. Again, this relates to understanding the nature of the artform. For example, in a theatrically driven musical, stage managers may have very similar relationships with a musical director or a choreographer as they do with the director in the theatre. Whereas their relationship with the same person may be very different when working with that choreographer on a ballet or that musical director as the conductor of an opera due to the increased formality of the genre. As Hawley pointed out earlier, it is not only stage managers who cross over artforms and stage managers need to consider how to manage their relationships with collaborators who are working outside their usual artform.

Rawlinson and Trott point out two cases that serve as a reminder that for stage managers the prime determiner of how to manage relationships is the specific production's needs, rather than its genre. Rawlinson suggests different productions within the same genre may dictate a very different relationship between production members.

> Rawlinson: It's a funny thing and I don't know whether you've noticed this. If you do a show that has lots of scene changes in it, the cast and the crew get on so much more as a team because everyone relies on each other more.
> Whereas if you're just doing a static parlour drama, the props are on the props table. Every now and again you page a door. There's not so much integration and banter or whatever.

On the contrary, Trott discusses how similarities in production methodologies on productions from very different genres may be more important for stage management to consider in their approach to managing the relationships involved rather than the genre itself.

> Trott: I found working with version 1.0 [a devised documentary theatre company] very much like working for Vulcana Women's Circus. It's the same kind of thing. There's a written script with version 1.0 as opposed to a physical script in circus but it's still a devised work, and you're still notating as you go along, and there's still changes and you're still dealing with the people, and the making. It does not matter whether the score is [movement or verbal], it is about how the work is made.

The preferences of each stage manager for, or affinity with, the differing methodologies of producing and presenting productions in different genres therefore are important. Studham suggests that stage managers benefit from seeking out the nuances of those genres they may be interested in early in their careers.

> Studham: Miscommunication can happen because terminology doesn't necessarily translate across the genres. And so if you're working in opera or dance, or you're working on something that's movement-based or music-based, rather than

theatre-based, your terminology is going to be different. You might use the same words but they could have different meanings. So I think it's really important that if you're interested in working in opera, you go and introduce yourself to an opera stage manager. See if you can shadow them. Listen to the terminology. Ask questions.

Hawley points out that a stage manager needs to accept the realities of the artform they are working in and also that, while a stage manager may have a preference for one genre over another, stage management largely remains the same.

> Hawley: You have to learn to be able to [treat those in 'high' art circles with the appropriate reverence as required], because that's just the way it is. So you either get on with it, learn how to do it, or you get out of it. There's no two ways about it. . . .
>
> People say, 'I'm a ballet stage manager, I'm an opera stage manager', and I personally think that's nonsense. I think you're a stage manager first and foremost, you happen to be working at that point for an opera or a ballet company, and you might prefer it.
>
> And as you get to be an older more experienced stage manager, you might only want to do that, but you started off knowing how to do everything, and that was your core training. So I think that's really important.

Mark Simpson weaves many of these threads together, discussing notions of the personal preferences of the stage manager influencing their approach to the work and distinctions between 'high' and 'low' artforms. The stage manager's preference for variety or stability in their career as well as their perspective on art and how it relates to audiences more broadly are also important considerations.

> Simpson: So I was at the Royal Opera House for 12 years. Probably too long. And then I left there thinking, 'I've done enough of this. There's nowhere for me to go.' And I think particularly as someone who was used to doing a lot of freelance work there's something very exciting . . . about moving from job to job and there's always something new. When you stay somewhere too long there's nothing exciting anymore and it ceases to become vocational. It just becomes a job and I think for us the balance of freelancing and employment is something you've got to judge quite carefully.
> Michael: Yeah and it would be different for different people.
> Simpson: Absolutely. Yeah some people are far better in long-term full-time employment. Anyway, I'd always wanted to become a Company Manager and so I did some company management. Took tours out around Europe and with companies like Cheek by Jowl, a season as a Company Manager for Garsington Opera, Company Manager for a panto – never again! I've done too many pantos in my life.

Michael: And too many operas? Or are you still enamoured with that form?

Simpson: Opera is sort of an artform that has its own variety built-in whereas panto is very formulaic. In opera you can do all sorts of different things and ... different ways of working so that, not necessarily about the way you manage it, but the production side is always quite dynamic. It's fresh, fluid.

Michael: In a way that panto isn't.

Simpson: In a way that panto can't be. Because of its function actually. What it strives to do involves having to cater to everybody from two to 102 and there's a formula to it.

Michael: And there's a huge sense of tradition that's bound up in it which is part of the experience right? That's why you go to a panto.

Simpson: That's right, but equally I think where opera had been steeped or baked in tradition up until probably the 1980s or 1990s there was a re-imagination of opera from new directors which happened alongside the development of classical music, popular music, and the development of theatre as an avant-garde artform. I remember seeing a production of Robert Lepage's *The Rake's Progress* at the Royal Opera House after I left and I thought 'This is just so completely different to anything that one might've expected from grand opera.'

At the heart of art is our shared experience of it. Are you aware of the Banksy gig at Sotheby's?

Michael: Oh the self-shredding –

Simpson: Yes, the self-shredding painting. It suddenly becomes a piece of performance art and the only reason it becomes a piece of performance art is because everybody is invested in it. Everybody gets it. And whilst you might see it as populist and 'serious' art lovers who are so far up themselves that they don't get that art is just a statement of the human condition (which I think is what it is) might not get it, but I think everybody else does. That's what makes art accessible and that's what art should be doing. That is bringing people together.

That's why I also have a slight problem with classical music and opera being seen as elitist. It's not. It happens to be very expensive to do. Because it involves huge numbers of people and in order to get those huge numbers of people on stage you've got to have big budgets and you've got to have enough space to do it and enough support. It's not the artform itself that's elitist. It's the people that can actually afford it that makes it elitist.

And so consequently I'm rather thrilled to see that there are all sorts of initiatives out there to allow any number of people to go and see it. I still don't think enough is being done to actually dispel the myth of the artform itself being elitist. There's a lot more work to do there.

Knowing about the traditions of different artforms, and the demands they are likely to make on stage management and the company members, can help a stage manager determine which genres or companies to pursue working with. This is especially the case if the stage manager is aware of their own 'interior culture',[3] preferences for different artforms and opinions about art in general (as Simpson demonstrates in the preceding extract). Reflecting on these factors can help a stage manager determine if they are likely to be suitable for, and enjoy, working in a specific genre or with a specific company.

Each different genre of performance is likely to partially determine the demands placed on stage management. The similarities are likely to come from the source of the score; the formality of the production; and the needs, personalities and type of relationships which need to be formed with the collaborators, especially the performers. These considerations are likely to impact the attractiveness of the project to the stage manager. Some of these considerations may be driven more from other aspects of the mounting of the production than the specific artform, whether the piece is being devised or is already scripted for example.

Different scales of production

The production's scale is another important aspect which leads to a variance in approach by stage managers. A production's scale is determined by the level of resources available to it. These resources include the production's budget; the number and level of expertise of human resources used; the level of infrastructure the producing entity and performance venues have; and the amount of time a production has. The intended audience reach (in terms of demographics of the target audience, capacity of the venue or venues and the season length) is another factor which determines the scale of a production. The production's resources and intended audience reach influence each other reflexively. While it may seem obvious that stage managing the smallest fringe show for a very limited season and stage managing a mega-musical with an open-ended run require different approaches, the caveats outlined for generic differences apply to scale as well. That is, while there are differences, much that is fundamental about stage management applies to all scales of production, and stage managing any production requires responding to that production's individual needs even on productions that theoretically have the same scale.

Despite these caveats, the stage managers interviewed offered interesting perspectives on the approach required by different scales of productions. Often these were offered in terms of stage managing small versus large productions, the tone of the producing entity, the specific demands of touring and whether stage managing for Broadway is different from stage managing elsewhere.

The smallest-scale productions are known by various names throughout the theatre industry. These names include fringe theatre, pub theatre, independent theatre, storefront theatre and off-off Broadway. Typically, they have only one stage manager in the stage management team, who may also be responsible for operation and/or designing production elements. Many stage managers discussed the demands these kind of productions place on stage management. For Freeburg they are the perfect training ground for a stage manager. Jo Alexander agrees that they are a 'young person's game' and suggests these productions can be frustrating for a more seasoned stage manager. According to Alexander, at this scale the cast and the director do not fully appreciate what stage management can offer. For Trott and Marich, in Australia at least, there seems to be the opposite problem. That is, the more corporate theatre companies seem to value the contributions of stage management less than the independent theatre companies. Legah points out that these differences may be more attributable to the tone of the producing entity, rather than purely a function of scale. Freeburg concurs, noting the specific tone of Steppenwolf Theatre Company and how the nature of an ensemble theatre company influences the approach to stage management.

Freeburg believes her time in storefront theatres was a formative part of her career. Her description paints a vivid picture of the scope of stage management at this small scale. Freeburg argues that working in this way is an excellent training ground for stage managers.

> Freeburg: Then I went to another theatre company . . . where I was essentially the only person that ran all of the shows. . . . It was a storefront theatre. It was in a strip mall above a frozen yogurt store. . . . It was me and a roll of gaff tape and 42 cents. . . .
>
> Usually those storefront theatres . . . the theatre's staff is very small. So it's some production managing, as well as being the only person on the production team, so you're also running the light board, you're also running the sound board. You're also the only person backstage, even though you're not backstage, so you have to do all the pre-set . . .
>
> I think it really gives you a great scope of the show on a nightly basis. . . . It really makes you think about the order in which you do stuff. When you're the only person, and you can't be backstage to do the handoffs, it's the creativity and having the forethought of, 'How can I make everyone's life better, even though I can't be back here?'
>
> I think it's great because you really get a really good idea of all of the pieces of stage management. You're sitting in rehearsal and you're taking blocking, you're doing prop tracking, you're doing costume tracking. You're also on book the whole time. It really helps you, it teaches you to split your focus and still be focused on everything all at one time. You can tell the people who have done that a lot, because they really can have a conversation with you while being on book, and they can go back and forth. It's a really great way to start your career. It's a lot of really good training. . . .
>
> Michael: Does that experience at a storefront level help you facilitate and coordinate different people when you do have a crew?
>
> Freeburg: I think it does, because I feel like I would never ask anyone to do anything that I wouldn't do myself, or I haven't done. When I send my apprentice off to go sharpen 400 pencils and make coffee, and these copies, that's part of where you are in your life, in your career, and that's what I need you to do. It's not sexy, but it's really supportive, and I really need that to happen. . . . I understand that there

are all these different cogs in the mechanism, because I've done them all. . . .
I think it helps me appreciate other people's talents and skills, and what they're doing too.

Alexander was not a fan of what in London are referred to as fringe productions. Her description of how people working at this scale perceive the role of stage management reminds me of the perceptions of stage management from dance and circus earlier in the chapter. It also accords with my direct experience of many, but not all, productions I have stage managed at this level, so I suspect her comments apply more generally than to this specific production.

> Alexander: I've not done a fringe show before [this one] and it's all a bit weird. I won't be doing it again. I think it's a young person's game. Because you're on your own. And in this particular instance, the cast's very young. I hate being on my own. I want a team. And I like being able to order people about.
> Michael: More than just the cast?
> Alexander: Yes. They don't understand why I'm ordering them about because I'm not the director. It's freaky. So, it has been weird. When you look back it's been fine. But it's not the experience where I really am going to think, 'I want to do that again.'
>
> I don't want to be driving for eight hours in the day to pick up seven different things that I've ordered because there is nobody else to do it. That's not what I want anymore. I've been there, done that, when I was an ASM.
> Michael: But is it good to get that experience, to know that that's not what you want to do?
> Alexander: Oh yes, absolutely. The other thing about being here is that I can be at home. So being a Londoner, it's good to be able to just go home at night. My cat's very happy. My husband's quite happy.

Contrarily, for Trott and Marich, smaller-scale productions allow for, and value, more creative input from stage management than larger-scale productions. This may be a product of the geographical distinctions already discussed, as both are based in Australia. It also may be a consequence of the more formal tone, and hierarchical structure, used by more corporate theatre companies as opposed to the independent theatre companies. In this aspect it bears some resemblance to the notions of 'high' and 'low' art considered earlier in the section regarding genre.

> Trott: I feel like maybe when I was working for smaller companies I had more technical and artistic capacity than if I was working for a big company.
> So maybe if I was working for STC [Sydney Theatre Company, one of the largest theatre companies in Australia] there was very little that I would contribute creatively. Yes, I made props, but if I was doing props I would work with the props team so I would have less agency. But also, I would never tell

the director what I thought. Whereas if I was working for a small company I'd probably tell the director what I thought if they asked my opinion.

But in a bigger company they would probably never even think to ask the stage manager. Even though the stage manager is a wealth of knowledge about theatre.

Marich agreed that smaller-scale companies are much more likely to have a collaborative ethic which places greater value on stage management's contribution to a production. Marich, quite rightly, took exception when I mistakenly referred to the more corporate theatre companies as more *professional.*

> Marich: What I think is different across the range of different scales of performing arts companies in Australia is not, for me, this notion of 'professionalism' but it is the nature of theatre practice, and my experience and observation would suggest to me that the better funded companies are more hierarchical and less inclined toward the collaborative ethic that I like to think is the ideal of theatre-making at its best.
> Michael: Yeah. I think that's what, when I was lazy with my words, I think that's what I was getting at with 'professionalism' in inverted commas.
> Marich: I wasn't trying to be critical but rather I think it gets back to the tropes in the whole system where big company equals more professional, and smaller company equals less professional and I think that is a totally misguided perception.
> Michael: Yes. I would agree with that.
> Marich: I think collaboration does not come at the expense of professionalism.
>
> The professionalism, so called, to me is often really a euphemism for factory process. It, to me, limits – I want to say – the creative scope. It's not quite the right phrase but it's in that territory . . . it limits the capacity for play and experimentation, particularly where new works are concerned.
> Michael: Certainly I find in companies with those more corporate – which I think is a better word than professional – cultures there's much more formality about things. That's been the biggest change of my communication style when I'm working for the state-subsidized theatre companies, they want a more formal tone in your paperwork.
> Marich: I've not ever been conscious of having to change the tone of my reporting because my manner in that regard is pretty . . . well let's say, I try to keep it as objective as possible. And I qualify anything and everything that might be perceived to be personal opinion.
>
> I've been criticized for things I consider to be really inconsequential. Unnecessary or unhelpful criticisms that I attribute to a lack of want or will by key individuals to be collaborative.
> Michael: Is that your experience throughout all of those levels or is it different when you've got those more collaborative workspaces?
> Marich: No, it's different at the smaller scale because communication is far more free and open.

> And there is this issue ... where the 'corporates' assume that when you've done a lot of independent and fringe work, that you don't have the capacity or capability to be a stage manager for those bigger, more corporate companies.
> Michael: From my experience, it depends on the nature of the company, and of course the demands of the production that you're working with, but usually it's actually easier to stage manage those shows from a corporate culture because you've got far more support, right? They generally require *less* of your capacities and capabilities.
> Marich: Yes! Thank you very much. It's that misconception that 'Why would you choose to work with X, Y and Z independent companies when you can work with A-B-C corporate major theatre company? There must be something wrong with you.' For a stage manager to make choices not based on prestige and income, but creative fulfilment and a belief in the creative output of a company is not de rigueur.

Legah also felt frustrated and hindered when working with larger theatre companies. Especially in comparison with his time at the Royal Court – which, while smaller, is hardly a fringe theatre company. This may suggest that these issues have more to do with how *corporate* or *institutional* the culture of the performing arts organization is, rather than the level of resources available. Although, I contend that the higher the level of resources the greater the tendency for corporatization or institutionalization. Legah here points out that the stage management approach in these more corporate or institutionalized environments needs to accommodate the comfortable nature of individuals who have been with the company for a long time and the siloed approach of departmental divisions.

> Legah: I was at a large institutional theatre company at the time that it was celebrating its 25th year anniversary. ... Whilst it was great, we had big budgets, we had all that type of stuff. People were getting rewarded for just having stayed in the same job the whole time!
> Michael: It becomes a fixed mentality.
> Legah: Absolutely. It's one of those things where you go, 'Crikey! There's no growth.'
>   You start that at the infancy of your career and you gradually work your way up. I'm not saying you can't stay as an ASM if you want, but go somewhere else, go to a different building. But all that happened is, people became comfortable.
>   I was in danger of getting comfortable. I was earning a lot of money. We also had access to perks, like travel expenses, that are not normal in the industry.
>   And in fact, the freelancers that we were getting in, would be working in regional theatres going, 'We're crying out for this money in the regions and we could employ more people.'
>   Did I get disillusioned there? Not disillusioned, but the fun and the family was taken away from it.

Michael: . . . It sounds almost the antithesis of what you were saying you enjoyed about the Royal Court.
Legah: Absolutely. There we were all a family and at this institutional company you were in your department. You only did your bit of it. You all went to your separate places.

Freeburg also discussed this notion of the tone of the company and how that changes stage management's approach to the work. In this case, the tone of working for Steppenwolf Theatre Company which is heavily influenced by its storefront beginnings and its commitment to an ensemble. The familiarity of working with ensemble members influences the depth of the relationships established among colleagues and the speed in which this rapport can be built.

Michael: You were talking about how Steppenwolf as a company has a less formal approach than, say, opera. . . . To be an effective stage manager, you need to be able to read that and adapt?
Freeburg: Exactly. One of the great things about working at Steppenwolf is that we do have this tremendous ensemble of actors, and directors and writers, many of whom we each have worked with a number of times. . . . I think that's the joy of working at Steppenwolf.
Michael: I imagine because of that ensemble that you'd get to know them much better than you would on say a typical short-run freelance contract?
Freeburg: Right, even if it's a cast of eight and you only have two ensemble members, that's two I don't have to learn. It helps, and it's an interesting dynamic when you have a show that's mainly ensemble members, with a couple of new people. It means adapting your communication style and what you do with who's in the room

In Freeburg's comments it is apparent that while the ensemble nature of the company is an important aspect of her stage management approach with Steppenwolf, the primary driver is still responding to the production's specific needs. Overall, the resources available to, and preferred working methodologies of, the producing entity are part of the many variables which influence stage management's approach to a particular production.

Some of these particular demands will be determined by whether or not the production is touring. Touring requires different resources than a production that is designed for one venue. In words that echo the refrain for most sections in Part 1 of this book Stern and Gold suggest 'that all moves are alike and all moves are different'[4] in theirs. They use the term 'moving' to cover both transfers and tours. Their discussion[5] concentrates on the administrative burden of tours providing templates for itineraries, letters and agreements and provides counsel to stage managers about how to try to prevent the touring company from 'making too much whoopee once out of town'.[6] Whereas, my conversations with the interviewees about touring productions concerned the additional demands for stage managers' flexibility and creativity as Loth and Marich point out. Touring can also bring into sharp relief that stage managers build relationships with audiences just like performers. Different venues allow for different kinds of relationships to be built between stage managers and audiences.

Regardless of how prepared a production is for touring, each venue will present slightly different circumstances that stage management must negotiate in order to maintain the artistic integrity of the production. Loth suggests that the need to accommodate different venues can become one of the most important considerations in terms of a touring show's aesthetics, especially if the venues' resources are widely different from those the production had assumed will be available.

> Loth: [I was the] SM for a new musical about Barbie that they were working with Mattel to develop.
> I think it was about eight weeks we were in L.A. to rehearse and build the show ... It was quite a large musical, with a very small team. Yes, that turned into a big job. It was a cast of 23 and 1 stage manager and 300 costumes and we were going to tour all of Asia.
> I got credited as the Resident Director and the Stage Manager for the show because every venue we went into was completely unsuitable for the show that we had built because they sold the tour before we'd built it. So stage managing was redirecting the show.

Marich also believes that touring allows for more scope for stage management to demonstrate creativity. Marich points out that this relies on the stage manager maintaining the artistic integrity of the production and keeping this in mind when making the necessary compromises to adapt staging elements to fit venues on a tour circuit.

> Michael: What's different about stage managing when you're on tour?
> Marich: I think that awareness of maintaining artistic integrity certainly comes to the fore. Inevitably, compromises have to be made. Yeah, so I think if you don't have that relationship with a director to understand their vision, hopefully a unified vision agreed to by all the artistic staff, without that, it would be very difficult to do it well. Certainly touring will force that hand ... or should force that hand.

Loth also discussed how the nature of the venue and the audience influences a stage manager's approach to the work. This is particularly apparent on touring productions. Venues and audiences, like other aspects of scale, can be more or less formal and stage management needs to be able to adapt. Theatre practitioners and researchers often consider venues from the perspective of the actor-audience relationship, but the stage management-audience relationship imposed by a venue's architecture is often not considered.

Loth: The tech box for that space was the back corner of the seating bank. So the window that I was looking through to operate and call that show from was behind a row of people. I could see their heads, I could touch their heads through the window. You were in the audience and you really did feel the reactions. It was the same with *My Name is Jimi*. You could really feel those days where the show was going off... and that's a really enjoyable and beautiful experience because you ride it with the audience...

Sometimes when you're backstage, calling shows off monitors, you can feel really removed. But that's just a different style of calling. You have to trust the operators... It's just a different way.

But doing the studio stuff is quite engaging. And then take that one step further and going to places like Bamaga and setting a show up in a basketball court with a trestle table and then putting chairs around you and having kids on the floor in front of you and not being able to hear the cast because the audience is so excited and the kids are playing tag at the back. They're not used to sitting in a theatre space and watching a 'nice' show.

Michael: Behaving 'appropriately'?

Loth: Yeah. But being a part of that is special.

It's a bit like on *Barbie*. When I was doing *Barbie*, I called the show from out the front. It was a musical and the kids would go off and we would dance. We'd be there dancing to the musical numbers, and we'd be calling cues, but you would be doing it in that vibe of you were part of the show too. And we would wear our sparkly little pink wings and I had pink hair by that point too. You just embraced it and got into it.

And I think depending on the show, you can become part of the audience and you can become part of the show. Or you are also completely separate because of where you are and what you have to do.

It seems touring exemplifies the old theatre maxim that no two performances are ever the same. The different energies of different venues and different audiences bring that into sharp relief. This is usually openly acknowledged for actors. Stage management is often viewed as imposing order and maintaining consistency despite these factors rather than being equally impacted and changed by them.

Some of the stage managers interviewed for this book had extensive experience working on Broadway. I sought out these stage managers and undertook a field trip to observe the stage management team of *The Phantom of the Opera* in order to see if Broadway's venerable status in the theatre world, or long-running open-ended musicals, resulted in markedly different stage management practice. Similarly to all of the content-driven differences considered in this chapter, while there were significant differences, it seemed that the core of stage management remained the same. Those interested in the detail and the specifics of the differences in stage managing on Broadway should refer to Lawrence's book.[7] The main theme in the conversations with Broadway stage managers revolved around the approaches to a production's maintenance.

Stage Management

Ira Mont and Abel both emphasized the similarities in working on Broadway and elsewhere. Mont acknowledged that the increased financial resources and the lengths of the run involved do have an impact on stage management, but the skills required are the same. Abel suggested there may be a mental divide from an outsider's perspective and that the commercial realities of Broadway dictated the kinds of material a stage manager will be working on.

> Mont: I firmly believe that there is very little difference in the theoretical skillset that one might need or want to stage manage a production at college or on Broadway. They are the same skills . . . they have many of the same requirements. The simple answers to the difference between them is one, the length of the run and two, the money that's involved.
>
> By money, it's not only or even mainly about how much you might be being remunerated as an individual, but just everything that might be at stake. In terms of the length of the run the difference is you are probably not investing so much thought in how to keep the thing going in the long term with a fixed run. . . .
>
> But back to your original question, I think that I view going into the endeavour the same way regardless.

For Abel, the economics translates into different sorts of productions being mounted. This, and the longer runs aimed for on Broadway, necessitates the need for her to seek out other opportunities while working on Broadway in order to keep fresh.

> Michael: Is there a big difference between Broadway and the rest of the theatre scene in the states?
>
> Abel: Look the bottom line is we're talking art versus commercial.
>
> I think that from a stage manager's point of view I sometimes long to go do some artsy-fartsy thing regionally. Something that will have no concern as to how much money it makes. Then, on the other hand, I love walking out of that stage door every night being on Broadway.
>
> So, I don't know if there's really that huge of a divide. I think it might look that way from the outside looking in.
>
> But I think all of us in the business feel that same way: 'Oh my god, I landed a Broadway show hallelujah!' But now that I'm in this Broadway show I'm still craving some kind of other thing and I'm not going to really find that here . . . And when you're on a long run like this, doing readings and workshops are absolutely the cherry on top. Because it's another avenue for keeping you fresh. I'm a real big advocate of that.

This notion of keeping something 'fresh' is part of maintaining a production. This maintenance is the aspect that most of the Broadway stage managers identified as a key distinction in their practice. The maintenance involved goes far beyond the requirement to tend to the upkeep of the resources needed for the production. A lot of these issues apply equally to open-ended productions wherever they are. However, because of stage management's increased role with artistic maintenance of a production in the North American system, there was a greater emphasis on this aspect of stage management practice in these conversations. Some other aspects of maintenance stage management must consider include the needs for cast rotations, the rotations necessary within their own team and maintaining the morale and atmosphere of the company.

Abel points out the need to rely on the crew for proactive maintenance and how cast replacement, both in terms of people leaving permanently and the use of understudies, is an important aspect of the maintenance cycle.

> Michael: What is the difference between stage managing a fixed run and open-ended run?
> Abel: So, it's the maintenance of the show itself. [*Wicked* is] fifteen years old, which means everything here is fifteen years old. So there's troubleshooting and planning ahead. How do we not have something happen? So we have an expert crew who will say 'we need to look at this before something happens'.
>
> By the time a year passes, you've definitely got cast replacement. And for me that's a wonderfully challenging aspect of what I do.

The specific approach to cast replacement adopted on Broadway and its related issues of working with Associate Directors is relatively new and is considered more fully in the next chapter regarding recent developments. This need to accommodate and celebrate the renewal provided by cast rotations is mirrored in stage management's approach to rotations within their own team on Broadway. Stage managers on Broadway need to adapt their approach when there is a permanent replacement in the team and, also, to accommodate rotations within the team itself. Both of these contribute to maintaining the production.

With regards to permanent replacements, Lawrence and Justin Scribner discussed the changes involved in their interviews. Lawrence outlined the process by which a permanent replacement is brought on board on a Broadway production. Scribner talked about the need to recalibrate the group dynamics in this situation.

> Michael: Can you talk me through the process for when stage management staff are leaving the show and getting replaced?
> Lawrence: Well, it takes two weeks usually. . . . The first thing that I always want them to do is I introduce them personally to everybody in the show. Then I also want them to watch the show a couple of times from the front of the house. Usually if it's a replacement there'll be an audio tape or video, and even before they come to view it for the first time I want them familiar with the music so they start to get the music into their bones. Then they'll watch the show a couple of times and then they'll start trailing backstage. I've found with most pros it doesn't take that long to learn the deck . . .

Stage Management

>Michael: I wasn't surprised to hear that one of the earliest parts of the process is to go and watch it from the audience, right? That's an important part of the process.
>Lawrence: It's crucial. You have to know what show you're doing.
>Michael: Even if you're just running the deck? You need to know the reason why you have to do it that way is so that it can look like that out the front?
>Lawrence: Exactly. But also, we're part of an artistic process. You have to learn how to fit into the artistic process. You're not working at General Motors, stamping. It's not happening like that. You're part of a bigger process.

Scribner points out that fitting into that bigger process is not just about the pragmatics of running the show but also recalibrating the personal relationships involved.

>Michael: You were saying you just had a rotation with your stage management team. Can you talk me through the dynamics of that?
>Scribner: It is quite a transition to change your stage management team on a long-running show, and recalibrate the balance, and the dynamics, and the relationships between people.
>
>There is no trumping one another, or voting. It's not a democracy, and it's not a hierarchy of power. It's a team, and we work together always. Upsetting the balance by losing a family member is taking us a second to adjust to ... We're still, I think, recalibrating. I'm glad I said that word earlier, because I'm feeling it. We're very much in that transition right now.

In addition to these permanent replacements, on Broadway stage management teams undertake rotations as a matter of course. They take turns to fulfil the various stage management functions within the week. This allows for freshness and redundancy within the team. Because of the greater need for artistic maintenance on an open-ended run and the greater financial resources available for a Broadway production, these rotations also allow for a member of the team to be free to watch the production from an audience's perspective when possible.

Greg Livoti outlined his weekly rotation for *The Phantom of the Opera*.

>Michael: So how do you do artistic maintenance? Do you make sure that you've watched a certain number of shows a week from the house?
>Livoti: Yeah. I set up every week to make sure I watch one show fully from beginning to end, to get the whole story. And then I probably watch throughout the rest of the week, nearly another full performance, but perhaps in smaller chunks ...
>I would say over the course of week my goal is to always watch nearly two full performances. One all the way through, and then most of another one. Some weeks are harder than others because stuff comes up, but that's always how I start off.
>Michael: And in the rotation you'll call a certain number of shows a week?
>Livoti: Yeah, I call two performances a week. And then with the other two-ish that I'm watching, that leaves four others. And that's when I'm really focusing on not only the schedule for the following week, but advanced scheduling. ...

And other day-to-day stuff that comes up that just pulls me away and needs my attention. Perhaps, we might be doing rehearsals off site, maybe I'll go to that for an incoming principal. If I need to teach anything. Seth [the Production Supervisor] does the majority of the teaching for new principals, but there are times when the schedule pulls him away. So I do get to help bring somebody along.

One goal of the rotation is to ensure that the stage management team does not become complacent. The rest of the stage management team at *Phantom* pointed out other ways that they achieved this goal. Firstly, understanding that there is always the potential for something new to happen even on the longest-running Broadway show of all time. Secondly, it is about adopting a mindset that every show is different and to allow themselves to feel that.

> Fenton: Even in the time I've been here we've had a number of occurrences that have never happened before. It always happens, there's going to be something new.
>
> One of the good things on a long-running show is that if you get certain situations you already have solutions. It's like, 'Oh yeah, we've done this, this is what we do.' For example, if certain people are called out and all of a sudden you have to do a cover, 'Oh yeah, we've done that, this is what happens and it works.'
>
> But there are still occurrences that will pop up where you go, 'I've never seen that before.' The hat, last night, was a good example of that.
>
> Athens: It landed on the candle!
>
> Fenton: . . . Everyone was saying, never seen that before. A simple thing like that, but every performance is different.
>
> And you have to be aware of that because you can't fall into the trap of thinking 'I know what this show is.'
>
> To my mind, this crew is very good at maintaining that. The people who are actually running the show, maintain it very well and they have a great respect for it and a great love for it and they really do work to make sure that it's as it should be.
>
> It's just not sliding into complacency, you can't. I still shake at the top of the show, it doesn't matter how many times I've called it.
>
> Athens: Me too.
>
> Oliver: Oh yeah!
>
> Fenton: Once I get past the first transition, I'm fine but there's still that unknown. We've all experienced too, doing a show and going, that was awful, that was not right to me.
>
> Athens: Yeah, absolutely.
>
> Oliver: Absolutely.
>
> Fenton: But that's not complacency, you just don't feel right about things. That's just being human and doing it, you get through it but it keeps you . . .
>
> Athens: On your toes. . . .

> Michael: I think if that nervous energy you've got at the top ever goes away then we've got problems. I think it would mean we don't care enough about our job enough anymore, right?
> Athens: Right. Absolutely.
> Oliver: Yeah.

Stage management also helps every member of the company to maintain the appropriate level of energy and mindset to allow them to commit fully to each performance. This is an important aspect of maintaining the morale of the company which Scribner and Abel highlighted as key to production maintenance, especially on long-running productions.

For Scribner, managing the emotional environment of the workspace through empathy is the key to maintaining company morale.

> Michael: So, for you, part of maintaining the artistic integrity of a production is maintaining the morale of the company?
> Scribner: Exactly. You're working with artists who are very sensitive, who are looking for ways to connect their personal experience to the work that they're doing onstage and have a tendency to embody characters from onstage offstage, and with empathic individuals, you have to make sure that you are really listening to what they are saying and also what they are not saying backstage. Even if you are providing a warm space, you're not done. Within the warm space, you have to always be juggling the needs of the company, both unspoken and clearly shouted, and that is not just my responsibility, it's my team's responsibility. So, we work together. I don't feel like that's only my job, but it's our job.
> I empower the people on my team as much as I can, to really be sensitive to the needs of others, and be thinking ahead in the ways that are maybe non-traditional to make people feel great about what we do and feel supported.

Abel similarly monitors the morale of the company and introduces changes to the backstage environment to prevent performers from getting stuck into patterns that may end up introducing any 'staleness' in the performance to the audience.

> Michael: So, part of maintenance is obviously the physical stuff. And replacing people. But, for the company that continues, how do you keep them fresh?
> Abel: Well, we try very hard to – I shouldn't say we try hard. Basically, we have a really great group of people. I think that when people get this job they know what sort of a golden opportunity it is. And so those who have sort of been here for a long time are very conscious of keeping themselves fresh.
> But it is a challenge. Morale is a situation which we really do try to manage. We're very aware of it. We try to do some morale builders. Food is a biggie as you can well imagine. A lot of times some of our principal players will just bring in

something to share. And we'll often do games like bring your baby picture in and see if people can guess who is who. Deep into the winter, around Christmas time, is when I always try to do something kind of challenging, like a scavenger hunt. Because that's the time when people can find it challenging. We need to be aware of the way that morale ebbs and flows.

Broadway places its own demands on productions. Many of these distinctions can be found in any open-ended commercial theatre productions. The key distinctions all revolve around the different approaches to maintain the artistic integrity of a production over a long run. As ever, though, the stage management team must respond to the specifics of each performance of each production.

Conclusions

Content-driven differences in approach to stage management result from productions having a different genre or scale. Generic considerations include the artform of the production (e.g. dance or music), its subgenre (e.g. ballet or contemporary dance) and the production methodology (e.g. devised or scripted). Different scales are defined by the different level of resources available to a production. This is partially determined by the desired target audience reach.

The genre of the production will provide some guidance to stage management as to what may be the primary focus for the audience and what some of the concerns of the performers and their other colleagues are likely to be. Depending on the specifics of the production, its artform, subgenre and production methodology will have different levels of influence over the stage management approach. All these factors will impact the kinds of relationships stage managers must build and maintain with the company.

The smallest-scale productions seem to be less formal and have a wider variety in their use of, demands on and respect for stage management. Typically though, stage managers at this scale are responsible for a wider variety of the production's needs than productions with more resources. Regardless of the level of resources available for a production, each producing entity has its own tone and level of formality which also has an influence on stage management approaches. Touring a production places specific demands on stage management in terms of preparation, administration, creativity and flexibility. The experience of touring can bring the relationship stage management has with an audience into focus. In commercial theatre with open-ended runs stage management must concentrate more on the maintenance of the production. This does not only mean the physical maintenance of the production's elements but also maintaining the artistic integrity of the performance. A large part of this involves enhancing the company's morale and guarding against complacency.

While it would be silly to deny that the artform of, or the resources available for, a production does not influence a stage manager's approach to their work, it would be equally ludicrous to suggest that every opera, for example, requires the same approach.

Stage Management

And that this operatic approach needs to be radically different from the approach required to stage manage any play. For any production, stage managers need to understand how it intends to connect with its audience, the resources available to it and the modus operandi of the people involved. Understanding the genre and scale of a production is important because it allows stage managers to make appropriate assumptions and decisions about how to manage these aspects of audience connection, resource deployment and relationship management. Stage managers also need to understand how their own strengths, weaknesses and personal preferences will intersect with these considerations. In short, stage managers respond to the specific needs of any production they work on and some of these needs are influenced by the content-driven aspects considered in this chapter, but the needs are by no means prescribed by these aspects alone. Some of the needs of a contemporary production are likely to be dictated by the recent developments influencing stage management practice which were identified by the interviewees. These are considered in the next chapter.

CHAPTER 4
RECENT DEVELOPMENTS

The preceding chapters have explored how differing approaches to stage management develop over time, in different places and according to different types of production content. This chapter will examine some of the recent developments which suggest that stage management's evolution continues. To discover these influences, I asked the stage managers interviewed for this book to comment on the changes that they have noticed during their careers and the implications these hold. While these answers were idiosyncratic and reflected the specific contexts and the expertise of those interviewed, several themes emerged. This suggests that some of the main factors driving changes in contemporary stage management practice transcend genre, scale or geographical boundaries. These factors include changes in technology, changes or challenges to labour divisions and health and safety management. While these changes are significant, a useful frame for this discussion was put most eloquently by Mont who, when asked about the changes he had noticed, responded:

> I would say a lot and very little all at the same time. And I would hazard a guess that many of my peers are probably going to give you a similar answer. How stage management hasn't changed: it is still about managing people for the most part. It is a people person job. Human beings are becoming more complex in some ways (or possibly less complex if you view staring at small screens in your hand as making us less and less complex!). So handling the situations that arise when people interact with each other and with things is still the focus.

This mirrors many of the discussions outlined in the previous chapters. The differences that result from considering these more recent influences are significant, but they remain similar enough to suggest that there is a common core to stage management practice. As such the contemporary influences outlined in this chapter can be seen as more of the context that stage managers must take into account as they respond to each production's needs.

Communication technology

A prominent point in Mont's summary alludes to recent developments in communication technology. These have had a major impact on stage management practice. This, of course, is something stage managers have always adapted to, from managing scarce access to printed materials and literacy in the earliest times through to the emergence of electricity giving rise to cue lights and, later, audio technology allowing for verbal cueing. These days, the ubiquitous presence of mobile, internet-connected, communication technologies are responsible for some of the largest changes in stage management practices. Pallin states that 'advancing technology [is giving] rise to smarter devices and applications' and goes on to point out 'some examples of technology that can assist [stage managers'] work'.[1] These devices offer the potential for easy, instantaneous recording of information and communication. Many of the stage managers interviewed stated the presence of these devices as the most readily identifiable recent development in stage management. For example, these are the initial reactions to the question provided by Mel Dyer and Hawley.

> Michael: Have there been any changes in the role of stage management during your career?
> Dyer: I guess technology is the big one. Especially with the use of smartphones: being instantly accessible, and, for example, being able to record fight choreography on your phone versus having to use blocking notation.
> Michael: I'm interested in the evolution of stage management over time. What changes are you aware of?
> Hawley: Well, certainly there are a lot more electronic devices. The nuts and bolts of stage management doesn't change. We still do rehearsal notes, we still take blocking, still do prompt copies and so on. But, there are a lot more electronic devices.

From an administrative viewpoint having the ability to record, copy and send information quicker and more easily results in more efficient (and therefore *better*) practice. However, most of the stage managers who discussed these issues felt the presence of these devices was not always beneficial. They pointed out that *immediate* communication is not always helpful, that it should not replace more *structured* communication, that these technologies can lead to difficulties with regards to timing and that their mere presence can be counterproductive at times.

When problems occur it is in how the tools have been used and the assumptions made about them. Here when the stage managers, including myself, speak of new, 'immediate' communication tools, the typical example is the smartphone. Because almost everyone has them, almost all the time, and it is much easier and faster to create, send and receive messages than before, they give the sense of being immediate. Ironically, when they are implicated in communication breakdowns it is often precisely because of their mediated nature. It is rare for some to misread the tone of face-to-face communication or for them to not receive it. These are comparatively common problems with the illusory immediacy of a text message.

This sense of immediacy also often relaxes the formalities of the communication protocol. This can happen through, for example, the use of text-speak and through the desire for rapid messaging. This contrasts with taking the time to craft what the interviewees have characterized as structured communication. That is where the messages have been constructed more thoughtfully with regards to their completeness and usefulness to those who receive it. Even when stage managers are aware of these issues, and use these tools judiciously, they need to be aware that others in the production team may have these assumptions about these communications devices. Taken altogether, these points suggest stage managers need to think critically when adopting new communication tools.

Hobden discusses the expectations that come along with the ability to communicate immediately. Stage management needs to be aware that many people working on the production can now communicate changes immediately with others. This opportunity needs to be managed appropriately because there are circumstances where this actually hinders the efficacy of the team, instead of enhancing it.

> Michael: It seems that the immediacy of communication now has come with a whole bunch of expectations that aren't necessarily helpful.
> Hobden: Yes! For example, getting props in a rehearsal room. If the director says something at 10:00, they want it there by 11:00, or 11:30. . . . When I started there was no email, no texting. Rehearsal notes came out at the end of the day. If you were lucky enough to have somebody else in the room with you, and they can nip down to the props store and get something, great. Otherwise, you sort of make do with what you've got. And often what happens is they make a request, but by the end of the day, they've changed their mind. With immediate communication now, they'll want something, and an ASM will text the prop supervisor, and they'll start getting that in motion. So then three hours later you're going 'Oh, stop, stop!' 'But I've already spent £50 on it!' Sometimes there's not the time to let an idea just settle.
> Other times it's great. Because you need something and it can be there, and it can facilitate a very productive rehearsal.
> Michael: Is it about knowing what needs to be done immediately and using the right communication tool for the job?
> Hobden: Yes, but sometimes you're not always in control of that because there are other people in the room, who've already taken it upon themselves to just do something. It depends on your team and how you get the team to work. One of the ways, obviously, is if you have ASMs in the room, when stuff like that comes up you always get them to check, 'do you want me to pass that on, or do you want me to wait?' It's a very simple thing. You have to set that up.
> Michael: A good ASM has initiative, and might hear it and just go for it?
> Hobden: And you want them to have initiative, absolutely. But sometimes it's quite useful to go, 'Actually, in my experience, let's just wait until the end of the rehearsal and I'll double check if they really want it.'
> Michael: Then you can have a lengthier conversation with the director to get more design specifics, or whatever. You're not passing on a little tiny bit of information, but more precise information through the rehearsal report. It depends on the director and the room, but also sometimes they're throwing objects at actors that they had no intention of being on the stage. . . .
> Hobden: . . . and it's just an exercise – exactly!

Stage Management

Using immediate communication tools can result in a loss of structured communication. This can impede rather than serve the production. As alluded to by Hobden earlier, this is often apparent in how this constant immediate communication can impact rehearsal reports. Both Maccoy and Hawley also discussed the need to balance immediate communication channels with more curated processes, especially in terms of structured rehearsal notes. Another important aspect of structuring the communication is ensuring the right people have the right information at the right time to be of use to the production.

> Maccoy: What I've seen is a move to just constant messages being sent out to different fora that not everybody gets. And there's a good reason for doing rehearsal notes at the end of rehearsal where you document everything that was discussed and decided and then everybody gets it and it's all in one format. It doesn't need to be bits of paper, it can be electronic but it's all there. Whereas with ten text messages during the day means you may lose some of it, or somebody may not know and it's a surprise. I just see that all the time.
> Michael: And text messages two and six of those ten may be contradictory because something has changed back.
> Maccoy: Yes and somebody didn't know that. . . . I think that this constant availability of communication is part of that problem.

> Hawley: So if you've all got laptops, and that's great, because you all need the information, but it's also bad, because it means that this beautiful thing of having the rehearsal note, as a central point, and everything radiates out from it, sometimes gets circumvented, and therefore it gets lost in translation.
> So I think that's something that's good and bad, and I think stage management these days ought to contend with that. When I first started, you literally typed your notes, and then you put it in somebody's pigeonhole, that was how we did it. But at least you knew that they got it, because it went straight into a pigeonhole. And nobody else could do it, because you were the only one with the information, so it was a much more structured environment for delivering information. Now, even though these days information can be delivered much faster it has got a propensity to be a bit wishy-washy, a bit grey around the edges.

I contend that this notion of the immediacy of communication channels providing *less* precision stems from two aspects that are easily overlooked – namely, the asynchronous and asymmetrical dimensions of the affordance of contemporary communication. Because it is so easy to send an email or a text, especially to a group of people (as opposed to printing notes and placing them in pigeonholes or even making phone calls), and because from experience we know that they (usually) arrive at their destination almost instantaneously after sending, it is easy to forget that this does not mean that the recipient has received, read or understood the message instantaneously. *The Phantom of the Opera* stage management team interviewed points out that this assumption can be problematic when an urgent message needs to be received.

The *Phantom* stage management team has lived through many of these changes since the Broadway production started in 1988. Perhaps it is more accurate to say that they have inherited the legacy of these changes, as none of the stage management team members interviewed were part of the original stage management team. The discussion with the team provided the useful reminder that even with instant communication devices now available, it may only be the sending of the message that is instantaneous, and that communication requires the reception of the message.

> Fenton: I think I've even read a note from Greg [Livoti] about the first time that the company had an email list. 'We've now come into the twenty-first century and we're going to email you the rehearsal report.' That's a big difference.
>
> But things can still slip through the cracks because people think they've sent something and just rely on the fact that you're going to receive an email or a text without talking to somebody. And we all know that it could come through three or four hours later.
>
> I think some of the best ways are the old ways. You make sure you talk to somebody, that's what you really should do. So somebody gets the message.
>
> Michael: There's something to be said for face-to-face communication.
>
> Fenton: Even on the phone.
>
> Athens: Just on the phone, that's just fine.
>
> Fenton: Yeah. You just actually had a conversation with somebody and you now know that the person who has to know something, does know it, rather than just relying on the technology.

The ease of sending these messages can also lead to the assumption that the recipient can decode and enact an appropriate response as easily as it was sent. Passaro outlined that this assumption can lead to unrealistic expectations, stating that while questions and requests can now be sent immediately, many of the responses required take much more time and this disconnect can cause frustration.

> Passaro: Answers to questions, resolutions to challenges – they don't come quite as quickly as you might like, because the theatre on some level is still a very mom-and-pop business. It's still handcrafted, it's still made by people, you can't replicate it like you can an mp3 or a movie or whatever. . . . We can't replicate it instantly, and that takes time, and can be frustrating to those who are not used to it. It's not like, control-C copy, control-V paste. It doesn't work that way.

Maccoy discussed how the mere presence of laptops and mobile phones can impede a production's progress. They can act as a distraction for stage management or the others in the room. They also have a distancing effect that hinders rather than helps communication.

> Maccoy: If you've got your laptop, while you're typing into it (unless you're a brilliant touch-typist), you aren't listening, you aren't watching, you are

concentrating on typing and I think that's interesting. I think psychologically, if you've got a laptop open in front of you in a rehearsal room and you're doing something, there is an element of both the cast and the Director thinking that you're on Facebook or not concentrating on what they're doing.

Michael: It has a distancing effect?

Maccoy: It is distancing.

Michael: Regardless of what you're doing on it. It either says to people 'oh I'm the most professional one in the room, look at me!' or it says that you are not listening, or not available, at least. Because there's a mediated sense to your presence then. It doesn't feel like you're immediately available in the room, which is one of those signals that you do want to be sending out. So even if you were brilliant at typing and could type and concentrate on the rehearsal at the same time the perception in the room is just as important. It's not a good look because it sends out signals that are getting in the way of the creative process.

Maccoy: Yes it does.

Kincman concurs by advising stage managers to minimize 'work on computers in smaller rooms where even the quietest typing will be heard or where the "wall" of a laptop screen can inadvertently communicate disinterest'.[2]

These concerns are not meant to dissuade stage management from using these technologies. But it is important to consider the implications of them to ensure that, on balance, the communication technologies and channels used contribute positively to the way productions are managed. Many of those interviewed celebrated their benefits as well, including those who pointed out their shortcomings. For example, Hobden and Maccoy outline that when used appropriately, using immediate communication technologies can enhance the sharing of information and resources.

Hobden: In other respects, immediate communication is great because you can email the Production Manager and say, 'Can you send a picture over of this, can you send a plan for this?' You can have the information that might have taken a day to get photocopied and sent to you, instantly.

Michael: There's this sense of immediate communication being better.

Maccoy: And it can be better, there are times where the Director says, 'can we get this for rehearsals?' You can text your Stage Manager and say, 'any chance of getting this into the rehearsal this afternoon?' and that's brilliant. I'm not against it, but you need to be very careful in that it shouldn't supersede the documentation of all those decisions and the discussions.

This latter point is key. In Hobden's and Maccoy's examples the immediate communication channel was requesting information or an item where the decisions, discussions and documentation already existed. Where these are yet to occur, like in the earlier example of adding a new prop, using such a channel may be inappropriate.

Abel also highlighted how choosing the correct channel was key when relating her journey from eschewing the use of immediate communication channels to becoming an enthusiastic user when they are used appropriately.

> Abel: When I first arrived here, I actually put a note on the board that said, 'I will not be texting. Do not text me. I'm an old-fashioned stage manager. Call me.' Now I live for texts! I've developed over the years.
> Michael: Technology changes?
> Abel: It totally changes. Let me compare the communication I had to do with *Les Mis* with this [*Wicked*]. With *Les Mis* I would go to every single person in the building. It would take me twenty minutes to a half an hour to go to wardrobe, sound, hair. 'We're setting up this next week, okay?' Now, I have a group text, a group email. It's so much more efficient. I get a response back that is written so I don't have to think 'Did I hear that correctly?' because now I can look: 'Oh that's right, they needed it like this.'
>
> So to me at first I was rejecting this technology because I thought everything had to be one-on-one personal communication. Now I embrace it so very much. Because it enables me to function better.

Abel was keen to point out that these methods of communication should not replace more personal forms.

> Abel: But I also make a conscious decision to go through and see the departments. Because I could end up in a bubble up here in the office. I could close the door – I've got the show through the monitor – and I could become a hermit with the technology. So I make a conscious effort to go out and greet the people. Just to say hello at the beginning of the day. And I think that that's important.

But the most important aspect seems to be in choosing the appropriate channel.

> Abel: Now, has it taken the art away of communication? I don't know, has it? Is there any art in the email? It's strictly factual. However, I do feel like there is art when I am communicating personally with them.
> Michael: And maybe the art is in knowing what's appropriate to email or text? Or needs . . .
> Abel: . . . an actual face-to-face conversation. Yes.
> Michael: And knowing which messages that you're sending out will be received well by which tool you're using?
> Abel: Exactly. Yeah.

The relatively recent ability stage managers have to send messages to individuals or groups almost instantaneously has had a large impact on stage management practice. Stage managers need to be aware of the implications of these technologies though, to ensure that their use is of benefit to their productions.

Stage Management

Performance technology

Another area where technological change has had an impact on stage management practice is in developments with performance technology itself. Designers within technical theatre disciplines can now create more nuanced cues. Show control technology has also developed so that there are new ways to coordinate the different departments. This makes different demands of the stage management team in terms of calling (and in some cases operating) the show. Mont states, 'I think that technology has certainly impacted what the job is. I am certainly aware from my predecessors how the calling of a show before the computerized lighting boards was a whole different craft and art than it is now'.

For Studham the more nuanced cueing of shows has led to stage management's expertise being valued and sought more from other theatre-makers. Marich feels that while digital show control allows for many more complicated sequences to be pre-programmed this comes at a cost of responsiveness to variations during different performances. Evans points out the rise of networking various technical disciplines together digitally can enable greater coordination.

> Studham: Technology has changed. You're not just calling a light or a sound cue or running the reel to reel in isolation anymore. There's so much more now. I think there's a new awareness of how all the different technologies are meant to be working together. There's a new level of awareness. It needs to be more specific in some ways. And there are not those broad cues that there used to be where you might have a bump at the end of a number or a snap to black. Cues are more nuanced because the technology can be.
>
> And you are a voice in the conversation. We didn't used to have that voice in the conversation. I think that's the change for stage management. We were note takers, organizers, timekeepers, and now we're part of a conversation. And we're brought into it; we're invited into the conversation. Because you need to understand what that conversation is to get the best production that you can. To get the production that all the collaborators are working towards. And if you don't understand that, then how can you make the choices that you have to make if something goes wrong?
>
> Marich: At the Stables [Theatre] back then, you had a cassette player and a CD player and a sound console where you were switching speaker-assign buttons, manually crossfading from one track to another . . .
> Michael: Does that level of technology gives you the ability to respond more organically to a changing performance?
> Marich: Absolutely, absolutely. So you are interacting quite directly from moment to moment with the performers, yeah.
> Michael: Which is something that, you know, in these days of QLab – we can certainly shift when the cue starts, when we say go – but if all you've got is pressing the space bar and the length of the fade's already pre-programmed,

> then you can't have that same level of response to the shifting nature of the performance.
>
> Marich: That's right. That's right. It's taken the 'rock and roll' out of it for me and now I don't get the adrenaline rush that I used to get. Because I'm a little bit more removed from it. You're less a part of the performance. You're more of a facilitator as opposed to being a part of it and integral to it.
>
> So, I think, with respect to all these technical effects having become more computerized and automated, I feel it restricts the interactivity of the stage manager with performance. I think that's a sad thing.
>
> Evans: One thing, the one area that's pulling lighting, sound, video, all together is digital networking. So, everything now is being connected together. That's where it's all happening.
>
> Michael: And that, to me – I don't know about the electronics of that – but theoretically, that means that it can be coordinated better?
>
> Evans: Yes it can, completely. I mean, in the 2012 Olympics, sound, light and video everything ran down one Cat5 cable. And there were days not long ago where even having lighting and sound on the same power supply was a no-go. But now, they're actually sharing the same data cables and make it all happen.

Again, it comes down to an issue of balance and responding appropriately to each production's specific needs. Like the discussion I had with Abel earlier about when to use which communication channel, achieving this balance involved notions of artistry. Marich coined the terms *technical perfection* and *performance perfection* when suggesting that, for her, live performance should always allow for more immediate responsiveness from all the technical elements of a production.

> Marich: I had a discussion with a lighting designer, in fact I had an argument with him, because there was an insistence on his part for programming all the lighting, all the sound effects, and all the A/V into QLab. But the argument came down to the designer wanting *technical perfection*. And I said, 'But that is not the same as *performance perfection*.' And we agreed to disagree on those two very different notions. And for me what he is seeking belongs to the world of film or computer games, whereas I still want those technical elements to be at the heart of live performance, to give it the full integrity of being a *live* performance.
>
> Michael: Yeah. To me and, from what it sounds like, to you, the joy of working in the theatre is, it's a shared space and it's a shared moment in time. Each performance – although it's usually a well-rehearsed and contrived experience – is still a unique experience.
>
> Marich: Absolutely. And where there is a reliance on . . . I mean, where does the value of *technical perfection* lie within the context of a *live* performance? You can ask a performer to do something the same way every time, but there will still be some degree of variation from performance to performance. And I would like to

be able to support the performance each night, not just in the technical rehearsal, where it's 'perfected' and you then assume that it will always be delivered that way for the performance season. And when you have lighting, sound, and AV cues that are all pre-programmed to happen on one press of a space bar, the playback of those cues are not adaptable, you can't change it. You can't vary your response to support the variability that a performer brings to the stage, night after night.

So, when special effects start to become the focal point of a production, that's when I start to lose interest, I have to say. As an audience member as well as a stage manager.

Michael: Because when a performance has to be moulded to the technical support of that performance, then it's not –

Marich: That's right, then it's not *live* performance for me, because the programmed effects are dictating it . . . and I don't think that's the way it should be. That's my feeling.

It is important to consider the implications of using these new techniques to ensure that they are servicing the needs of the production as a whole. Stage managers, and other theatre-makers, should consider that just because something is now possible, it does not mean that it is required. With increasingly computerized and pre-programmed effects much more complicated and coordinated cue sequences are possible, but theatre-makers need to understand that while automation provides efficiency and reproducibility it necessarily limits flexibility and interactivity. Marich's notions of *technical perfection* and *performance perfection* are key in considering the liveness aspect of the performance arts.

New approaches to maintaining productions

Chapter 3 outlined that a key distinction to stage managing on Broadway was taking into account how to maintain an open-ended production. This approach has changed relatively recently in terms of adopting a new philosophy of how to approach cast replacements and with the introduction of Associate Directors.

Abel outlines the approach they take to bringing in new cast members for *Wicked*. Passaro details that this is a relatively new approach, and that Abel is one of those at the vanguard of it.

Abel: Because they hire people and it's not like you're just hiring a carbon copy and putting them in. You've got to work with the director, the choreographer, the musical director and ask, 'how can we incorporate this person's talent into something that we've already done?' I really love that part of it. I also love teaching the understudies. And I'm really fortunate because the creative team here is very willing to allow us to try things and that's essential. You have to be able to do that on a long run . . . But the challenge of the long run, seriously, is in the maintenance of it.

Passaro points out that this renewal approach to cast replacements is relatively new and earlier approaches sought to replicate the same performance.

> Michael: I was talking about long runs with Marybeth [Abel] and she explained there is a continual renewal and refreshment cycle built in. Whenever there's a new person on that stage, because they are human beings and because it is a live experience, and that's to be celebrated in the theatre still, hopefully . . .
> Passaro: Yes. Hopefully.
> Michael: . . . then that injection of a new talent onstage refreshes everybody.
> Passaro: I think that she is very good at the overall landscape of a long-running show, because she really understands and has moulded that position to be the executive in charge over there. And she's involved in the artistic maintenance and continued development of that show, and she's also rooted in the supply chain operation, if you will.
>
> The job has evolved from some of the London transfers, from the 80s and early 90s . . . when it was like, 'No, you have to have your hand here, and you have to move at this angle, and you have to make sure you're standing like this.' That was out of necessity no doubt, that they had to maintain the shows in that way because they were figuring out that methodology because the commercial theatre had never had the volume – the supply chain – that those shows provided. But I think that something like *Wicked* shows just how far we've come in the development of that methodology. I think they cycle actors in and out of those principal roles in an attempt to keep things fresh.
>
> We're still learning and evolving on Broadway as to how we deal with these unbelievably long runs, which are incredible not just because they provide so much work, but they also bring incredible enjoyment to people all over the world. But we're still learning how to deal with some management effects of those long runs.

Part of that evolution on Broadway has involved the introduction of Associate Directors. Associate Directors are charged with maintaining the artistic integrity of the show over the life of its run, including managing cast replacements and monitoring the ongoing performances. Lawrence and Passaro discuss the history of the position and how they were imported from the UK. Perhaps this was partly because of the relatively lesser role stage managers have with regards to maintaining artistic integrity and giving notes to the cast in the UK as outlined in Chapter 2. Lawrence, Passaro, Livoti and Abel all have different stances on the role, but the common thread is that maintaining the artistic vision of a production on Broadway now involves managing this key relationship.

> Passaro: There was a time when Production Stage Managers on Broadway were at the very top of a hierarchical, top-down organizational chart. But as the shows became more complicated, things became more targeted and splintered, a lot of that artistic and management control was redistributed amongst other

members of the producing team and the stage manager was left – here I'm talking specifically about Broadway – with a much smaller artistic voice in the process.

    The Associate Director position became very widespread when what I call the 'London invasion' started in the early 80s with *Cats* and *Les Miserables* and *Phantom* and *Miss Saigon*, because the Associate Director is a position that is specifically associated with the original London productions of those shows. And when they were transferred to Broadway, these positions became institutionalized for a time on the Broadway versions of those over the years. Home-grown Broadway shows tried to adopt that method but it didn't really work as intended and now there's sort of a hybrid of that.

    The job of stage managing on Broadway, in the thirty-plus years that I have been doing it, has changed and evolved. I think that the generation before me had a real conflict with the introduction of the Associate Directors, but it was never something that I had an issue with. And, in fact, because the shows nowadays are so complicated technically that a lot of my time as a Production Stage Manager, is dealing with personnel matters and all that. For myself it leaves very little energy at the end of the day to be maintaining the show. So, I always hope that the shows that I'm working will have some kind of an associate or resident director to help carry that load.

Lawrence's comments typify the generation Passaro mentions as the one before him.

> Lawrence: I'm part of a tradition in the US that basically says that everything upstage of the proscenium arch is controlled by the Stage Manager. Which means that the Stage Manager not only was responsible technically for the show, but also artistically. That is, that there was no Associate Director. What's changed is that the Brits came in with their model, which is that there is always an Associate Director. So, for instance . . . when I did *Gypsy* with Sam Mendes, which was fifteen years ago, I was the Associate Director as well as the Production Stage Manager. I've also done a number of jobs where I've just been the Associate Director a number of times. Which on its own is a boring job because you can't control anything really. All you can do is whine! But I think more and more in this country, the tendency is to hire an Associate Director. Even on shows that have nothing to do with any British creative team.

Due to quirks of history, *The Phantom of the Opera* now has a Production Stage Manager from the generation after Passaro's who is as uncomfortable with Associate Directors as Lawrence. However, despite *Phantom* being almost the archetype of the 'British Invasion', it does not have an Associate Director but a Production Supervisor. Livoti explains the difference and points out that the balance in the relationship is the key thing.

Livoti: Day-to-day, at least how it's set up on *Phantom* is the Production Stage Manager takes on what we often describe as an old school PSM approach, which is the one that notes and maintains the show. A lot of shows may have their own resident [director] now who's doing things like that.

Michael: Peter Lawrence was not a fan of that development.

Livoti: Nor am I. I really relish the opportunity to be able to do what I feel is my job. I don't need to be the one that makes casting decisions. But to help the show run properly, I believe that is part of our responsibility. And [our Production Supervisor] is very good about this. But that allows the Production Stage Manager to see something from the front and say, 'that's not reading quite right'. And that to me is what gives me the most joy of the show.

For Abel it is important for stage management not to lose sight of the artistic maintenance of the production even when they are working with resident directors.

Abel: I am so thankful that we have a creative team that is attentive. There is no way I could do this on my own. But I am also very, very happy that they allow me that opportunity [to maintain the show artistically] and then they come in and polish it up. And I really believe that that is something that we're losing in stage managing now because of this business of the resident director. And I just feel like it should definitely be a tandem thing. . . . I have had resident directors in shows over the years and we work in tandem. I'll say to them 'Look, I'll get the understudies all through the first two weeks. You come in week three and drop nuggets of gold. And then we'll polish it the week after.'

And that to me is really a beautiful way to keep the show running. Because what it does is it involves the stage manager in knowing how the show keeps its direction. To me the most important thing on a long run is keeping the essence of the direction. That's what can go askew. If you've sort of distanced yourself from that by going 'Well, we have an Associate Director' and you just call and deck the show then you're losing an enormous part of what stage management is. If you're just calling and decking a show, then it becomes rote. Who wants to stay on a show like that?

I try to empower my whole team that way. I don't want robots in the wings going 'Clear. Clear. Clear.' I want people in the wings who are watching the show, seeing what's happening, fessing up where they think there's an issue. Coming up and going 'Hey, did this change?'

Michael: It's hard to catch those changes over a long run. The little ones. It's amazing what can happen as you keep doing eight shows a week. Little subtle changes build up over time, whereas an Associate Director, can come back and see the show after a period of time.

Abel: And that's what's brilliant about having that. You've got that outside eye and they can call it. Absolutely. That is the advantage of having an Associate Director.

Stage Management

These ideas of how to manage the relationship between a Production Stage Manager and an Associate Director represent a specific instance of best practice in stage management when working with teams made up of slightly different production roles. Stage managers are encouraged to understand the pros and cons of this situation and clearly communicate the expectations to all involved and continually monitor the situation to enhance the strengths and minimize the weaknesses. This is yet another example of how stage management's approach to a production is always slightly different based on the specific needs of that production.

Developments in health and safety management

The differences in the stage management approach to coordinating the health and safety requirements of a production were another major recent development that many of the stage managers interviewed identified. These changes were seen as having both positive and negative impacts on the practice of stage management. The recent developments have seen a rise in the formality of managing the health and safety of production companies. Another relatively recent development includes broadening the scope of health and safety to explicitly include aspects of mental and emotional well-being. These developments are reflected in some recent stage management literature. As examples, Porter and Alcorn advise stage managers: 'production processes that are civil, communicative, fair, supportive, and free of harassment and hostility can create an environment where team members feel safe and collaboration and creativity can thrive',[3] and one of the major changes to Kincman's third edition is a discussion on safety in the rehearsal room which includes advice for working with challenging material and how to work with intimacy directors.[4]

To the extent that the health and safety of all team members has been enhanced, all of those interviewed were in full support of these developments. Hobden summarizes the increased formality of contemporary health and safety management. Maccoy points out that the way these new formalities are implemented can also have negative impacts in terms of the flow of a production and in placing the emphasis on the bureaucracy of risk management rather than on managing the risks themselves. Hawley suggests that the formalities involved, while offering much-needed protections to individuals, can have the effect of lowering people's resilience and ability to share their vulnerabilities and therefore the ability to work collaboratively in a creative environment. Stage managers need to ensure that the balance between bureaucracy and creativity, and protection and freedom, is appropriately set, communicated and maintained in response to each production's needs.

Hobden outlined the increasing formal approach to managing health and safety as a major change during her time as a stage manager.

> Hobden: One of the things that has changed is general workplace attitude to health and safety. When I trained, there was no formal health and safety. There was in

as much as: using a safety chain when you rig a lantern, coiling cables this way, taping things down so people don't trip. It was all common-sense. You were expected to do most of it, because why wouldn't you? Whereas all of that has become completely formalized over the time that I've been working, and people are required to have certificates and different government courses.

The reality is it can only be for the better. Because you shouldn't be doing something that has a risk of injury. It's not that we didn't do those things when I first started, but it wasn't as formal as it is now. We certainly didn't have somebody to write a risk assessment that I have any recollection of.

Maccoy outlines that the problems of implementing the increasing bureaucracy incorrectly can include interrupting the workflow and not reducing the risk of injury by shifting focus to the administrative documentation of the process rather than the actions taken.

> Michael: Is there anything else that's changed massively?
> Maccoy: I think technology in terms of what goes into shows is a huge change: what we can do is way more complex and therefore probably dangerous, therefore there's a responsibility there. . . . Within the UK, health and safety is a big thing and when I started working, we didn't write up risk assessments in the rehearsal. If the Director and actors decided they were going to jump up and down on chairs, you didn't risk assess it. You did, but you didn't have to do the paperwork. Now you would have to say, 'I think we need to check that we can do this safely.' Then you would have to do a risk assessment and you would have to make sure that all of that process gets done. And there's an element of that being a good thing, but also you can get bogged down in bureaucracy.
> Michael: Well I have two problems with the increasingly bureaucratic approach in health and safety and one of those is that, as you were saying, you can bogged down in the rehearsal process and it can get in the way. But if that makes people safer, then that's a good thing because that's more important than the show.
>
> The second thing is there's a kind of almost counterintuitive dissolution of responsibility once that piece of paperwork has been filed.
> Maccoy: . . . I agree with you, it's always been something that concerns me and I've seen it happening: 'well, we've done a risk assessment' but you haven't put precautions into it. The piece of paper should be documenting what you have done. And you need to be able to demonstrate that you've put that into practice.
>
> There's a real danger that people interrupt the workflow. I see this with students because they want to go away and do the risk assessment and write it down and then put it into place. If you can put it into place and then record it then it is better, because then you don't slow the process down. I agree the paper trail component sometimes becomes the task rather than improving safety.

Stage Management

Hawley advocates a balance between protection and resilience.

> Hawley: I think younger stage managers perhaps aren't as resilient these days. They are not willing to put up with as much as I did – and I don't know if that's a bad thing or not. In my time I think perhaps we put up with too much actually. There were no risk assessments, there were no health and safety regulations, you just worked and got on with it, and there were no policies that protected you as individuals, like we're seeing from all the campaigns that are going on at the moment. You just sucked it up and got on with it really. So that was my background very much to start with anyway. So maybe we could do with a little bit more of that, a little bit more of the school of hard knocks, but with a bit of what they've got now as well. We need stage managers who are resilient *and* protected. As I say, if we get the balance right, then that would be good.

Stage managers need to be aware of both the positive and negative implications the changes in the industry have for their productions and to adjust their approach based on this awareness. To strike the right balance stage managers seeking best practice in their approach need to adopt flexible systems that continually try to enhance the strengths of new developments and minimize the impact of their weaknesses.

Conclusions

Recent developments in the theatre industry that have had the largest impact on stage management practice include the technological developments of both communications technology and show control technology; the flux in the roles of the production team including the introduction of Associate Directors on Broadway; and the evolution of health and safety management. Each of these changes presents both opportunities and threats to the effective stage management of productions. Stage management teams that exhibit best practice typically seek to understand the implications of these changes in relation to the needs of the specific production they are working on. From this understanding, stage managers can adapt their approach so that the production benefits from the opportunities and avoids the threats as much as possible. In this way, the adaptations stage managers make due to these recent developments are similar in how they adapt to the differing demands placed on their productions by cultural or content-driven differences.

All these differing approaches are a continuation of the adaptations stage managers have always made in response to changes to theatre production throughout history. Despite these changes to the world of stage management, I return to Mont's words that in some respects very little has changed as well. It seems to me that the focus of the Ordinary of the Miracle Play and a contemporary stage management team, and at every stage in between, remains the same. How this focus is described leads to particular conceptual models of stage management's function. Three of these models will be explored in the next chapter. They are administrative, managerial and artistic stage management.

CHAPTER 5
THREE MODELS OF STAGE MANAGEMENT PRACTICE

The analysis of the interview material regarding the various approaches to stage management reveals many recurrent themes. These themes coalesce into what I call models of stage management practice. Many of these models are possible.

This chapter outlines three such models. Firstly, an administrative model of stage management which emphasizes stage management's role in ensuring the rules and norms of mounting a production are followed. The second model explored here is the managerial model. This model views stage management as a particular context within the broader field of business management practices. Finally, an artistic model of stage management is proposed. The artistic stage management model emphasizes the creativity of stage management and its potential to influence the audience's experience.

Presenting these three conceptions of stage management is not meant to signify completeness. Rather, it is hoped to start other theoretical explorations of the practice. Nor is presenting them separately intended to suggest that stage managers must subscribe to only one conception or another. Indeed, I suggest that the best stage management practice can be found at the intersection of these models.

The administrative model

This administrative model of stage management is the predominant one in current stage management literature. It also seems to have been the predominant paradigm for the training of the stage managers interviewed. The assumptions that when grouped together are indicative of administrative stage management are that stage management practice is task-driven and process-oriented; celebrates the 'correct' way of mounting a production; and is learnt best by doing it because it is too practical to be the subject of academic research. From this perspective, stage management is valued in terms of its efficiency.

While all of those interviewed agreed that stage management's administrative role is essential, many disagreed that it was a sufficient model to capture all of stage management practice. Further, they argued that viewing stage management solely through the lens of administration often leads to problems in the theatre-making process rather than enhancing it. The limitations cited included a too-narrow focus on the personal qualities needed for stage management and the potential to inhibit collaboration with other team members.

Stage Management

The predominance of an administrative model of stage management and its typical format was noted by Schneider when she describes the field as largely consisting of 'instruction manuals' for the learning stage manager, framed around a personal account of the author's approach to the practice.[1] In the generation since this was written, nothing much has changed as Abigail McMillan's response attests.

> Michael: Some of the stage management textbooks that I've read kind of present communication as 'here is a template for this document' and 'here is an agenda for your first production meeting'. As if it's a how-to book and if you just follow this along, then you will have stage managed a perfect production.
> McMillan: (dubious) Okay.
> Michael: Your reaction is heartening. You obviously don't believe that that's the case?
> McMillan: I think it's a starting point. I think it's absolutely a starting point . . . Is it [a leading stage management author]'s book? A new edition has come out. And it is about templates and it has a template structure.

Why this model predominates is easy to understand. Firstly, it reflects the wider culture's understanding of stage management. The term 'stage management' when used outside of a theatrical setting demonstrates the baseline assumptions about the role. In fields such as public relations or politics where something is 'stage managed' it is tightly controlled, manufactured and not allowed to flow organically. This use of the term stage management came up in discussion with Simpson.

> Simpson: You see examples in the newspapers or on the news about how something was 'stage-managed'. Whilst we're not talking about what we know as stage management. We're talking about a general understanding of stage management is that we are the people who make things happen.
> Michael: Yes, and control it and lock it down and make sure that it is exactly the same every time and presented in the way that it's 'supposed' to be.
> Simpson: Absolutely. And in some ways it's true. But again, it's like so many things about this. It's not everything. It's an angle on it.
> Michael: And it's the angle that kind of says that we're the creativity police and clamp down on other people's creativity.
> Simpson: I think that's absolutely right.

This model also predominates because it is useful by virtue of being easy to teach, explain, measure and is largely accurate. The administrative model conceptualizes the production process linearly and emphasizes the communication tools stage managers typically use to monitor that process. Marich believes those tools that are written and easily accessible become proxies for measuring the quality of stage management, and this is one reason why the administrative model predominates.

> Marich: [The administrative approach] is easily measurable by way of a tangible document, the rehearsal report. Whereas other approaches remains unseen

> by your production manager. So their own measure of your work becomes the paperwork, and the paperwork to me is only a tool.
>
> Michael: It's one of many communication tools that we have. But effective stage management cannot be judged by how pretty the paperwork is or whether it fits this template or that template?
>
> Marich: And yet it is. Too much.

By breaking the production process into phases and offering up examples of best practice in terms of paperwork, these books offer a convenient overview that can easily be converted into a classroom curriculum and guidelines for assessment. These can form the basis of a stage management degree which is a new enough phenomenon that many of those interviewed, like Abel, remember them beginning.

> Abel: Okay, so now what we've got is a degree in stage management. And they all know how to do beautiful paperwork. They all know how to call a very clean show. And I'm not saying that isn't important. . . . But from what I am experiencing in interviewing the upcoming stage managers now that I'm an older person, it's that – a lot of us talk about this – there's a sense of having shut themselves off from the emotional and caring part of the performer.

Mont and Scribner were also among those who emphasized that the administration of a production is definitely an important aspect of stage management's role.

> Mont: It could translate into the way they do their administrative part of the job because there is no denying that a tremendous part of stage management is indeed administrative, regardless as to how artistic we want to, or do, feel.
>
> Scribner: I feel like the stage manager's ability to create timelines, and simply execute schedules can go a very long way in helping people feel supported. Very simple, organizational tools can help.
>
> Michael: All the things that you find in the textbooks are essential?
>
> Scribner: That's right. Running the meeting properly, remembering people's names, understanding how to read a ground plan, and creating a fabulously complex puzzle of a schedule. Those are all great, and they do have an impact on people's happiness, and their ability to do a good job, but they're really only a part. But some folks, I feel, forget that even though you can write an entire book on the duties and responsibilities of the stage manager, it will never fully encapsulate what the stage manager's job entails.

Features

Which aspects of stage management can the administrative model fully encapsulate? In other words, does this model have strengths beyond its predominance and ease of teaching, learning and measurement? I believe this model's strengths lie in explaining those aspects of stage management that are task-driven, process-oriented and that work well with a linear conception of the production process. For problems where there is one correct solution, and accuracy, perfection, predictability and repeatability are the objectives, the administrative model comes to the fore. Indeed, these are so strongly represented in the administrative model that these can be taken to be the model's assumptions of what represents effective stage management.

The stage management literature reviewed suggests that these assumptions are widespread. Perhaps the best example of this is *Stage Managing the Arts in Canada* which largely consists of checklists of tasks to be performed by the stage manager throughout the production process.[2] See, for example, the checklist of daily duties for stage managers during rehearsals.[3] Stern and Gold's first chapter emphasizes the administrative nature of the role, defining the role as being 'responsible for making the entire production run smoothly'.[4] *The Stage Manager's Handbook* consists mainly of the forms and the paperwork required for effective production administration.[5] The philosophy of *Stage Management and Theatre Administration* is suitably reflected in its title and in its opening statements that a 'good stage management team can turn a potentially embarrassing production into a smooth-running, trouble-free success'.[6] This emphasis on process resonated with Dyer as what was valued about stage management particularly early in her career.

> Dyer: Because when I first graduated it was all about, 'Just do what you're told. Keep your head down. Do your paperwork.' You know? 'Be a part of the process but, you know, be *this* part of the process.'

Implicit in this focus on effective administration is the goal of doing things *correctly*. The assumption that one of stage management's primary concerns involves creating and enforcing systems that constitute the 'correct' way of mounting a production is also made explicit by much of the stage management literature. Often these systems exhibit a policing and controlling function over the other people involved in the production: with the implicit message that the best way of mounting a production relies mainly on sticking to rules and schedules. In Stern and Gold's book this assumption is displayed from the contents page onward with chapter titles such as 'Scheduling and Company Rules', 'Keeping the Cast on Time', and 'Keeping the Show in Hand' being illustrative of this focus.[7] Menear and Hawkins claim, 'The stage management team . . . are the organizers who ensure that everybody and everything is in its *right* place at the *right* time [emphasis added].'[8] As Trott points out this is still a key aspect of stage management today.

> Michael: How do you know in that situation that you're doing a good job? How are you assessing your own work?
> Trott: I guess when all the things and all the people are in the right place at the right time.

Fazio asserts that '*perfection* is the difference between doing a good job and a great job' [emphasis added].[9] In the administrative model, 'perfection' is attained by doing things 'properly' and 'accurately' (similar to what Marich referred to as technical perfection in Chapter 5) which is a view Lawrence largely subscribes to.

> Lawrence: Early on when I was doing the National tour of *Annie*, I came as a replacement on that show. Each of the Stage Managers called the show slightly differently. They felt it differently. I came in as the PSM. I stopped all that. You are going to call the show exactly where the Lighting Designer wanted it and no place else. Because the Lighting Designer is the artist in charge of that. I feel strongly that in this way ours is not a creative job. Ours is an accuracy job.

While there is this constant focus on doing things 'properly', these titles also advocate for ensuring there is a degree of flexibility. For example, Menear and Hawkins warn that stage managers 'need to be adaptable, flexible and mentally alert. In the theatre things rarely go exactly as planned, and there will always be last-minute problems and changes to be coped with'.[10] This seems to be a paradox. If things are planned and executed perfectly, why are there always last-minute problems? Perhaps this paradox is why the stage management literature largely advocates that stage management is a highly 'practical' endeavour – one that is resistant to the theorization of academic study and learnt best by 'doing'.

This distrust of theory or academic study, emphasis on the practical and belief that stage management is best learnt by doing it are all aspects of administrative stage management which are present within the literature. One of the more potent examples is Stern and Gold's apology for departing from the practical, 'I'll take a few paragraphs here to throw in a little philosophy – the Gospel according to Stern – very little and not too deep.'[11] The philosophical statement that is such a departure from the practical concerns of the rest of the book is that 'play production is a process of compromise' and this concept is presented in order to give stage managers an insight into a very practical concern: 'the inevitable compromises are sometimes preceded by confrontations that disrupt rehearsals or preproduction work and/or demoralize cast members'.[12] This is followed by a very practical guide to resolving these confrontations so that any disruption is minimized. This 'process of compromise' assumes that the ideal production realizes a director's vision perfectly – Stern is equating collaboration with compromise and lists everyone involved in the production as being a potential source of compromises except for stage management (whose job is not to contribute to this process but to limit the damage it causes). This is echoed in the interviews by Lawrence's comment earlier and Trott's comment: 'I think there is an administrative role in that it's your job to make sure the work is as close to what the director wanted as possible.'

According to Stern and Gold it seems that stage managers' interest in the play production process is limited to the practical and procedural implications that need to be executed. There appears to be no awareness that a deeper understanding of the play production process could enhance stage managers' creative agency, collaborative ability or understanding of theatre. Other demonstrations of practicing stage managers' resistance to theory and the academic study of their role can be found in responses to

Stage Management

SM-Sim surveys conducted by McGraw.[13] This survey examines different trends amongst practicing stage managers every two years. While the survey tracks certain aspects longitudinally, each survey also explores some aspects of stage management practice as a special focus unique to that survey. In 2009 one of the special focus aspects concentrated on was education. The 2009 survey received these comments about stage management education from different respondents:

> MFAs are diplma [sic] mills so schools don't have to hire AEA SMs. Waste of time!
>
> Education gives you the nuts & bolts – but to really manage a stage takes a good mentor and the opportunity to practice the craft.
>
> An MFA in Stage Management stands for 'Moving Furniture Around'
>
> The best SM education is doing it! I find school to be a waste except for paperwork.[14]

This lack of intellectual rigour in, and distrust of, an educational program's suitability for stage management was also reflected in many of the interviews during discussions about training.

> Michael: My training was very much: 'this is *the* way that you stage manage a production'. There was no real allowance made or discussion made about how to adapt that range of skills to different production environments or different artistic personnel. Is that similar to your experience?
>
> Marich: Absolutely. The emphasis was: systems, processes, and administration – which are all essential.
>
> McMillan: As part of my training, I was told never to have an opinion as a stage manager. You don't have an opinion, and you don't talk about what you think about what's happening on stage or how people are acting.
>
> Franklin: But when I was [my students'] age, it wasn't like that. We didn't think about it, we just did it. I would have said 20 years ago, 'Just do it. It's just a set of skills that you have, and you just learn. It's just common sense.' I would never say that now, because it's so much more than what a first-year student thinks it is. You know, they think I'm going to say, 'Set up a props table, do some blocking, organize the schedule, now you're a stage manager.' And yes, that's all important, but it's how you do it, it's your interactions, it's the filling in the gaps.
>
> Michael: When I was trained consideration of the audience wasn't really talked about.
>
> Studham: It was talked about to a degree when I was trained in that we were told that in the moment things could go wrong, but we needed to problem-solve them in a way that the audience didn't know that something was wrong. So, we were trained in consideration of the audience. I think it's slightly changed how much we consider them.

Arguably, there is a link between this poor reputation of stage management education amongst stage managers and its bias towards administrative stage management. If stage management is essentially procedural and there is one correct way to stage manage a production, then there is limited advantage to learning it in a university setting over on-the-job training. Further, stage managers in this model are always caught in the paradox outlined earlier where they are trained to expect that there is a correct way of doing things, and to commit to perfect execution of these correct procedures, but that despite these efforts, they will have to be flexible and react to last-minute changes. This paradox leaves stage managers wondering if either their process or training, or that of their colleagues, is flawed. This is due to the limitations of the administrative model of stage management.

Limitations

These limitations seem to stem from the fact that because this model predominates it is either assumed or argued that it is the only model of stage management possible. The most obvious example of this is Fazio's claim that 'The SMs' work is neither technical nor artistic. There is no part of the job that requires the SMs to make a contribution in either area.'[15] This focus on the administrative aspects results in much that is part of stage management being left out of the discussion normally found in stage management literature. The chief omissions in this approach that the interviewees identified revolve around the character traits of stage managers and the nature of the collaboration stage managers have with the other theatre-makers involved.

From an administrative perspective the main character traits required of stage managers revolve around communication, organization and an ability to take responsibility while remaining what I shall term *invisible*. Stern and Gold's list of characteristics (good stage managers accept responsibility; keep their cool; keep their mouths shut, their eyes and ears open; think ahead; are considerate; keep their sense of humour; are organized and efficient; and are punctual and dependable) provides a typical example.[16] A further example of how they typify the administrative stage management model is found in their commentary on this list that the emphasis for the remainder of the book will be on the singular item of how a stage manager can be organized and efficient. This notion of *invisibility* is perhaps the site where the administrative model best demonstrates the need for alternative models of stage management.

Praising a stage manager's ability to remain invisible is not limited to Stern and Gold's advice that a good stage manager must keep their mouth shut. It can be seen in the comments earlier regarding training from McMillan (that she was trained that stage managers ought not to have opinions) and Studham (that the appropriate consideration of audiences for stage management revolved around how to solve problems without them noticing the problem or its solution). Trott also mentioned this assumption in the stage management literature.

> Trott: I think a classic stage management textbook would say the stage manager should almost be invisible, but I don't think they can be invisible.

Of course, the textbooks and training rooted in an administrative paradigm acknowledge that this is not literally remaining invisible or silent – they proceed to exhort stage managers to communicate effectively, efficiently and constantly. The goal, it seems, is for the stage manager to have as little creative agency as possible and where a stage manager may accidentally have an impact on the production that goes beyond facilitating others' work to cover it up as best as possible. This notion of the desirability of stage managers to remain invisible has merit. However, viewing stage management from a managerial or artistic perspective allows for more helpful descriptions of this objective as I propose later in this chapter, rather than the paradox of say nothing but communicate effectively.

The other reason this list of characteristics is problematic is because it leaves out some key components of what the interviewees identified as being the character traits required for stage managers. When asked to identify key qualities that make individuals likely to succeed in stage management, those interviewed all listed those traits that the administrative model of stage management values. Hawley's response 'I teach the stage management students here to base everything around good communication and good organization, because the two go hand in hand, and then everything else comes from that' serves as a good exemplar. Many of those interviewed, however, problematized the way the administrative paradigm values the adaptability of stage managers. They also advocated that stage managers must understand the artform they are working in. This trait is remarkably conspicuous in its absence in most treatments which view stage management as administration.

As outlined earlier, from an administrative perspective, stage managers are exhorted to remain flexible because, despite their best efforts, things may need to change. Many of those interviewed also listed flexibility of stage management as a necessary quality for effective stage management. However, this was presented in terms of being foundational in a stage manager's approach, with Freeburg's comment that 'Flexibility and adaptability, I think as a stage manager, the better you are at those skills the better off you will be' serving as a typical example. This notion of flexibility was not seen as something stage managers only relied upon to correct mistakes but integral throughout the process, with McMillan commenting, 'Being flexible. I think you have to be . . . A lot of stage management is about creative thought and about problem solving.' Rawlinson thought of this flexibility in opposition to being an administrator.

> Rawlinson: You have to . . . just be very, very flexible. You can't be at all set in your ways. We're not always right.
> Michael: So it sounds like you see stage managers as creative artists in much the same mould as most other people working in theatre. Is that fair to say?
> Rawlinson: Absolutely. As a stage manager you can help steer things and I think that it's a very flexible practice.
> Michael: Even those most formalized and formulaic stage management jobs, I would argue allow for and benefit from a creatively minded stage manager, is that something you would agree with?

> Rawlinson: Absolutely, and also if you're . . . creating art, to do that in a boring and mundane fashion, I don't see how you can do it. You then become an administrator.

In these descriptions a stage manager uses their flexibility and adaptability to drive their creativity and positive contribution to a production, rather than relying on them for course correction.

The interviews also revealed a set of key traits for stage managers that are often omitted completely by the administrative model. These revolve around the stage managers' relationship with, and understanding of, the material they are working on. Many of those interviewed suggested that caring deeply about the material and the process can greatly benefit stage managers. Dyer and Rawlinson argue that stage managers need to be passionate, with Dyer suggesting that this is one of the hardest things to teach (which may be why the administrative model omits it). Hawley, on the other hand, counsels that stage managers must retain some level of professional distance with their material to do their jobs effectively.

> Dyer: But I think the biggest thing I can't teach is just a passion for wanting to work in the artform. Quite frankly. You either do or you don't.
> Michael: And how does that express itself in students?
> Dyer: I think it comes down to how they talk about theatre. I think it comes down to if they see shows. Or if they actively go and actually watch theatre just in terms of having a toolkit for themselves to be able to be a part of the theatre community through just being an audience member. I think it's definitely something that I've seen a few students kind of develop. . . . But stage management is also that job . . . that if you don't love it you don't do it. Because when the times get tough . . . the passion for theatre, the passion for the project that you're working on, and the passion for the job is the thing that will get you through that moment. And if you don't have that you're just going to hit that wall and you're not going to be able to pull yourself out of it.

Rawlinson again eschews an administrative approach when she discusses passion and being a part of a creative process rather than 'being quiet in the corner' like stage managers 'used to be'.

> Michael: [You said] you've found a passion for theatre for young audiences, do you think that that helps as a stage manager? If you've got a passion for the work or the kind of work that you're working on? Or does it not matter?
> Rawlinson: No, it completely does. One of the things that I talked to the first years about is that stage managers are creative. We aren't the people with socks that match our waistcoats, as we used to be, in rehearsal rooms with big earrings. You know, being quiet in the corner!
> Michael: [Laughs]

Rawlinson: We're a part of the team . . . I think what's really important now is that we do a lot of work that anybody can access . . . and to enable those shows to happen, to be a part of that team, you have to be on board with the whole creative process.

And I think that's where stage managers have the real opportunity to be a part of the creative process and really enjoy their work a lot more and feel a real passion for it.

Hawley reminds us that stage managers must remain balanced and in control even when they are deeply moved by the pieces they are working on.

Michael: How sensitive to the material does a stage manager need to be?

Hawley: I think there are two camps here. I think personally, it can be quite dangerous for stage managers to get too personally and emotionally involved in a piece . . . because actually you need to be the voice of common sense. You need to be the one that keeps everybody else calm, and on a nice, straight, even line. So I think if you've got a stage manager who's getting too emotionally involved with something, then they're losing a bit of control.

Now another stage manager would probably disagree with me. They'll say, 'Well, how can you possibly enjoy something if you're not emotionally involved in it?' I understand that, but I think my argument is I still enjoy it, but I still am able to step back from it and go, 'Okay, that was a really intense rehearsal you had today, actually we're now going to the pub.' You know, 'that's the end of the working day. I've done what I needed to do.' . . . and cut off from it.

I think the danger is, particularly for young stage managers, if you get yourself so emotionally entangled with everything that it becomes unbalanced for you. You need to be grounded. You need to sort of go, 'Yes, I love my job, but ultimately it finishes at this time', whether it finishes at ten o'clock at night, midnight, four in the morning, sometimes, or five o'clock in the afternoon, it's still only a part of you. And there's another part of you that has to be able to flourish at the same time, in order for longevity of career.

Despite being absent from most descriptions of personal qualities that effective stage managers need in the administrative paradigm, throughout the interviews there was broad consensus that understanding the nature of the artform was crucial. Scribner, Mont and Freeburg made the point that knowledge of art and the human experience more broadly was also beneficial for stage managers. Scribner sees this as a reflexive process.

Michael: How necessary is it for stage managers to understand theatre and audiences?

Scribner: Oh yeah, imperative. You cannot be a quality stage manager if you don't understand the medium, you don't understand the artists within it, and you don't understand the material. So, you have to really be a student of the theatre history, and I would venture to say art history, theology, politics, the human experience. Psychology, relationships. It's not just theatre. It's all of the things that theatre ventures into, and there really is no place that theatre can't access. So, being a good stage manager is being a student of human experience, and being a constant consumer of news, and experience, and being a voracious reader. These are all things that have helped me become a better stage manager, and also I feel like theatre helps the other way, as well. Being invested in theatre encourages you to read more, to look outside of your experience, to connect with others, to study the world at large. It offers you a window. I have learned, through working on certain shows, the history of people that I would never have otherwise understood. People of different ages, and the experiences that they will have. Different genders, countries, origin stories, and these are all the avenues I have been able to walk because I have worked on a production and been a student of whatever it is that the author is hoping we will experience and question.

Mont also alludes to the breadth of artistic knowledge that is useful to stage managers.

Mont: I think stage managers, just like actors, need as broad a palate of human experience to inform their practice. You should take advantage of everything that life presents and, for example, go to museums. I've had the good fortune to stage manage for Trevor Nunn on more than one occasion. Well, how sad for me it would have been – and I probably wouldn't have had multiple occasions if it were true – if when Trevor starts talking about historical Shakespearian references I had no idea what he was talking about.

And I know now you can just go and run to your phone and Google anything, but it's just not the same. So I think it is very important to not only the personal experience of the stage manager, but also to allow them to bring the broadest scope of involvement and offering to a project. They need to know more than how to hang a leko. So whatever opportunity, so going to all different kinds of theatre and film and television, reading and travelling and just all the things that make a person a better person because theatre is the reflection of life. And if you choose as an individual to be a different kind of a stage manager and really just enjoy the administrative and technical aspect and feel that that's your job, well fine. I wouldn't diminish that. But I'm not sure I would hire you as an assistant because I want more in the room and I wouldn't work that way myself.

Freeburg reminds us that theatre is a composite artform and stage managers benefit from knowing how each of those component artforms speaks to an audience individually and when blended.

Michael: Do you think that it's essential for a theatre stage manager to know about theatre, and even more broadly than that art in general?

> Freeburg: I think it is. I think to be able to execute these different design elements, I think to be able to know artistically, this is what it wants to look like, this is the feeling that I want to have as an audience member. So my job, again, is to take those pieces, those paints on the palette, and swirl them in a way that gets the painting that the designers want. Sometimes part of the artistry of stage management is to know, on this night, these human actors on stage are a little bit different, so I have to call all the cues just slightly different to accommodate what they're doing, to still get the artistic experience that I want for the audience. You can tell when things aren't right. The lighting designer really wants you to call this light cue here. You know what it's supposed to do, and so part of the artistry to me is to say, 'I know what you want it to do, I'm going to call it on this word. Let me just call it there and see what you think. If it is what you want, then that's what we'll do. If not, I'll go back to calling it where you were.'
>
> Michael: What we're trying to do is get what you want.
>
> Freeburg: Exactly. My job is to make your art look beautiful, and I'm trying to execute your art. Usually, they'll say, 'You were right, that's what it's supposed to look like.' If I don't have a general aesthetic of what the play wants to look like I couldn't do that. I think the more you know about that, the more effective you are as a stage manager.

This knowledge enhances stage managers' abilities to work within their artform, on the material at hand and with their fellow theatre-makers. The type of collaboration discussed here is of a very different quality from the typical approach we saw from the administrative paradigm which views collaboration suspiciously as a source of compromise, and the stage managers' role to ensure such compromises and delays are minimized.

This creative approach to collaboration is the other major element which is missing from the administrative paradigm of stage management. When stage managers and other theatre-makers view the function of stage management as being purely administrative, in opposition to a creative role, it can lead to a lack of respect, as Hobden points out.

> Hobden: It astounds me when I see people that have a little 'us and them' attitude. Because I think this is not an industry to have 'us and them'. The best theatre is one that is completely collaborative.

The flexibility and adaptability required for stage management to commit to building systems appropriate for effective collaboration was emphasized by many of those interviewed. McMillan and Mont highlight this as a distinction from the administrative approach.

> McMillan: I think a textbook can give you a template, but I think it's the personalities that are in the room that will dictate how you as a project manager or production manager or stage manager then manages whatever's happening. Absolutely.

> Mont: From an administrative perspective, there are similarities in every room . . . That being said, every show is different and the personalities that make that show happen are different. And you simply can't run the room, so to speak, in the same manner with different people. . . . There is no such thing as a cookie cutter approach, I don't think there is.

Freeburg makes the point that effective collaboration even within the same team demands flexibility and adaptability from stage management on a day-to-day basis. She regards this as part of the artistry of stage management.

> Michael: It's not like there's one ideal way a room needs to be run? That changes?
> Freeburg: Every director, every process, every group of people, on a day-to-day basis it can change. Theatre is peopled with people who have very different backgrounds . . . but who are all incredibly passionate about what they do. If . . . one of them is having a bad day, you're going to know. How do you adjust how that room feels, as opposed to the next day when everybody's having a great day? I think that is absolutely part of the artistry.
>
> There's a basic way I like to have my room feel, but it depends on who the director is, and who's in the cast, and what the time commitment is, and how emotionally heavy the show is. All of those factors come into the room every day.

Simpson discusses how building relationships that operate on many levels is key. He also discusses the potential for richer collaboration if all theatre-makers recognized that stage management's role is broader than administrative service to other theatre-makers.

> Simpson: I build relationships between myself and the cast and the director. Nick Hytner in the introduction to Maccoy's *Essentials of Stage Management* talks of the stage manager being everybody's best friend.[17] In some ways that's true but I think he rather undermines that relationship because it's much much more than that. It's PA at one level, it's general manager at another level, it's assistant director at another level and it's all of these things and they're rolled up into this because you are, in some ways the director's eyes, ears, nose and throat. You are everything because without you the director's work on that production could go for nothing. So, you have to recognize that what you do as a stage manager in terms of the relationships you build and the communication you maintain is central to that work being realized in the way that the director and the designers' creative visions require.
>
> I think there is a balance to be struck between the creative and the administrative. In the same way as not all of the work of the director is creative and, of course, not all the work that stage managers do is creative, but lots of it is. We need to recognize that as stage managers, but equally we need to encourage

others to recognize it as well so that the perception of stage management being purely a service industry is defeated. That perception is not great for us but equally it's not great for everyone else because if they don't actually fully understand what we do and what our impact is then they can't actually respond effectively to what we are asking of them. So understanding why we're asking something is vital.

The administrative model captures much of *what* stage managers are expected to do. It is unsurprising perhaps that much of stage management literature and education focuses on these aspects. When this model's predominance implies, or some of its advocates argue, that this is the only paradigm appropriate for describing stage management practice its limitations can cause problems. I have identified two alternative models that are present within the interview material.

While sometimes harder to find, evidence for these two models is also present within the stage management literature, often lying latently, obscured by the weight of the administrative assumptions. This is not to suggest those administratively focused books aren't useful to stage managers. No book can hope to capture everything. I have chosen to reference the titles included in this book, even those that I suggest have limitations, because they have been the most useful to me during my stage management and teaching career.

The two alternative models considered here attempt to address some of the limitations of the administrative model. Of course, they have limitations too. As many of the interviewees pointed out earlier, a lot of stage management is administrative in nature and the administrative model is predominant because of its accuracy and usefulness. I propose that stage management as *management* may be the most effective model for describing *how* stage managers do things, and that viewing stage management as *art* may be the most effective model for describing *why* stage managers do things.

The managerial model

If the chief tension in the administrative model of stage management can be seen between the competing needs for accuracy and flexibility, then the chief tension in the management paradigm could be described as the competing methodologies of business and art. In both models, resolving these tensions is not formulaic, and the resolutions tend to occur at points of intersection and overlap than on either end of the spectrum.

This model views stage management as a particular instance of organizational management. It encourages stage managers to view themselves as managers, filling in the gaps of the administrative model by learning management theory which benefits from a much more extensive literature than the field of stage management. It asks stage managers to consider their practice with regards to concepts such as how they exercise power and the impact they have on morale.

Many of those interviewed discussed these aspects of stage management. For Passaro and Maccoy managerial stage management was their main paradigm for conceptualizing stage management practice.

> Michael: You often describe a stage manager as a hybrid CEO-COO of a business. Is that fair to say?
>
> Passaro: Most working stage managers would agree with this to some degree if not entirely. Because as the productions have become not only more technically complicated, they've become more expensive. And the lead producers of these shows are very often from environments that are completely outside the theatre world. Same with the creative teams: they can come from many other disciplines. All of this means that the expectation now is a level of leadership, management, executive technique and skill that wasn't ever part of the tacit 'mentor/apprenticeship' relationship that has existed for years for stage managers.
>
> Also, Broadway in particular has become a global brand – our shows like *Wicked* and *Jersey Boys* and *Mamma Mia* and *Phantom* and all those very, very long-running shows have really become our version of a Fortune 500 companies – and as such require a level of management and leadership expertise that you wouldn't necessarily get by having somebody just pass it down to you.
>
> Michael: Another thing that I really liked in *Essentials of Stage Management* is that management seems to be central in the approach that you take.[18] And that it's about leadership, collaboration, managing people, and communication; that hasn't changed I presume?
>
> Maccoy: No. For me that is the really interesting bit. It is the fascination of different people who you work with, how you manage them, and how you have to approach people differently. You talk in terms of communication but I think in terms of actually managing.

While stage management involves managing lots of different resources and processes, the area of management which is central to the practice is human resource management. For many of those interviewed how to manage people was *the* key aspect of stage management practice. These comments from Mont and Passaro highlight this:

> Mont: I think that managing people is the key element of stage management. And by managing people that's in a broad sense, you can specify the different pieces of it.
>
> Passaro: When you think of stage management and the word 'management', to some practitioners and to some outside of the field, it tends to focus on the technical side of things. Which is no doubt a major pillar and foundation of our work, but I have found since I started working as a stage manager that the technical area tends to – not necessarily take care of itself but become something that becomes routine in a way – especially over the course of a long run on Broadway. But no matter where you are employed as a stage manager, I have found that the

technical issues usually aren't the primary focus for stage managers. Either in the rehearsal process or in maintaining the run of a show, what becomes the primary focus is the people management.

Much of the discussion around management centred on different management styles. Livoti and Passaro both discussed the need for striking a balance between a hard-nosed business approach and a softer people-centred artistic approach.

> Livoti: For example, let's say, I'm going to put a new Phantom into the show. Well, the actor playing Christine, and the understudies, are going to have a long stretch of rehearsals for several weeks. Before I put up the official notice, I'll seek out the women playing Christine and say, 'Just so you know, I'm putting something up on the board. There's going to be a lot of rehearsal for you, and it's going to be these weeks. I'm going to try and spread it out between all of you, but just be prepared. Schedule things in your life before or after then.' And I find that goes a long way.
>
> And for the person leaving the show, it's an emotional experience for them. So, before I put that sign up, I'll tell them 'Just so you know I'm putting up the notice to say that we're announcing your final performance.' So, they're ready for 25 people to come to them and say, 'I'm so sorry you're leaving.' I feel like it's a professional courtesy to them to say, 'I realize this is going to be hard for you, but I need to tell people, so it's going to happen.'
>
> Michael: It is a professional courtesy, and you're doing it because you're a nice person, and you care for the people that you work with. But also, you're doing it because that's what's best for the show?
>
> Livoti: But not everyone takes that approach. They say, 'Okay I'm not going to get involved in the day-to-day. And you're a professional, and I expect you to understand that' . . . They're the type of person who has the managerial attitude of: 'it's a job, it's a business. You come in and you do your job, and you're a professional. And however the chips fall, I'm going to do my job by saying, "This is what's happening." And it isn't my problem or my responsibility to manage your emotions, or to make you feel better about something.'
>
> And the flip side is a more hands-on approach that does deal with the emotional aspect of it. So, I think that's for me the difference in the type of person, the type of leadership personality. It's just different management styles.

Passaro discusses the appropriate management style in terms of the balance required in managing a creative process which has the demands of an industrial one.

> Passaro: But I think in terms of stage managing, you're managing something that is incredibly fragile, you know. And you look at these big musicals you have a sense of just the machinery, the gears, the girders, the steel, all kind of grinding away to present the experience. But when you actually think about it as an

experience, or how the people who are presenting that experience relate to one another, it's really as fragile as like a Fabergé egg. And I think it's that dichotomy that you have to be keenly aware of as a stage manager. Because the actress could be standing out there belting out 'Let It Go' – a character in charge of her own destiny – but if she's having vocal issues, or problems at home, or whatever challenges, you have to be aware of how to take care of those people in a way that they can do what they're supposed to do.

Michael: Yeah. . . . That fragility I think is part of the magic. It's part of the liveness of the experience. So, you can't manage the fragility away.

Passaro: You can't manage the fragility away, but you can't completely disregard the fact that it could be a threat. People sometimes kind of frown when I make the comparisons to working at McDonald's and Broadway, and that you are working in some sense on a factory floor. But I don't think you can completely disregard that. We can't completely disregard that *Wicked* or *Phantom* tonight has to feel, taste, and smell like it does tomorrow in some sense, whether it's the understudy or whether there's technical issues, whatever. You have to give the experience that people are expecting – and they know what that is even if they have never seen the show before.

Michael: Yeah! People have bought their hamburger, they need their hamburger. Like you said, it's managing the dichotomy. You can't just be all fragile and precious. There's still a show that needs to be delivered, and people have got to eat their hamburger.

Passaro: Exactly, exactly right!

One aspect of management style that came up in many interviews was the relationship that stage managers have with power. Because stage managers are ultimately responsible for a production and are often the final arbiter of decisions during a performance season, it can be tempting for some stage managers to wield this power with an authoritarian style. Lawrence spoke against this tendency.

Lawrence: I don't like road Nazis. I don't like it at all. When I was directing *Sunset Boulevard* on tour, I won't say names, but I had a difficult Stage Manager on that. I let him go because he treated the company so badly. I don't like it.

Michael: Sometimes I've had student Stage Managers who think that the job is about power and about being authoritarian, and they tend not to survive very long in, either in the course, or either in the industry if they manage to get through the course somehow. As a Stage Manager, I think that would be the worst position to kind of have that attitude towards the company?

Lawrence: As far as I'm concerned it is.

Dyer suggests where this tendency comes from, especially amongst student stage managers.

Dyer: I think the position of power comes because they are privy to those conversations that perhaps other people aren't privy to. They are in the room when sensitive work is being made. They are expected to know the ins and outs of every single detail of their show. And they are in charge of discipline, and they are in charge of making things run on time, and they are in charge of what happens on a daily basis. For students in particular, when they're suddenly in control, and have to find their management style, it becomes all about them. This sense of, 'Well, *I'm* running it now', can sometimes overshadow the needs of what the show necessarily are.

Simpson describes the balance between being in charge and in service of the production's needs as a duality stage managers need to be aware of.

> Simpson: There's a number of dualities I recognize within stage management. One of them is the balance that we strive to strike between – it's what I call the PH balance – it's the balance between power and humility. I'm in charge of this process because I'm in service to it.

For Maccoy effective people management revolves around understanding the needs of the different people involved and taking the time to get to any underlying issues.

> Maccoy: I don't believe particularly that 'difficult people' exist. I think there's always an underlying issue, that is causing somebody to be 'difficult' and I like to try and get to the bottom of it, I think that that is really important.
> Michael: You mentioned a stage manager needs to be sympathetic to actors and what they're going through but that would probably extend to the rest –
> Maccoy: Oh yeah I think so, everybody. Definitely. I mean all the different personalities and roles and what they're doing.

Lawrence's advice is to adopt a management style that increases ownership of decisions across the company as this will enhance their morale.

> Lawrence: One of the things Nichols taught me is that when he's directing, he comes in with very specific ideas but he doesn't let the company know. He lets the company feel that he is slogging through it the same way they are. So, it's a mutual discovery as opposed to his teaching the company something.
>
> It really helped me. If we feel as a company, 'Well, what do you guys think? What's the best way to solve this? If you were doing this, what would you do?' Even though I already know how it's going to come out sometimes. Letting people feel they are a part of the process is the most valuable thing to do. It gives them a sense of ownership, a sense of bonding and it increases morale.

Evidence of the managerial stage management paradigm is latently acknowledged even in the most administratively focused stage management books. Unsurprisingly, since management is a field with a much larger publication history, much of the existing literature refers stage managers to seek out further publications. Stern and Gold serve as typical examples of the approach when they state after the brief section dedicated to 'communication/management skills' and 'effective committee work', 'These few ideas about communication and management skills are an eyedropper's worth in an ocean of possible self-improvement.'[19] Pallin's chapter on management techniques also is rooted in the administrative paradigm covering 'systems management', 'points of order' to keeping various spaces at their most efficient and 'managing time' in more detail than 'managing others'.[20] There are signs that as stage management practice increasingly acknowledges this model, so too does the literature. For example, Maccoy's book came out in 2004 after the first editions of both Stern's (1974) and Pallin's (2000). Maccoy's second chapter, entitled 'the stage manager as manager' concludes with the claim that 'The successful stage manager must be good with people; they must be able to be assertive, yet to empathise with and be able to nurture, the creative process . . . Above all, they must be good managers'.[21] Perhaps the most useful approach to management for stage managers today comes from Porter and Alcorn's much more recent (2019) book. In it management style is considered as part of the ethical framework adopted by stage managers.[22] The authors introduce their readers to (and encourage them to read further about) utilitarianism, the ethics of care[23] and servant leadership[24] as being particularly appropriate. This last approach resonates with Simpson's notion of 'the PH balance' noted earlier.

One of the chief limitations discussed with the administrative model was that it limited the collaborative capacity of stage management from other theatre-makers by separating them from a creative function and placing them in the position of policing the decisions made. All of the interviewees who view stage management through the paradigm of management have advocated for a methodology of stage management which narrows this distinction between stage managers and others. They argue for a management style which seeks to empower team members, shares a common purpose and increases morale. One which calls for collaboration and for all those involved to wield their power and expertise to the service of what is best for the production. This, of course, begs the questions what is best for the production and how does a stage manager decide. From an administrative perspective, the answer to both of those questions usually is whatever is closest to what the director wants and is achievable within the current process and resources. In terms of a purely managerial perspective, the answer would be whatever makes the team most productive. While these are both useful perspectives, I suggest these questions are ultimately artistic and the answers revolve around considering whatever gets us closest to the desired experience for the audience.

In truth, for the vast majority of decisions a stage manager makes all three perspectives would yield the same outcome. This partly explains why the administrative and managerial models are so useful. While the distinction may be nuanced, I argue that the best resolution of the tensions between accuracy and flexibility, between authority and service and the problem of how to most effectively enhance collaboration requires an artistic model of stage management.

Stage Management

The artistic model

An artistic model would regard stage management as a conceptually reflexive and creative artform. In this model the 'correct' procedural approaches are contextually specific and open to change throughout the production process. An artistic approach to stage management would be one which embraces creative flexibility and empowers stage managers to anticipate and participate in the process, rather than viewing changes as problems 'to be coped with'[25] as the administrative model holds. Such a model would run counter to the predominant administrative model's implications (and some of its advocates explicitly arguing, like in the earlier Fazio quote) that stage management is not artistic.

In the interviews there was much greater acceptance that there is an artistry involved in stage management than in the literature. However, the power of the administrative model can be seen in the reluctance of many theatre-makers, stage managers included, to call stage managers artists. Thus, often these discussions revolved around the extent to which stage management could be considered artistic. In those conversations where the artistry of stage management was explored further, two central nexus points emerged. The stage managers interviewed were most likely to consider their practice artistic when discussing their choices regarding how to adapt their communication and as the directness of the relationship between their choices and the audience's experience increases.

Artistry

In considering the question of whether stage management is artistic, it would help to have some common ground about what constitutes art. Like most terms in the humanities, the precise definition of art is complicated, and I did not spend any time during the interviews trying to define it, leaving it up to the interviewees to decide what the term meant for them. From their answers, they seem to concur with my preferred definitions from Dewey who regards art as a distillation of experience, commenting, 'In short, art, in its form, unites the very same relation of doing and undergoing, outgoing and incoming energy that makes an experience to be an experience'[26] and Langer's 'pattern of sentience'.[27] Both titles taught me a lot about art and helped me gain confidence as describing myself as an artist as a stage manager.

Studham establishes the parameters of the discussion and acts as a useful summary of some common responses. There is a reluctance as stage managers, partly based on our training in the administrative model, to call ourselves artists. However, there is far less resistance to the notion that stage managers apply that training in a creative fashion.

> Michael: We've spoken before about the artistry of stage management and whether or not people are comfortable with the term artist as a stage manager. What's your take on that?

Studham: Look, it's a really interesting discussion. And my take on the word artist? Or whether stage managers are creative?

Michael: Well, they're two different questions, right? So, answer both of them now that you've posed both of them.

Studham: Thanks! So, when I was trained, we were taught we were the organizers.... And we *are* the organizers. However, you can creatively organize. There is a lot of creativity that goes into how you're going to schedule, how you're going to make everything work, how you're problem-solving to support the production itself. So, what we're doing is supporting the production in different ways.

And so, I believe that stage managers are creative and I believe that they are artists or can be artists, depending on what their definition of artist is. For myself, having it drummed into my head all those years that you're an organizer, I don't know if I would say I'm an artist, but I definitely feel that I'm part of the creative team.

Michael: Great! I think you've answered both questions in one answer.

Studham: And that's not to say that anyone who says 'I'm an artist' is incorrect. Absolutely, you're an artist. It depends on how you're defining it. I guess in my mind I think of a visual artist, but what we do is artistic.

Evans also likes to make a distinction between being artistic and being creative and echoes the assumption that a visual artist is the archetypal version of an artist.

Michael: Another slightly contentious word that I've been bandying about in these interviews is artist. How do you and your students sit with this term, artist? Would you regard yourself as an artist? Would you regard your students as artists?

Evans: I prefer the word, creative. Within our program, we teach design as well. At the first class I sit down with the sound design students and I say, 'Hands up, all of those who think that they are not creative.' And a majority of them put their hand up.

And I say, 'Is that because at some point, a parent, a teacher has told you that you can't draw?' And most of them say 'Yes.' Then I say, 'Okay, you don't have to draw to be creative.'

Scribner was comfortable with viewing stage managers as artists, seeing the artistic in the most administrative of tasks and arguing that stage managers who view this work like this can be more fulfilled as a result.

Michael: It sounds like you are comfortable with stage managers being called an artist?

Scribner: Yes. I don't think that all stage managers are artists, and I don't think that a stage manager has to be an artist, but I am an artist, and I believe that all stage managers can be artists. So, there's also so many different types of jobs we can have, and I have seen stage managers work corporate events as an artist. And

I have seen stage managers work on Shakespearean revivals of Shakespearean shows that are so deep, and beautiful, and they are not artists, because the way they view themselves is not as an artist. It's up to you how you want to portray yourself, and also experience your job, I think.

Michael: So for you, being an artistic stage manager, what does that mean?

Scribner: Because it's about a sense of self, and a way of being, which manifests in how you speak to people, and how you feel about your role in calling a show, your role in creating a schedule. I think there is an art to creating a schedule, not just in how it looks, or how it flows, but actually in knowing what is needed for each moment.

Michael: So, if I'm understanding you correctly, even those stage managers who don't describe themselves as artists still need to understand the artistry of those around them, and the artform of theatre in order to be effective?

Scribner: The artform, yeah. I think I have a very broad kind of definition of artist which allows me to embrace all of these ideas about how a stage manager could be an artist. I don't think it is undercutting a stage manager's abilities to call them an artist. I don't think artist is a dirty word. I think that being an artist is understanding the process and being an integral part of the process. We are not outside of the process, we are within the process, and that's what makes us artists. If we are so removed from it that we don't see ourselves as an artist, and we think of it as just a job, we're missing a big part of what we can take home from the job. I feel like I am so lucky to have a job that offers me an intellectual and artistic fulfilment.

Marich suggests that for practicing stage managers in Australia today it still may be risky for stage managers to view themselves as creative or artistic. Even in this landscape, though, there is some concession given that calling the show may be a creative act.

Marich: There are risks with making creative observations and of making creative offers as an Australian stage manager. So, when you ask me if I think I'm a more effective stage manager because of my eclectic creative background. . . . Perhaps I should never have become a stage manager or maybe I could've pursued a more – what's deemed to be a more – creative role. But I think there is room for creative thinking within a stage management role.

Michael: In your experience, is that an unusual approach to stage management?

Marich: I get the feeling that it is. But you still do need to have some creative sensibility in calling or operating cues with respect to timing and rhythm, that kind of stuff. That's still important.

Michael: So even in the least creative manifestations of stage management, there's still an expectation that stage managers have a sensitivity to what theatre is and how theatre talks to an audience?

Marich: I think so, but I'm not convinced that all directors understand that. And I certainly think in this day and age where everything is becoming more and more automated, I think that feeds into the perception that stage managers aren't creative.

For Dyer, the recognition of stage manager's artistic contribution is growing in Australia. The most overtly creative act of stage managers of calling the show is highlighted again in this extract as she compares the stage manager's art to that of an actor.

> Dyer: I think the way stage management is viewed, in terms of it not being just a facilitator but actually being an artistic practice is definitely changing. Because while we do a lot of scheduling, admin work, supporting, making sure people have what they need, actually, a lot of times if I'm calling or operating a show, the rhythm of the show is up to me.
> If I wait an extra beat to trigger that cue that changes the dynamic of the show. That's about being so involved in the artistic process of the show and knowing what the director's vision of the show is to make those decisions about the rhythm of the show on any given performance and responding to the audience. The same way an actor responds to the audience, I think stage management needs to respond to the audience. I'll just let this applause go for a little bit longer or, actually, there was no laugh there so I really have to move this along. We get to dictate, in some respects, how that show works on a nightly basis. And I think stage management is shifting more into being an artistic collaborator rather than just a facilitator and doing what you're told.

For Trott, too, the similarity between the artistry of acting and stage managing was clear.

> Trott: I guess it's as creative or it's as artistic as an actor is artistic. You're still just a cog in someone else's vision, to some degree. There's definitely creativity, and nuance, and sensitivity in how you get the things in the right place at the right time.
> Michael: Actors are often described as interpretive artists. And I think that stage management is an interpretive artform as well.
> Trott: Stage management is a somewhat interpretive art. Yes. Definitely.

According to Simpson, the divide between 'the creatives' and the rest of a production team is a false one. Similarly, Simpson minimizes the distinction between the art of the stage manager and a visual artist and argues that all artists are interpretive artists.

> Simpson: No one particular piece of this process is necessarily creative in its own right. A lot of the work of the director is not creative per se in what we understand by that term but then what is the definition of creativity? For me it is about problem-solving. Because in any other discipline, in any other industry,

creativity is defined as problem-solving or vice versa. Problem-solving is the most creative activity within any organization, any other industry. Isn't that what stage managers do on a daily basis?

Carl Sagan was famously quoted as saying, 'In order to make an apple pie from scratch you must first create the universe.' We are not talking about creativity as starting something from scratch. None of us can. We can only use what's available to us at the time and the same is as true of fine art as it is with theatre-making. In that I have a palette, and this is the palette I'm going to use. I didn't create this palette. This palette was given to me by the planet. And I'm using this and I'm now going to move these colours around in order to create something fresh. I'm seeing it with fresh eyes, but those eyes are not creating it.

Even scheduling is creative because you're making it work for everybody. And you're gathering time slots and you're moving them around so that actually it's like a painting. You're just moving paint around on a canvas in exactly the same way you're making the picture.

However, the medium of a stage manager's art is less discernible and this, I contend, plays into the sense of invisibility being a virtue for stage managers. Simpson here points out that the invisibility of a stage manager is celebrated within the management paradigm as well.

Michael: I think where the analogy falls down is that the medium of our artform, our creativity, and our problem-solving isn't as tangible as that.

Simpson: It isn't. It's that old adage about no one sees good management. You only see bad management. I use an example in class about if you see a production as a problematic and then you consider that when the lighting designer comes in to light that production they're solving that problematic: 'How do I ensure that this production can be seen?' . . . And light is the medium of the lighting designer.

Then you can start to expand that thinking and you start, 'Okay what's the function of the stage manager or the stage management within that problematic?' It's to solve 'these problems' which are part of the creative process. Now, the thing about that is, as you previously said, this is all behind the scenes as far as the audience is concerned.

The part of the problem that the audience sees is the set, the actors, the lighting, the costumes. The bit of the problem they don't see is the bit at the back of the washing machine. It doesn't mean it's not important because the washing machine wouldn't work with all that wiring at the back.

Communication design

From my analysis of the interviews, I contend that what Simpson would call the 'problematic' stage managers are trying to solve is 'How do I ensure the information about this production is shared?' In other words, the *medium* of the art of stage management is *communication*. Stage managers design the communication for a production in much the same way that lighting designers design the light.

All of those interviewed discussed the importance of communication to stage management. Of course, communication is at the heart of the administrative and managerial models as well. From an administrative perspective, communication relies on structuring information so that it can be transmitted efficiently, reliably and predictably. Pallin typifies the approach with the claim that 'to communicate effectively is to pass on all information as quickly and accurately as possible with the least amount of negative interaction'.[28] From a management perspective, communication skills are how you share purpose, enhance morale and support effective collaboration. Both models view stage management at the hub of the communications wheel.[29] But this is too passive an analogy for the artistic model, which would instead cast the stage manager in the role of an unorthodox wheelwright actively building the relationship between the hub and the spokes in a fluid and reflexive manner. Precisely how a stage manager designs this communication is taken up in Part 2 of this book.

When talking about what is artistic in stage management, the interviewees emphasized these reflexive adaptations of their communication. Here Scribner talks about the artistic process involved in compiling the rehearsal report which, on the surface, appears to be one of the most administrative tasks of stage management.

> Scribner: But as stage manager you need to understand how the process unfolds for each person and speak their language. To be able to hear, and assess what is going on for each person, and then be able to communicate other people's needs back to them. The idea of a rehearsal report, for instance, is such a direct and simple, clear, daily duty, but there's so much more to it. Because you aren't just disseminating information in a 'Just the facts, ma'am,' way.
>
> You're also aware that different people are reading it, looking for different things. So, how you word it is vital. What order you put things in, how you sparingly needle, and follow-up through the report is important . . . So, I like to think that the report looks very simple from the outside, but has a lot of layers from the inside, and there is an art to communicating in the report.

Scribner's reference to speaking the language of different people relates to the translation objective of stage management detailed in Chapter 7. These adaptations often represented departures from an administratively driven model that values efficiency, as Abel suggests, 'You can be giving the same general note to three different actors in three different ways. Again, I feel like that is an artform. I really do.'

Freeburg also thought the adaptation of stage management communication was central to its artistry.

> Michael: That's a theme that's running through these interviews. That stage management is adapting your communication style and that's really the artistry involved in stage management. Is that something you would agree with?

> Freeburg: Absolutely.
>
> Michael: And we need to know enough about everyone involved in it, so that even if we're giving everyone exactly the same piece of information we can think through how and when do I give it to them in the best way possible for *them*?
>
> Freeburg: Absolutely, yeah. There's always that one person that needs to think it's their idea, so how do you pitch it so that they come to the conclusion that you want them to? Then there's this department that wants to know why you made all these decisions like this. Then there's this person who just wants to know what the information is in the fewest words possible. You may have to adapt the same piece of information three or four different ways to get everyone to come to the same conclusion. Yeah, I absolutely think adaptable communications is huge.

Scribner points out that the reason why stage managers adapt their communication is to help the production.

> Scribner: But depending on the person and the situation, I will be communicating completely differently, and it's that flexibility, adaptability . . . that allows any good stage manager to respond in the most helpful way. Because it's not just about being clear, it's not just about being direct. It's about being helpful, and sometimes being helpful is not being the most direct. It's letting other people figure it out for themselves.
>
> Michael: So, you're constantly designing the communications based on each individual company member's needs?
>
> Scribner: Correct.
>
> Michael: You're going to do what is most helpful for the production?
>
> Scribner: Correct, and there are times when that feels inefficient, and sometimes inconvenient for me. And that doesn't matter because it's actually about the bigger picture. That doesn't bother me. I know that's the game. The game is, make everyone feel important, get things done, and do whatever it takes.
>
> Ultimately, it is all our job. Everything falls on our shoulders to make sure that the show is smoothly run, and that everyone backstage is content and able to do their best, and that the production is the best experience for an audience that we can make.

In this last statement, Scribner neatly sums up the goal of stage management communication from the perspective of each of the three models. The administrative goal is to ensure 'the show is smoothly run'. Making sure that everyone is 'content and able to do their best' is the goal of the communication from a management perspective. From an artistic perspective, the reason why stage managers adapt their communication is to ensure 'that the production is the best experience for an audience'.

Audience experience

This notion of the audience's experience being central to stage management artistry recurred in two common themes throughout the interviews. The first theme was stage management trying to make decisions that were best for the show overall. The second theme was the ease with which stage management's involvement with calling a show was identified as their most artistic contribution to a production. Both of these themes warrant further exploration.

Many of those interviewed expressed ideas similar to Scribner's comment earlier regarding behaving in ways that are the most helpful for the production which, ultimately, is about the audience's experience. The most common phrasing in the interviews is that stage managers make decisions based on what they regard as 'best for the show'. As a typical example, Mont said, 'Doing what's best for the show is the key [to effective stage management] and that is a simple statement that I think is quite easy to understand even though it's going to have different definitions in almost every case.' When expressing this notion, the concept of the audience's experience is usually implied, as in the case of this comment from Freeburg:

> Michael: How do we make those choices about prioritizing our time?
> Freeburg: What is best for the show. Sometimes it may not be best for the cast, but it's best for the show, as an overall entity . . . I think our job, too, is to keep an eye on the whole thing. The different designers are looking at their part of the product, and how their part of the product fits in with the whole. My job is to look at the whole, everybody involved in it, and the thing itself.

Equating what is best for the show with the audience's experience often required me to explicitly label it as such. Typical examples can be seen in the following comments from Abel and Evans:

> Michael: What's the arbiter there? Is it what you determine is going to be the best for the production? And therefore good for an audience?
> Abel: Always. Always. Yeah. I mean, listen, that's my main goal always.
>
> Evans: So, when a designer says, 'I need you to do this', they [automation engineers without theatre training] go, 'I can't'. The designer says, 'But I need it to do this because of this, this and this', and they just don't get it. But if somebody has got a theatre training, they'll come in there and say, 'Right, let's see how we can make it do that.' So, it makes a difference.
> Michael: Or, 'We can't do that, but we can have a similar impact on the audience by doing it this way.'
> Evans: You said it, yes. Exactly that, yes.

When I equated the concept of best for the show with what is best for the audience's experience, most of the interviewees agreed with the concept. I suspect stage management training, predominantly in the administrative model, with its concept of the invisible, unartistic stage manager who is nevertheless responsible for the whole production leads neatly to the concept of doing what is best for the production. This leaves implicit that 'the creatives' know and create the audience experience and we as stage managers need only serve these creatives and their production without needing to worry about the audience directly.

An artistic model of stage management argues that the impact of stage management's decisions on an audience should be their central concern and that it is the audience's experience which is the determiner of what is best for the production, not the experience of the stage manager's collaborators. Like with the managerial model, the evidence for an artistic model in the literature has grown recently. For example, Pallin has included a new chapter in the latest edition entitled 'creativity in stage management' which aims 'to cultivate a new climate of understanding which places communication, problem-solving, creative and soft skills at the heart of the stage management experience'.[30] Vitale in 2019 advises that 'when you can see how you have impacted an audience, cherish it, because at the end of the day that is why we do the job'.[31] The area of stage management practice that has the most direct impact on the audience is the calling of cues during a performance.

This is because the calling of cues is the aspect of stage management that is most directly linked to the audience's experience. More evidence that recent stage management literature is increasingly acknowledging the creative and artistic aspects of the role concerns this specific aspect of cue calling. In Fazio's second edition the claim 'The SM's work is neither technical nor artistic' still exists, but where in the first edition this claim was strengthened by the subsequent words, it is now considerably tempered by 'though knowledgeable in both areas. . . . The SM's greatest artistic contribution to the show comes during each performance as they call the cues for the show.'[32] The artistry involved in cue calling was most commonly referred to in the interviews as the distinction between doing it correctly (from an administrative model's perspective by calling a cue where it appears in the prompt copy) and doing it well (fulfilling the artistic intention of the cue by giving the audience the desired experience).

Abel was emphatic about the importance of this distinction:

Michael: So, to your point, calling and decking a show, to my mind, there's a difference between doing it clean and doing it well.
Abel: Yes. Oh Absolutely. Absolutely. Absolutely. Yeah. Absolutely!
Michael: If you do it clean –
Abel: Terrific, right? Okay so it doesn't have any mistakes. That's an excellent point. And so there we go again: you have to know what that director and that designer want.
Michael: Because you can do it on that word because that's what the prompt copy says . . .
Abel: Or you can feel it and do it well! I agree with you.
Michael: Because if you know that the lighting designer or the director wants it there to have this impact on the audience.
Abel: When you're saying like a clean show and a good show, you're absolutely right with that. Because you have to know the show. For example, you have to know like 'Oh, so-and-so is on this evening.' So, if you know that, you know that you've got to change this cue a little bit here for this.

Michael: Yeah. And you can't record that in a prompt . . .
Abel: . . . copy anywhere. That's right.
Michael: It's understanding the intention of that cue?
Abel: Absolutely. It is the first step. And then we're able to recreate it every night.
Michael: Even to the point where, if you understand that this shift starts happening, (so this is where I'm going to call the cue) when Elphaba has this thought then, you know as the calling stage manager, that you need to be clued into Elphaba's thoughts. Not that word on the piece of paper, right? Because next time she does it, the thought might not happen in her head, until . . .
Abel: Two words later. Right. Yes. Absolutely. Absolutely. So, it's about understanding why the shift happens there.
Michael: So, sometimes to recreate and to maintain it, you have to do it differently?
Abel: Absolutely. No, but that's interesting, because it's exactly what happens!

Similarly, Freeburg pointed out that it is the audience's experience which determines when a stage manager should call the cue.

Freeburg: I think to be able to execute these different design elements, I think to be able to know artistically, this is what it wants to look like, this is the feeling that I want to have as an audience member. So, my job, again, is to take those pieces, those paints on the palette, and swirl them in a way that gets the painting that the designers want. Sometimes part of the artistry of stage management is to know, on this night, these human actors on stage are a little bit different, so I have to call all the cues just slightly different to accommodate what they're doing, to still get the artistic experience that I want the audience to have.
Michael: So, if you know what the lighting designer wants to do with that cue, and you know that today the actors are presenting slightly different shades of colour on their palette –
Freeburg: Yes, that's a nice way to say it, yes.
Michael: I'm using your metaphor here. The way that you swirl it together for that show is something that you know, because you know the show. If I come in because you're sick, and I have to call from your prompt copy, I'm going to call it formulaically, and it will be approximately right.
Freeburg: Right, it will be 99% right. It won't have the finesse.
Michael: The audience won't go, 'oh, that's a mistake', but they won't – it depends on the lighting cue, of course, and how integral it is to the production – they won't have that 'aha moment', of beautiful art executed beautifully, because it doesn't land in the audience in exactly the same way. That's what we're trying to do.
Freeburg: That's what we're trying to do, yeah.

In pointing out that the audience will not notice a 'clean' call but will miss out on some of the experience without a cue called 'well', we are challenging the notion of invisibility

Stage Management

as a stage manager. For an artistic stage manager, the goal is not simply to be unnoticed but to also contribute to what the audience *is* noticing.

I contend that having the desired audience's experience as the guiding principle for all stage management decisions is the hallmark of an artistic model of stage management. Dyer, who, while taking stage management's impact on the audience very seriously, reminded me that not all models of stage management hold this as necessary for its effective practice. For Dyer doing what is best for the production does not equate simply with the audience's experience and their experience need not be the primary focus of effective stage managers.

> Dyer: We always have the audience, you know, for me, the audience experience is a big part of our job. It's to make sure every audience gets to experience the play as it was intended. . . . Everyone else leaves after opening, the show suddenly becomes ours to sit with and of course the show's going to move slightly as people discover and try things, and all that kind of thing. But when it goes really off-kilter, we're the ones who pull it back because . . . we understand exactly what the . . . overall vision is, and then it's our job to make sure that that stays.
>
> Obviously, I think the audience experience is really important. I have a really big problem with crew walking on to the set to start packing up before the audience has left. . . . I don't care how long they sit there for; we'll wait. Because they've just experienced something and maybe they just need a minute to sit, and kind of ponder, and dissect, and work out what they've just seen . . . Because the post-show vision is just as important, I think, in terms of the experience that they have. . . .
>
> I guess where I differ from you, slightly, is that I don't always think that theatre is for the audience. I think, absolutely, you need to have an audience to tell those stories, but I don't always know that my focus is on their experience as a stage manager. I try and make sure that the show, as a whole, is actually what I'm focused on, and I guess the audience is part of what the show is and what the show becomes on a daily basis. But they're never at the forefront of my mind when I'm on productions. I become very aware of them when something does go wrong, or something does change their experience. That's when it definitely draws into light.
>
> Michael: I'm interested in unpacking that distinction. Can you give me an example where concentrating on the show is different from concentrating on the audience's experience?
>
> Dyer: Yes. I did a show once where it got very bad reviews. Extremely bad reviews. I had a disgruntled cast that didn't want to do it anymore . . . And for me, it became less about the audience and more making sure that the show itself was the best possible version of the show it could be . . . And so, in that instance, it became about looking after the cast. It became about presenting the show that was intended. And not allowing the cast to deviate from that, regardless of things going on. It became about pulling together as a company. I can still make sure that the ASM and I are working together to make the work environment the best environment that we can, regardless of everything else going on.

Dyer's comments here portray all three perspectives: stage management's role in pulling a show back when it goes off-kilter and maintaining it as intended comes from what I am calling an administrative model; the desire to make the work environment the best it could be comes from the managerial paradigm; and the desire to allow the audience to have their post-show experience demonstrates the artistic model. All three paradigms presented here are equally valid conceptions of stage management, and their relative utility will depend on the specific circumstances a stage manager faces.

Conclusions

This chapter has presented outlines of three conceptions of stage management: administrative, managerial and artistic. These serve as useful summaries of the different approaches to stage management throughout Part 1 of this book. Earlier I suggested that those interested in stage management may best be served to look at the administrative model to learn about what stage managers do, the managerial model for how they do it and the artistic model for why they do those things. While this provides a useful perspective, it is important to note that each model is complete within itself. That is, each offers a perspective on what, how and why stage managers do the things they do. Specifically, in the administrative model stage managers perform tasks as efficiently as possible to ensure the correct procedures are followed to enable the smooth running of productions. While in the managerial paradigm stage managers ensure resources are used effectively, especially human resources, by motivating colleagues and ensuring workspaces are productive environments. Finally, in the artistic conception stage managers creatively interpret and balance colleagues' needs through designing communication strategies that enhance the audience's experience.

Part 2 of this book will examine how stage managers design this communication in more detail. In so doing, it will argue that stage managers are scenographic artists and use scenography to guide their design decisions. Stage management and scenography can both be enhanced by understanding this. Concentrating on the artistic model is not meant to suggest that it is more important than the other two models. It is done because it is the model for which there is the least information. As we have seen, where it is acknowledged in the interviews and in the literature, much of what is artistic about stage management has been left implied in notions of flexibility, adaptability, creativity and doing what is best for the production. There remains a need to be explicit in specifying what an artistic model of stage management looks like. Part 2 of this book is an attempt to address that need.

PART TWO
SCENOGRAPHIC STAGE MANAGEMENT

This part examines what an artistic model of stage management might look like in greater detail. The model is developed from taking a few of the conclusions from the last chapter as a leaping-off point. Namely, that all approaches to stage management revolve around the idea of effective communication, and that the artistry of stage management can be seen in its impact on the audience's experience.

Other technical theatre disciplines are already more widely acknowledged as being artistic and their artistry already evaluated in terms of their audience impact. It follows that adopting the language, concepts and methodologies already applied to these other technical theatre disciplines could be useful in describing an artistic model of stage management in three ways. Firstly, in following a path that has already been accepted as demonstrating artistry. Secondly, by using common elements it is envisaged that the potential for mutual understanding is increased and collaboration is enhanced. Finally, by placing stage management within the same academic field as other technical disciplines, it is hoped that more academic enquiry, critical thinking about the practice and relevant interdisciplinary research may result. For these reasons, this section will commence with a consideration of which current ways of thinking about technical theatre's impact on an audience are most relevant to stage management and, in effect, reverse engineer stage management practice from this viewpoint.

Chapter 6 takes Simpson's comment regarding the 'problematic' of the lighting designer noted in Chapter 5 as its inspiration and briefly outlines how lighting design demonstrates its artistry. It follows Pilbrow's argument that the artform has a medium, the medium has various properties, which can be manipulated to reach certain objectives.[1] Currently, the way these objectives have an impact on the audience is considered mainly through the critical lens of scenography. This is similar to how the artistry of other technical theatre disciplines is currently conceived. Therefore, scenography is the most relevant critical lens through which to view stage management's artistry. This is despite a marked absence of stage management practice in current surveys of scenography and, reciprocally, despite many practicing stage managers being unaware of the field. Nevertheless, by comparing key definitions and analytical approaches of scenography with the comments made by the stage managers in the interviews, the suitability of placing stage management within the field of scenography will become apparent. An artistic stage manager is a scenographic one. From this perspective, stage management consists of designing communication which influences the performance environment in order to shape the audience's experience.

Stage Management

Chapter 7 examines how the *objectives* of stage management communication enable this influence on the performance. These objectives form a hierarchy with each later objective depending on, at least partially, the realization of the former. The objectives outlined are selective information flow; targeted information flow; distributed cognition; mood and atmosphere; and translation. Reaching these objectives in order to manage a production's relational semiotics is a scenographic practice and constitutes the artistry of stage management.

Chapter 8 advocates that the medium of the art of stage management is communication and examines how stage managers manipulate the *properties* of communication to reach the objectives. The properties of communication discussed are the message, the medium, distribution and updates. Using the tools and techniques available to stage managers to manipulate a production's communication in order to reach the objectives is a design practice. Concentrating on the tools and techniques themselves is the craft of stage management and is the central focus of the administrative model.

Using this scenographic model stage managers may be better equipped to collaborate effectively and gain a deeper understanding of their role in the creative process because it parallels how other technical theatre disciplines are practiced and discussed. This approach would also allow stage management to be treated in a similar way to other aspects of theatre by the academy and the pedagogy and research of stage management would be more suited to a university context.

CHAPTER 6
SCENOGRAPHIC STAGE MANAGEMENT

This chapter is more theoretical and hypothetical than the other chapters in this book. The hypothesis being tested is whether stage management is scenographic. Spoiler alert: this chapter concludes and contends that it is! This is not widely accepted among either other scenographers or stage managers, so some detours away from stage management must be undertaken to discover where these fields intersect. This means that the references for this chapter will come from a wide range of fields with the interview material being used to offer how similar concepts are expressed in stage management. Due to this difference from the other chapters, I will start with a more thorough outline of the argument before proceeding to the details and the evidence which support it. Hopefully, this will provide a sense of where the detours are leading and some assurance that there are connections to stage management.

In the last chapter it was suggested that if artistry was involved in stage management, it involves contributing to the audience's experience. For those less inclined to view stage management as artistic there was often talk about the distinction between stage management and the 'creative' team which creates this experience for the audience. This version of 'the creatives' typically includes 'directors' of the performers (depending on the genre such positions may include a director, choreographer or musical director, for example) and the 'designers' of various technical theatre elements. Therefore, examining the way designers are considered creative or artistic and comparing this to stage management can test whether such a distinction is justified.

If this distinction is not justified and stage management can be conceptualized using similar language and methodologies as other technical theatre artists, then there are potentially many benefits. Using a common language and methodology may enhance mutual understanding among theatre-makers and therefore enhance collaboration. Stage management may be open to similar levels and methodologies of critical enquiry that other technical theatre disciplines attract. This could make stage management a site for interdisciplinary research with reflexive improvements between the understanding of stage management, theatre-making, theatre pedagogy and the broader fields involved in such research.

How lighting design describes itself as artistic is examined as the basis from which to make a comparison with stage management. The choice of lighting design over the other technical theatre disciplines was partly inspired by Simpson's comment discussed in the last chapter about lighting designers solving the problematic of how a production can be seen. In particular, Pilbrow's[1] articulation of a theoretical framework for lighting design has been the most influential here. This is partially because this framework makes the relationship between the technical and the design process explicit, simple and transferable to other disciplines. In brief, Pilbrow explains that the medium of light has particular properties and that the lighting designer manipulates these in the pursuit of certain objectives. These objectives relate to the audience's experience.

This framework allows us to reverse engineer a similar model for stage management. Reverse engineering is appropriate because Pilbrow's framework starts from that which is particular about lighting design and builds to the audience experience. Therefore, it is most likely to resemble other disciplines which are concerned about the audience's experience in the latter aspect. This reverse engineered approach is also the most appropriate for an artistic model of stage management as it builds from the rationale (the audience experience) to the methodology (objectives) which then inform the tasks to be completed (controlling the medium's properties). This is the opposite direction of conceptualizing stage management to the administrative model.

What this means for this book is that this chapter firstly explores how the framework of medium, properties and objectives relates to the audience's experience for other technical theatre artforms as a way for practitioners to demonstrate their artistry. Some consideration of why stage management may not have had this framework applied to it previously is considered.

At this level of the audience experience, scenography is a common critical lens used to explore the artistry of these other disciplines, especially when they interact to create a cohesive performance. Because the development of scenography shares much in common with the development of stage management practice, a brief overview of this development and its relationship with stage management will be outlined. Why stage management and scenography are mutually absent in each other's fields will be considered, as will adopting a definition of scenography that seems to bring the two together.

Having thus demonstrated that artistic stage management may be scenographic in nature, this chapter will then turn to presenting some of the most common ways of analysing scenography. These analytical methodologies will be compared with comments made during the interviews to demonstrate their applicability to the field of stage management. This comparison, it is hoped, will offer some more concrete guidance to stage managers, and those interested in stage management, for how to evaluate their practice in terms of its contribution to an audience's experience.

Such an evaluation may involve applying the other parts of the theoretical framework of technical theatre artistry to stage management. That is to say, having understood how stage management contributes to the overall audience experience in the same manner as the other technical theatre disciplines, it is time to consider stage management's particularities in detail. This is done in the remaining chapters of Part 2. Chapter 7 sets out what the objectives of stage management are. Chapter 8 takes communication as the medium of the artform of stage management and explores how a stage manager manipulates the properties of communication to meet these objectives. Taken together these three chapters attempt to demonstrate stage management as a design practice which is technical, artistic and scenographic like the other technical theatre disciplines.

Therefore, stage management is available to the same critiques and methodologies and contributes to an audience's experience in the same manner as these other disciplines.

Other technical theatre disciplines

Unlike stage management writing, it seems that many practitioners from other technical theatre disciplines are prepared to write about their work from a theoretical and artistic point of view. While this chapter employs lighting design as an example it is important to realize that many technical theatre disciplines, apart from stage management, seem to have established their artistic and academic credentials. There are historical reasons for this which mirror the recent history of the development of stage management teams outlined in Chapter 1.

Baugh details the reflexive developments between technology, technical theatre artistry and theatrical styles.[2] The process outlined is as 'technologies and workshop skills became more complex and sophisticated ... [there is] an enlargement and gradual fragmentation of the ... team'.[3] This is the same process that gave rise to the stage management teams we recognize today. However, in other technical theatre disciplines such fragmentation resulted in a new role for each discipline: the designer. In this way, other technical theatre disciplines have not suffered a schism which has been interpreted to be a separation from their aesthetic considerations like the one which saw stage management become separate from direction. Once established, the designer remains the aesthetic decision-maker for that discipline and oversees any future fragmentation within the discipline.

Given this history, it is unsurprising to find that much of the literature from other technical theatre disciplines appear to be much more comfortable framing their work as artistic than the literature from stage management. Examples can be drawn from any technical theatre discipline.[4] Of these, I have chosen to interrogate Pilbrow's[5] work as a way of investigating whether this distinction between stage management and design is justified. This choice was inspired by Simpson commenting that the lighting designer's role was solving the 'problematic of "How do I ensure that this production can be seen?"' and because Pilbrow's explanation of that process is so explicit, clear and transferable to other design disciplines. That is to say, my interpretation of Pilbrow's explication of lighting design has served me as a useful model for understanding how design works generically.

My interpretation of Pilbrow's model is outlined here and shown diagrammatically in Figure 1. A design practice involves the medium of the artform. This medium has properties which the designer controls in order to meet certain objectives. Analysing Pilbrow's model suggests the equipment, tools and processes which lighting designers use to understand the medium of light and manipulate its properties constitute the technical aspect of their work. Similarly, the choices of how and why to manipulate these properties in the pursuit of the objectives constitute the artistic aspects of their work. These objectives, properties and their relationships, and their analogues in

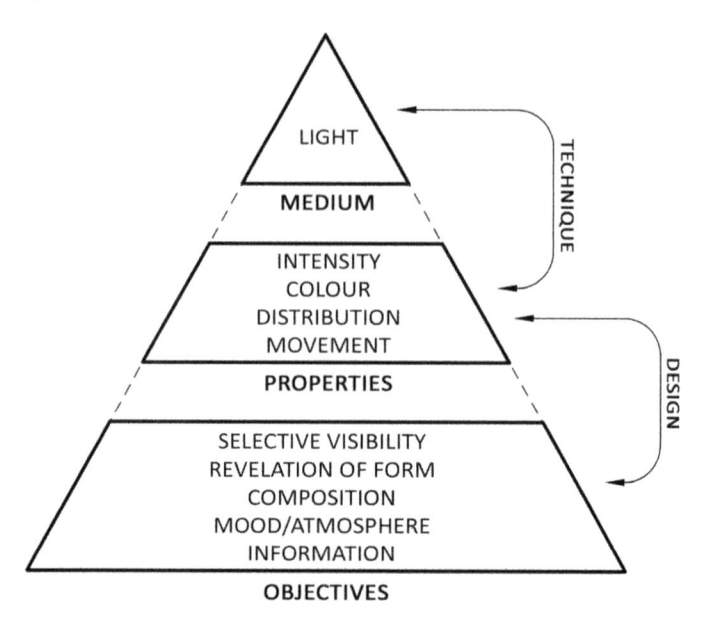

```
              /\
             /  \
            /LIGHT\
           /--------\
          /  MEDIUM  \         ↑
         /------------\        TECHNIQUE
        /  INTENSITY   \       
       /    COLOUR      \      
      /   DISTRIBUTION    \    
     /     MOVEMENT        \   
    /------------------------\ 
   /       PROPERTIES         \   ↑ DESIGN
  /----------------------------\
 /    SELECTIVE VISIBILITY      \
/      REVELATION OF FORM        \
         COMPOSITION
        MOOD/ATMOSPHERE
          INFORMATION
         OBJECTIVES
```

Figure 1 Lighting design: medium, properties and objectives (after Pilbrow). Graphic design by Eduardo Canalejo.

stage management, will be discussed in more detail in Chapter 7 which outlines stage management's objectives and Chapter 8 which considers the medium of the artform of stage management and its properties. Pilbrow also emphasizes the flexibility that artistic practice requires throughout the production process counselling lighting designers even during the dress rehearsals that 'theatre is never a static and final piece of work; it is alive and open to change'.[6] In emphasizing this reflexive nature of the production process, Pilbrow distinguishes that in theatrical lighting design (unlike in architectural lighting design, for example) this artistry and its effectiveness in meeting its objectives forms part of, and can only be evaluated with reference to, the audience's experience of a complete theatrical production.

It is perhaps not surprising given their similar names that theatrical set, costume, lighting and sound design could all be described by a similar framework for their practice. That is, one that consists of: the medium of their artform; the techniques available to manipulate its properties; the artistry of manipulating those properties to meet certain objectives for an audience; all in a reflexive, iterative process. In comparison, the emphasis on management in the job title 'stage management' implies the different approaches outlined earlier in this book. However, it is the audience's experience which is the common ground for all theatre-makers. This is why, as demonstrated in the interview material presented in the last chapter, notions of stage management artistry are so closely associated with the audience's experience.

It is not merely the differing job titles that makes it easier to assume that stage management is divorced from the audience experience. Generally speaking, stage management's contribution to the audience experience is far less perceptible to that audience than those of the designers. Audiences are generally aware at least of the existence (or absence) of set, costumes, lighting, sound and other designed elements even if they are not aware of how these influenced their experience of a production. The relative lack of awareness of stage management by audiences can lead administrative stage managers into the trap of thinking that their sole remit is ensuring a production is well administered. Conversely, the very discernible outcomes of designers' work can lead them into the trap of thinking that their sole remit is ensuring that their control over their medium (lighting in the example of a lighting designer) is effective. These traps can lead to designers and stage managers alike concentrating too much on the tools and techniques of their art, rather than its reception. These traps stem from the nature of the audience's experience itself.

Observing that an artistic model of stage management concentrates on the audience's experience is, by itself, even less useful to stage managers, or those who want to understand their practice, than concentrating solely on its administrative function. It is only through interrogating the nature of the audience's experience, and how this experience can be analysed, that this observation can become useful. This is because this analysis will allow the relationship between the audience's experience, stage management objectives and the properties of the medium to be ascertained.

The most salient point of the audience's experience is that an audience does not perceive the production as a set of discrete elements. They experience all the elements over the same span of time. Because of this, their evaluation of that experience is usually a result of the relationship between the various elements that constituted the production. Freeburg observed stage management's role within this.

> Freeburg: [Stage management is] also negotiating between those two designers. They want it to do different things, and so it's coming to a compromise. I can't do both of those things for you, but let's see if we can find a way that we can all get to the same place and get your art to look good with each other as well.
> Michael: Because that's what theatre is, right? The audience doesn't . . .
> Freeburg: That's what it's about, yes. The audience doesn't go, 'This is the sound and this is the lighting'. They don't deconstruct it in their head while they're experiencing it. It's one experience for them, that's what we're aiming for, unless we're aiming for, for effect, a particularly disjointed experience.

In effect, all theatre-makers' artistic contributions are taken from their original artform and placed within, and subjugated to, the needs of the theatrical artform. This is a key distinction between, for example, a scenic artist and a painter; or a sound designer and a composer. This is not to say that any individual artist could only be effective as one or the other but to argue that they are at their best when working in a theatrical context if they understand that their work will not be judged in isolation. This is what is meant by the cliché of theatre being a collaborative art.

Stage Management

Scenography

This distinction between designing exclusively within one's own medium and using the same medium for a theatrical design is often characterized by the term 'scenography'. Svoboda advocated this position in 1971 when he stated, 'Scenography must draw inspiration from the play, its author, all of theatre. The scenographer must be in command of the theatre, its master. The average designer is simply not that concerned with theatre.'[7]

Aronson details this ongoing shift from design to scenography, including Svoboda's influential role in it.[8] The emphasis on the lived experience of the audience can be seen in Svoboda's maxim: 'true scenography is what happens when the curtain opens and can't be judged in any other way.'[9] The distinction between designer and scenography is characterized elsewhere by Aronson when he states scenography is 'more than creating scenery or costumes or lights. It carries a connotation of an all-encompassing visual-spatial construct as well as the process of change and transformation that is an inherent part of the physical vocabulary of the stage.'[10] In short, scenography is the potential for the relationship that each technical theatre design element creates with each other, and with the other elements of a performance text, to be not just the sum of their parts. This relationship requires significant attention and focus from theatre-makers, which is why scenography is important for contemporary practitioners.

Baugh[11] demonstrates that this history of the coalescence of various technical theatre disciplines being recognized as artistry under the banner of design, and then scenography, roughly corresponds to the order in which the various tools used to manipulate the properties of their respective medium became so sophisticated as to demand a specialist approach in the first place. However, the continued absence of stage management under the heading scenography is palpable in Baugh's statement that the term scenographer is now 'used to describe the artists who have responsibility for all the visual and aural contributions of theatre and performance: the stage setting and properties, costume design, sound and lighting design.'[12] Perhaps this absence is because stage management is not currently seen to have a design function, so the need for it to be included within a field that coalesces the different design processes may have been missed.

Certainly, the term scenography was not well known among the stage managers interviewed. Those who were aware of the term typically had extensive experience teaching stage management at a tertiary institution and had encountered it with reference to other technical theatre disciplines. Within those who were aware of the term it is not universally well regarded. Evans and Franklin point out that in some circles the term scenography can be seen as pretentious and overly academic; while, in others, it can be seen to be passé and outdated.

> Michael: Can you give me a flavour of some of the contention around the word scenography?
> Evans: Some of the contention is that around the world, in some countries, it's seen as an old-fashioned term and in other countries, it's seen as the 'now'

word to use. The other debate of it is literally about defining what it is and what it means. And as I mentioned to you earlier, within the OISTAT organization, we now have the Performance Design Commission, which was once the Scenography Commission. And that debate is huge because it all came down to somebody saying that we'd have to define what scenography is. And other people saying, 'No, we don't.' So, it literally came down to a vote that was very, very close.

Michael: What are the issues with the term scenography in the UK?
Franklin: I think there is an anti-intellectual suspicion, to some extent, in the British theatre. 'We're just getting a show on, right?' Like a musical, a variety or whatever. It's not all 'art'. We don't do 'art'. The crew might say, 'What are you like Russian?' There is a sort of an inherent suspicion of anything that might be seen as artsy or pretentious, if that makes sense. I think the term scenography has for a lot of people fallen into that artsy, pretentious, category and they ask 'What is that? It's just the set.'

And I think that's unfortunate, because I do understand why certain people are arguing for a concept of scenography as integral to theatre and how we experience it. . . . It's a really useful concept, actually. But the word itself is so loaded with suspicion in the business. . . . I think there's problems on two sides. People on the more, 'Oh, it's a load of nonsense' side are a bit reluctant to open their minds to actually think about it, and really engage with it, and think what it might be. And people on the scenography side, 'Let's write and think about scenography and what it is', don't necessarily explain it very well.

As Evans pointed out, like in many fields of the humanities, a precise definition of scenography is yet to be settled on. Rather than viewing this as a weakness, I suspect that if it were to be definitively settled that would signal the end of the utility of the field. However, because it is likely to be a new concept for many stage managers, having one definition in mind may help to fix it in place for long enough for the relationship between scenography and stage management to be established. Also, given the anti-academic suspicion already present among technical theatre practitioners, as Franklin mentioned, and exacerbated by the prominence of the administrative approach to stage management, I thought offering a concrete definition rooted in theatre practice that offered some scope for stage managers to see themselves within the field might prove beneficial to the interviews. McKinney and Butterworth's definition of scenography as 'the manipulation and orchestration of the performance environment'[13] seemed fit for these purposes and became the definition I relied upon during the interviews. This conceptual history and definition comes from the Anglophone perspective of the word scenography which is only one of many as Hann explains.[14] For many of the interviewees, this not only seemed to leave room for stage managers but also seemed to be a job description of them. Alexander and Freeburg, in particular, seemed to embrace this as a definition of stage management itself.

Michael: I know that you asked me before what scenography is about. There's lots of different definitions but the one that I'm using is, 'scenography is the manipulation and orchestration of the performance environment.'
Alexander: Oh, okay. That's what we do. That's stage management, yeah.
Michael: Typically, though, it's applied to designers more so. It's applied to set designers, and lighting designers, and most recently sound designers as well, and stage management kind of gets left out a little bit, of that conversation.
Alexander: Because we're not seen as creatives.
Michael: But my point is that we are creative. And that we're creative in pretty much the same way as those designers are. If that's the definition that we're using, then we should be in that conversation, is basically the thrust of the argument.
Alexander: I agree with that wholeheartedly.

Michael: I don't know if you've heard the term scenography at all.
Freeburg: No.
Michael: That's of interest to me because I hadn't heard of it either. Once I found it and started reading about it, I was asking, 'Why haven't I heard of this? This is what we do.' The definition that I'm using is the 'manipulation and orchestration of the performance environment'. There's other definitions out there - but the reason why I chose that one is because when I read that, I thought that sounds like a job description for stage management.
Freeburg: Yeah, it really does. Yeah, it really does. Yeah, absolutely! Manipulation always has a negative connotation, but you really do. You manipulate the schedule, and the feeling in the room. You do a lot of that. The performance environment, you are sort of the master manipulator of it.
Michael: Why I bring that up now is because you were talking about directors looking after the artistic vision, and designers looking after their part of the product. That obviously has a contribution to this thing called scenography. But, in a sense, stage managers are mainly concerned with the performance environment as a whole.
Freeburg: Exactly! The director leaves once a show opens, and we have to maintain the performance and the production. The scope of the performance environment is our entire thing, from the first day of rehearsal to the very last day of performance. You're maintaining their artistic vision, and how do you do that? By manipulating certain things and orchestrating other things. I think absolutely it works.

Abel suggested that the initial understanding that scenography is more directly applicable to design fields rather than stage management is because stage management's contribution to performance environments is, in some senses, reliant on that of the designers.

Michael: Have you ever come across the term 'scenography'?
Abel: No.

Michael: The definition that I'm using is scenography is the 'orchestration and manipulation of the performance environment'.
Abel: The manipulation of the space. Absolutely. Yeah.
Michael: So those people who talk about scenography initially tended to be scenic designers.
Abel: Okay. Well, yeah, because they're manipulating the space. Absolutely.
Michael: They are. And then eventually costume design got rolled into that. Then lighting. And then, most recently, audio. But still . . .
Abel: Still no stage managing.
Michael: No. Stage management is conspicuous in its absence.
Abel: Well, in order for us to manipulate that space we have to have those designs. So, I sort of understand why. Now if you wanted to get really base about it, what I always think of is when you're setting up your rehearsal space. Where are we putting our table? Where does the director want the lip of the stage? And then how are we going to manage that space? But again, we're dictated by whatever the design is, right?

So, I don't know. I mean I don't know whether stage management is included in that.
Michael: Do we have some role to play in orchestrating and manipulating it?
Abel: Absolutely. Absolutely. Alright well so, yes. Then I understand. Yes.

Yeah that's what we do, right? We have to take whatever they give us, figure out how to put it in a space.
Michael: In some respects, I think stage management has more to do with the orchestration and manipulation of it. Whereas the designers create it.
Abel: Oh absolutely. So, they create it, absolutely. But in terms of absolutely putting it into process . . . Yeah, I would definitely agree with that . . . The more I'm thinking about this the more I'm in agreement with you.

This anecdote from Hobden about a writer observing stage management in action and equating it with the conducting of an orchestra serves to suggest that even people outside of the field of stage management can see that it contributes to the manipulation and orchestration of a performance environment.

Hobden: Once we had a writer who was fascinated about how all the tech worked and when we were running the show he wanted to listen on cans one night. So afterwards, he was like 'It's amazing!' He said of the show calling position 'You're like the conductor backstage, because you are conducting all of this wonderful stuff that is happening, and everybody's doing their thing at the right time in the right place, in order to make the magic happen.'

I suppose in that respect, I think certainly that is something that we do. How much we create it, I don't know. Because we usually are given the things which we then have to manipulate and make do what they want. We don't create the things, we make the things that they have created work.

If stage managers, and those observing stage management, accept that the role involves manipulation and orchestration of the performance environment and this is an accepted

Stage Management

definition of scenography, it seems reasonable to conclude that stage management is scenographic. Moreover, if scenography is accepted as a field which is concerned with the artistry of technical theatre practices, especially design, it seems reasonable to conclude that stage management is a technical theatre art and that, perhaps, the distinction between it and design is not justified. While interesting academic points, these conclusions also have concrete implications for the practice of stage management. They suggest that stage management as an art has its own objectives and its own medium with controllable properties. These will be explored in Chapters 7 and 8, respectively. These conclusions also suggest that stage management contributes to the audience's experience in the same way as design and is therefore able to be analysed using the same methodologies.

Analysing scenography

Just as scenography has the power to coalesce the disparate approaches of various technical theatre disciplines around their united purpose in creating and controlling a performance environment for audiences to experience, it also has the potential to coalesce a disparate variety of academic approaches to analysing how meaning is made in theatrical performances. A scenographic approach to technical theatre practice does not seek to deny that there are significant differences between, for example, lighting and costume design but, instead, seeks to point out the significance of their common purpose and at the point of their interaction. Similarly, a scenographic approach to the study of theatre, drama and performance should not seek to deny the validity of the variety of methodological and theoretical frameworks that are commonly brought to bear in these fields but, instead, should attempt to highlight their commonalities and explore their interactions.

Two analytical methods commonly applied to scenography are semiotics and phenomenology. The semiotic approach to theatre as detailed in Aston and Savona,[15] Elam,[16] Esslin[17] and Pavis[18] is useful in discussing and categorizing a total theatre production in terms of its component elements and identifying how a single scenographic choice operates symbolically. There is evidence that stage managers instinctively understand and use semiotics throughout the interviews. Two particularly potent examples come from Abel and Freeburg. Abel points out how the smoke is used (in conjunction with less bright lighting) to signify the more serious moments in *Wicked*.

> Abel: Even in [*Wicked*] which is a musical comedy theatre piece. It is a lot of fun, but several of these characters have very serious things they have to deal with.
> Michael: Those moments are a big contrast from the light, fun comedic approach that we're introduced to at the start. So, you've talked already about how you contribute to that backstage, with those actors who need support. But what is going on scenographically?

Abel: It's all supporting that tone. So when you get a lot of smoke, and a lot of darker lights come up, you know what the audience is going to feel.

Freeburg demonstrates how colour can be used semiotically to indicate place or period.

Freeburg: If you're trying to help the audience go, 'Oh, we're back at that same place.' This is where we are, or this time period is all in a sort of an orange tone, and the orange lights are coming up so now we're back in the past. We're helping them understand the story of what we're trying to present.

In both examples the focus on the audience experience is apparent. A formal understanding of semiotics can enhance stage management practice considerably. For those new to the field, Tyson's accessible introduction may prove a good starting point.[19] This provides an overview of how a sign is the union of a signifier (something which the audience perceives) and a signified (a concept referred to by the signifier). Tyson explains the three classes of sign as index, icon and symbol which denote a different relationship between the signified and signifier.[20] Understanding the significance of scenographic choices is very helpful for stage managers. For example, if something is added in rehearsal, rather than simply reporting this bald fact, a scenographic stage manager may also report its semiotic intent. For example, adding a handkerchief because it is offered by one character to another to signify the first character's compassion, or so that a character can wave it to symbolize their surrender to something may suggest two very different handkerchiefs.

The main limitation of semiotics in analysing scenography (at least how it is often used – as McKinney and Butterworth point out there is a 'tendency for semiotic theories to be applied too mechanistically'[21]) is that it concentrates on breaking down a production into its component parts, rather than the totality of the experience. This reflects the fragmentation and specialization inherent in technical theatre training and literature which emphasizes the technical rather than the artistry discussed earlier.

Phenomenology avoids this limitation by placing the audience's experience at the centre of any theatrical analysis. The embodied experience of the audience is central to a phenomenological approach to scenography. Perhaps the most influential phenomenologist for scenography is Merleau-Ponty who emphasizes the relationship between the various sensorial inputs and their ability to refer to other senses synaesthetically in the claim,

The form of objects is not their geometrical shape: the form has a certain relation with their very nature and it speaks to all of our senses at the same time as it speaks to vision. The form of a fold in a fabric of linen or of cotton shows us the softness or the dryness of the fiber, and the coolness or the warmth of the fabric.[22]

McKinney and Butterworth point out phenomenology 'suggests that audiences can appreciate what they see on stage in ways that are embodied and precognitive.'[23]

Phenomenology is inherent in the way artistic stage management works. I have no desire to laden practitioners with extraneous theories (or theorists with irrelevant practices). However, where theory already exists, and is helpful in describing and diagnosing the practice, it can be of enormous benefit to know about it. The most common and direct way phenomenology is expressed in stage management practice, and in the interviews, is through the expression 'feeling the cues' which we have already seen in discussions about artistry and the distinction between calling a 'clean' show and calling a show 'well'. Studham offers a further example here and in her reference to understanding how the different elements are supposed to seamlessly intertwine for the audience she is invoking Merleau-Ponty's synaesthesia in a way that stage managers may recognize regardless of whether they are aware of phenomenology.

> Studham: I think it's feeling the cues. I think there's a difference between calling the cues as placed [in the prompt copy] and placing them where they need to be for what the designer was intending. Like if they tell you 'I want it to land here.' Okay, you want the cue to land here, but you've asked me to call it over here. Depending on what's happening on stage, I may need to adjust that to make the landing happen properly. So that's a creative decision that I have to make in the show in the moment, as opposed to I'm going to call it [as placed and] . . . not understanding the outcome of it . . . how all of the different elements have to seamlessly intertwine.

The limitations of phenomenology in analysing scenography revolve around its lack of concern with individual scenographic choices. For example, knowing what the audience is experiencing as a whole does not, of itself, tell a lighting designer that a particular lighting state is too bright. This is precisely the strength of a semiotic approach: this bright lighting state is not symbolically linked with a spooky night-time scene. Thus it is important to balance the two approaches as States argues, 'semiotics and phenomenology are best seen as complementary perspectives . . . if we think of semiotics and phenomenology as modes of seeing, we might say that they constitute a kind of binocular vision: one eye enables us to see the world phenomenally; the other eye enables us to see it significantly.'[24] In other words, phenomenology is about the experience of something, semiotics is about the meaning of something. Scenographers, including stage managers, are interested in both and the relationship between them.

One area of focus that semiotics, phenomenology and scenography all share is the significance and experience of space. Elam suggests that from a semiotic perspective 'analysis of performance systems and codes might well turn first, therefore, to the organization of architectural, scenic and interpersonal space'.[25] Merleau-Ponty claims that 'to be a body is to be tied to a certain world, and our body is not primarily *in* space, but is rather *of* space'.[26] Collins and Nisbet state space 'underpin[s] all aspects of scenographic practice' and emphasize 'the importance of space and spatial practice both in the abstract sense, the way we think about space, and in the concrete way in which space is used, organized and experienced'.[27] McAuley's study of space and its significance in theatre has been the most influential for this project.[28] McAuley proposes 'a taxonomy of spatial function' within the meaning-making process of theatre which incorporates space (both physical and conceptual) as encountered by theatre-makers, audiences and the broader societal spaces it inhabits and constructs.[29] It is a forceful argument that space is the defining feature of theatrical performance and both proves and explores the implications of the claim that the 'specificity of theatre is not to be found in its relationship to the dramatic, as film and television have shown . . . but in that it consists essentially of the interaction between performers and spectators in a given space'.[30] McAuley's work explores space's functioning in the theatre using theories and methods derived from semiotics, phenomenology, ethnography and sociology. Combining such approaches is typical for the field of performance studies in 'response to the complexity of the performance phenomena that are being explored'.[31]

Scholarship from the fields of performance studies and scenographic practice largely remain distanced from each other. This is somewhat surprising given their commonalities: incorporating both phenomenological and semiotic approaches, but with an awareness of the limitations of both, and holding the notion of space to be of fundamental significance. However, from the viewpoint of the scenographic practitioner who (even in disciplines such as set design where the term is most widely used) is still largely trained and paid as a specialist in a technical theatre area,[32] the field of performance studies may be a theoretical bridge too far. Carlson acknowledges:

> The term 'performance' has become extremely popular in . . . the arts, in literature, and in the social sciences. As its popularity and usage have grown so has a complex body of writing about performance . . . So much has been written by experts in such a wide range of disciplines, and such a complex web of specialized critical vocabulary has been developed in the course of this analysis, that a newcomer seeking a way into the discussion may feel confused and overwhelmed.[33]

In my experience, for practitioners who are used to expressing ideas visually, aurally and spatially, this written body of material seems, at first, even more impenetrable. Franklin agrees that performance studies, and indeed some scenographic theory which could offer a bridge to the field, can be viewed with suspicion among theatre-makers.

> Franklin: I think some of the problems people have with it is when you're talking about scenography that's not in a theatre, you know? Academics are not great at explaining this in a way that people can understand or get on board with, and it starts floating into notions that are related to things like sociology. Theatre-makers just go, 'That's not theatre', because it's not a show.
>   That's the problem with a lot of theatre-based research. I've worked in theatre my whole life. There is a portion of theatre-based research that I don't understand. As somebody who has worked in theatre all my life, what hope has anybody else got?

When Franklin refers to 'scenography that's not in a theatre' she is referring to recent scenographic scholarship which offers connections between scenography and performance studies, but in claiming this academic territory its relevance to practitioners may become somewhat obscured. The titles and contents of McKinney and Palmer's *Scenography Expanded*[34] and Hann's *Beyond Scenography*[35] serve as examples. Both of these titles identify Lehman's concept of a 'visual dramaturgy' in the work *Postdramatic Theatre*[36] as a key moment in the rise in status of the practice and study of scenography. All these titles have much to offer to scenographic practitioners, including stage management.

For those new to the field, though, perhaps the titles from McKinney and Butterworth[37] and Collins and Nisbet[38] are more accessible. The former provides an overview very heavily linked to scenography in practice. The latter provides an introduction to, and a context informed by, practice for a wide variety of critical material. This variety spans from densely written cultural and literary theorists to rehearsal sketches of practitioners – and from as ancient as Plato to as contemporary as sound design as scenography. It also includes work from the academic approaches of semiotics, phenomenology and performance studies.

The perceived distance between theatre practice and the theory of performance studies is not all one way. From a performance studies perspective, theatre, in general, and technical theatre, in particular, is often seen as lacking the generalities (and academic rigour) which make the field separate from 'traditional theatre studies'.[39] Even in McAuley's work which offers the potential for many connections to be made between these two fields she specifically defines much of scenography outside the scope of her work as she chooses to not deal with 'visual communication per se'.[40] In so doing, McAuley dismisses many of the sign systems and phenomena audiences 'read' in a performance and which, I contend, inform their ability to 'read' the organization and use of space. That said, narrowing the scope of this investigation to the fundamental and multifaceted use of space in theatre was necessary to elucidate its significative potency. Making the connections between this work and with scenographic theory and practice explicit may answer precisely McAuley's call for 'more work of an empirical sort is needed before it will be possible to theorize with confidence about how spectators read performance. It can, however, be posited as a working hypothesis that they do combine elements of the performance into units of some sort and, further, that the performance provides a good deal of guidance about how to do this.'[41]

This detour into some differing critical approaches to space was taken because space is fundamental to the practice of stage management as well. This can be seen in much of the interview material already presented, perhaps most potently from the comments from Abel in this chapter. Upon being introduced to the concept of the 'performance environment' Abel immediately took this to mean 'space'. In Abel's comments it was clear that stage managers' conceptions of space include some of the less obvious spaces in McAuley's taxonomy, such as the rehearsal space and practitioner space. I hope to make the connections between some of these theories of analysing scenography and the practice of scenography, specifically stage management, more concrete by sharing the framework I use for self-analysis.

The coordinates model of scenography

The framework I adopt for analysing scenography is one I call the *coordinates model of scenography*. This model, even more so than most, is intentionally reductive. It serves as an introduction to more complex theories, including those listed earlier. It is designed to be applied in practice. While it is my personal approach, it was shared, strengthened and changed during the interviews with the stage managers in this book. These conversations make me confident that the model could prove useful for stage managers wishing to understand and improve the scenographic aspects of their practice.

This model argues that audiences derive meaning of a theatrical experience mainly through recognizing patterns in the relationship between all the component parts of that experience. I call this *relational semiotics*. I suggest that it is the relationship between the different sign systems which creates the audience's embodied experiences. This, it shares, with Pavis's concept of integrated semiotics which was another influence in its development which, according to Taylor,[42] emphasizes that 'progress lies in the whole'. As can be seen in Figure 2, the three main relationships or patterns audiences recognize are concordance, dissonance and topology. These patterns are called coordinates because just as locating something in three-dimensional space requires latitude, longitude and elevation, each scenographic decision has an impact on all three relationships at once. This is true even if they are most noteworthy for their impact on one of these relationships. For example, we tend to focus on the elevation of Sagarmatha (also known as Chomolungma or Mount Everest), but it still has a latitude and longitude.

Concordance is the potential for, and potency of, significance to be attributed to an aspect of the performance environment due to the audience's understanding that it belongs with other performance elements. At the simplest level the concept of unity, where multiple elements share an exactly matched characteristic, is a useful example. Abel and I discussed how the different costumes for Glinda in *Wicked* concorded with the character's age in the various scenes.

> Michael: Concordance is about stuff belonging together. So, we know where we are in Glinda's life story by the costumes that she's wearing? Because, you know, we jump backwards and forwards through time, but we know . . .
> Abel: . . . by which costume how old she is. Right!

The potency is impacted by a number of factors. Firstly, as the number of elements belonging together increases, so too does the likelihood that an audience will ascribe meaning to it. For example, the more things on stage that appear to represent Ancient Egypt, the more likely the audience is to conclude that the location being presented to them is set there, all other things being equal.

Secondly, as the level of contrivance of those elements sharing that characteristic becomes more apparent, the audience is more likely to ascribe meaning to it. If a chosen dining table and chairs have matching materials and colours that are commonly encountered by an audience it may not mean much for them. The more that same set of

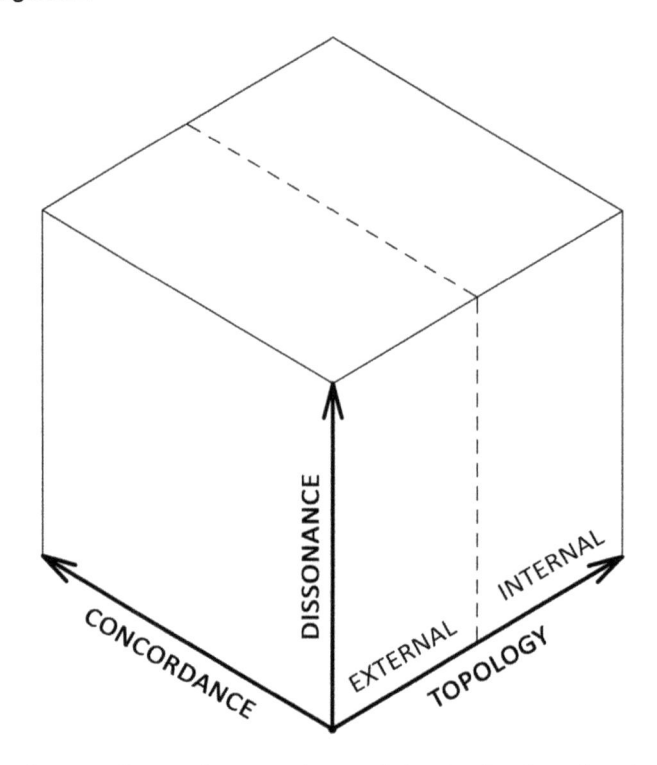

Figure 2 The three coordinates of scenographic possibility. Graphic design by Eduardo Canalejo.

table and chairs was all modified in a particular way (e.g. if they were twice, or five times, or ten times the normal size), the likelihood of the audience ascribing meaning to the fact that they all share this modification increases.

Thirdly, the nature of the characteristic that they share can have an impact. In the case of these table and chairs, if they are all painted a matte black (especially if most of the other elements in the performance environment are as well) the audience is likely to ascribe minimal meaning to this shared characteristic. This works on a number of levels. Phenomenologically, audience's eyes are drawn to the brightest objects on stage (all else being equal). Semiotically, in the theatre, matte black symbolizes neutrality: black box studios and dressing technicians in black signify to the audience not to ascribe meaning to them. This is often a very useful tactic that scenographers use to make something blend into the background.

If, however, these table and chairs were all painted a matching bright yellow when everything else remains matte black, the audience is much more likely to ascribe meaning to the table and chairs and to relate this meaning to their 'yellowness'. Of course, what their 'yellowness' may mean would rely on the relationships created with all the other aspects of the performance. In this last aspect, while the concordance of the yellow objects will group them together, so the audience is likely to ascribe a similar meaning to them, it is also their dissonance with the matte black background which marks them as significant.

Dissonance, at first glance, seems to be just the opposite of concordance. However, the opposite of both concordance and dissonance is a random chaos which lacks contrivance. Dissonance is defined as the potential for, and potency of, significance to be attributed to an aspect of the performance environment due to the audience's understanding that it challenges other performance elements. Just because a particular element does not belong with others, it is not automatically dissonant. This is why I use the word 'challenge'. It needs to 'not belong' in a particular way that relates to the other elements in order for the audience to ascribe meaning to it. At its simplest level, dissonance can be thought of as the use of contrast.

To use our table and chairs as examples, if only one of the chairs was painted yellow, while the rest remained black, its dissonance would be enhanced. However, if all the pieces of furniture were each different bright colours, the dissonance would dissipate. In this case, the audience is more likely to ascribe meaning to the concordance of the 'rainbow furniture' on stage than to the dissonance of the one yellow chair. In such a performance environment, a matte black chair would suddenly be highly dissonant and therefore significant to an audience. This is why in some productions, technicians who are meant to blend into the background wear costumes rather than stage blacks. The relationship between the elements of the performance environment is always more significant than any one element in isolation. The potency of dissonance then depends on both the nature of the characteristic that is doing the challenging (how bright the yellow of our one yellow chair is) and the degree to which this challenges the convention established (the colours of the other chairs). In other words, these two coordinates are interrelated.

Dramaturgically, concordance serves to establish the conventions of the performance text, laying out the limits of what is to be explored and the production's internal logic (or lack thereof). Associations by repetition can become symbols through their concordance. Freeburg gave an example of this in the discussion of semiotics earlier: always using the orange tone in the lights to represent the scenes from the past. Dissonance is used to identify departures from these conventions and/or variations within the limits established. Freeburg also demonstrated that stage managers are used to monitoring and discussing such departures or variations and ensuring that they are chosen in such a way that the audience may ascribe the intended meaning.

> Michael: And if we want the audience to think something differently, or be moved differently?
> Freeburg: Then we change it up, and then all of a sudden they're like, 'Oh, this is not the way we have been here. Something is wrong here this time.'
> Michael: Is knowing that's a part of how audiences respond important so that you can ask the designers 'That's not how we did it last time, so why are we changing it this time?'
> Freeburg: Right, exactly. 'You want to change it this time, is that for a reason? Is this the right way to change it, or should we keep it this way, but then the look of it is different? Or put it in a minor key?'

Freeburg here demonstrates the understanding that the fact that something has changed and what the change is are both significant for the audience in ascribing meaning to their dissonant experiences. If only one aspect has changed, this may heighten the dissonance and the change itself will be ascribed meaning (like the minor key in the example). But, if instead, it is a completely different piece of music, the dissonance may not be as potent, as the relationship between the two choices may be harder to discern.

Every scenographic choice establishes both concordant and dissonant relationships with all the other aspects of the performance environment. This is because there are many different sign systems that each scenographic choice participates in. For example, a production set in a particular period uses this period to unify (the sets, props and costumes will largely concord with this period), but the costume designer may use contrasting materials, colours and patterns of dress from this period for dissonance to signify a character's different social status, for example. Ball's example of an anachronistic prop[43] of a 1970s toy spinning top in an otherwise highly historically accurate period presentation of *The Three Sisters* set in Russia in 1900 would be highly dissonant. Ball called this an example of what he calls 'breaking systems' because this choice meant that all the director's 'work to achieve integrated naturalism was destroyed. That one moment of disbelief suddenly brought the whole act crashing to the floor.'[44] Because this production was supposed to be naturalistic this dissonance disturbed the spatial and temporal relationships of the production, which is precisely the third dimension of this model: topology.

Topology is the potential for, and potency of, significance to be attributed to an aspect of the performance environment due to the audience's understanding of how it relates to others in terms of space and time. At its simplest level, it can be thought of as the use of locations, periods and transitions. As I have borrowed, and probably misused, the word topology from mathematics, its use here may need to be explained. It is closely related to Svoboda's concept of 'polyscenic-ness' which harnesses the potential of a stage space to represent single or multiple places over single or multiple times.[45] In mathematics, topology is the study of continuous distortions of space over time that do not result in breaking or tearing. Each element of this definition has its analogue in scenography.

Every scenographic choice distorts the spatial and temporal relationships of the performance environment. One of the joys of theatre is the fact that these distortions of space and time can be much larger than we experience in our daily lives. However, a distortion is simply any change. Placing an object on stage distorts the space. So too does a lighting cue, a sound cue or any other scenographic intervention. This distortion has a relationship with all the other choices that have been made, or will be made, as part of the performance, both spatially and temporally.

Placing our hard-working yellow chair on the stage immediately imbues the performance environment with a different sense of place. Changing where it is placed on the stage will have a different impact on the audience. Likewise, moving the chair further distorts the spatial and temporal relationships. Both because of its two different positions on our stage and due to the qualities of the movement. Its materials may give the fictional location a sense of period. Placing it neatly around a table with three other matching chairs may establish an ordered sense to the space through the concordance. If these chairs are all slightly out of place and there are three bowls of porridge on the table, we may get a specific sense of time of day or of what might have happened before or what is about to come. If one of the chairs is far away from the others, and broken in pieces, this dissonance, informed by our phenomenological understanding of the force required to break a chair, and semiotic reading of this as an index of violence, changes the atmosphere of the space and leaves a keen sense of what might have happened earlier. The three dimensions are all interrelated, and the audience reads these relationships through their semiotic and phenomenological understanding of those relationships.

This distortion of space and time has two aspects: the internal and external topology of a production. Internal topology relates to any distortions of space and time contained within the fictional world being presented. External topology is the distortion of space and time between the audience's world and the fictional world. The division between the two is represented by the concept of the fourth wall.

While stage managers don't use this language, or necessarily see themselves as scenographers, orchestrating and manipulating the topology of a performance environment is already a part of their practice. The most obvious scenographic distortion of internal topology for stage management is a scene change. The most obvious scenographic distortion of external topology for stage management, in realistic styles of theatre at least, occurs at the starts and ends of acts. These cue sequences can be very complicated because they are doing the heavy lifting of taking the audience from their world into the world of the play, or vice versa. Often, they also establish conventions of the world of the play and make a comment about the distance (spatial, temporal and/or conceptual) between the two worlds *en route*. Other uses of topology that may be familiar to stage management involve considering a request to change a cue placement which both Freeburg and Abel mentioned in their interviews. In these moments from the interviews, I am also reminded of the earlier conversations about the artistry of calling a show 'well' as opposed to 'cleanly', which requires understanding what triggers each cue which necessarily fixes the start point for a transition. Some cues do not necessarily have a fixed trigger point. For them, the cue placement is then determined by the length of the transition and when the transition needs to be completed by. Calling a cue well requires understanding both the source and the magnitude of the topological distortion it represents.

> Freeburg: I find myself differentiating between 'sooner' and 'faster'. The director says, 'I want to get to that scene faster.' I ask 'Do you mean faster, like the lights come up faster? Or do you mean sooner, as in we start to do that sooner?' They are two very different things. I want to make sure that we understand what the director wants. I can call the cues sooner, but if you want them to actually happen faster, that's different.
> Michael: That's different. Yeah, it's about how long does the transition take, which reads differently to an audience, as opposed to . . .
> Freeburg: . . . when it starts and when it ends. Yeah.

Abel, upon hearing about the patterns of concordance, dissonance and topology, wanted to understand how stage managers could use them, only to discover that their use is part of what we normally do. Here, Abel clearly demonstrates that the point of managing these relationships is their impact on the audience.

> Abel: How do we keep those relationships [concordance, dissonance, and topology] under control? . . . And when do you step in and say, 'Oh, I don't think this is working.'
> Michael: So, if you're teching a show, and you've got a lighting designer who wants the cue here, and a sound designer who wants the cue there, so that's where you're calling them, but it doesn't . . .
> Abel: Jive.
> Michael: It doesn't jive, because those two things aren't working together. So, I'm sure I'm not the only person who steps in . . .
> Abel: Oh, no, no. Absolutely. We've all experienced that. It's not just a weird Aussie thing that you made up.
> Michael: So then, you say, 'Well, you know, that lighting cue's only two seconds long whereas that sound cue is ten seconds.'
> Abel: And hopefully when you do that, they will all go, 'Uh oh,' right? 'Oh, those lights change too quickly. We're going to adjust them.'
> Michael: So, we'll make the lighting cue last for as long as the sound cue lasts right?
> Abel: Exactly.
> Michael: And so they change it on the board to ten seconds. And then you run it again. But because our ears and our eyes respond differently, even though the computers say it's exactly the same time . . .
> Abel: The director says, 'No.' And it doesn't feel right. So, you have to change the lights to, I don't know, fifteen seconds. And then it feels like the lighting transition is taking the same amount of time as the sound.
> Michael: Because the important thing is what the audience experiences and not what the numbers are?
> Abel: Exactly. Absolutely.
> Michael: That's the important thing that we need to look out for, as stage managers.
> Abel: The thing is you're absolutely right.
> Michael: And that's part of what we're doing in a technical rehearsal?
> Abel: Watching how it's affecting that topology? Absolutely.

Reducing the elements of space and time to internal and external topology, and the dividing line between them, is not an attempt to reduce McAuley's very useful taxonomy of spatial function in the theatre to only two categories but rather (along with the other coordinates) an attempt to propose one way the performance provides the guidance as to how an audience may 'combine elements of the performance into units'.[46] All of the different categories of space McAuley identifies form part of the topological relationship.

In our context, as opposed to mathematics, what represents breaking or tearing is the production losing control of whether or not they can engage an audience. For example, in a realistic play the defining feature of the relationship of external topology is represented by the audience's willing suspension of disbelief. This enables them to be engaged with the fictional world as real. If, through a comedy of errors, the fireplace façade unintentionally falls apart revealing all its theatricality, then the members of the audience may find it impossible to remain engaged in the desired way. The external topology has been distorted so much it has been torn. In Ball's example noted earlier, the system that is broken would be represented in this model by internal topology. A prop suddenly appearing from the future breaks the internal logic of space and time that was being presented. Of course, such devices may be fully intended in a self-referential farce or epic styles to amuse or alienate the audience and thus would demonstrate their continued control of audience engagement.

This is a point that Abel, having just been introduced to the model, could immediately see was relevant to the practice of stage management.

> Abel: You can take [the audience] anywhere, but you have got to have started somewhere. And it has to start with those three elements [concordance, dissonance and topology], absolutely. Those elements have to be substantiated, and now as an audience member I'm willing to suspend the disbelief into whatever direction you're going to take me with it.
> Michael: Excellent. And then, and from there, we can . . . as long as we show you the shifts . . .
> Abel: Exactly.
> Michael: . . . then we can go anywhere in space and time. That's what theatre does.
> Abel: Yeah, and I'm sure you've seen things also, where you go like, 'Why would they do that? That took me totally out of the show.'
> Michael: That's right.
> Abel: And so therefore, you go, they've veered from these relationships that I'm now going to start applying to everything.
> Michael: I mean, someone like Brecht will often choose to do that. And remind us that we are an audience watching a show. Right?
> Abel: Yes. Yes.
> Michael: So you can do it on purpose.
> Abel: Sure. But it has to be done on purpose and correctly.

Scenographic possibility exists within this three-dimensional space. Each scenographic decision establishes a concordant, dissonant and topological relationship with all the others at the same time. It is these relationships any scenographic decision has with every other aspect of the performance that an audience ascribes meaning to, rather than the specifics of that decision. For example, exactly the same object could signify very different things to an audience depending on its concordant, dissonant and topological relationships with the other elements. An ornate throne considered by itself might signify wealth, power and opulence. But if that throne is presented in a cramped space filled with lots of other ornate, historical objects, then this concordance may signify a museum storeroom or a sense of history. If the throne sits atop a very large pile of rubbish then this dissonance may represent corruption. If the throne hangs precariously upside down from a rope that looks like it may break, then this topological relationship may be read by an audience to signify an impending revolution.

This model consciously simplifies and overgeneralizes much seminal work in the fields of performance studies, semiotics, phenomenology and scenography. It is precisely this simplicity that has rendered it useful for me in a wide variety of contexts. Two of these contexts are relevant here. Firstly, the model has been helpful in understanding and describing various theatrical styles. It has also enhanced my ability to talk about and practice scenography as a stage manager.

In this model, different theatrical styles can be defined in terms of being restricted to specific parts of this three-dimensional space. Naturalism could be categorized as highly concordant, with a low range of dissonance, limited room for shifts in space and time internally and a strong divide between the external and internal topology. However, even in realistic styles, how this fictional reality is portrayed is partially determined by the external topological distance that scenographers will seek to negotiate. That is, how to 'transport' the audience of the production from the place and time they are attending the performance to the time and place in which the performance is set. This often leads scenographers to, for example, choose props with iconic designs from the period because these will more clearly signify the period represented to an audience which is distant from that time and place. This is true even if these are outside of what those characters would 'actually' own because of their lack of ability or interest to own fashionable or the latest objects.

Maccoy mentioned an example of precisely this during our conversation which demonstrates its relevance to stage management.

> Maccoy: One of the notes that my students will get on the show that you've just sat in on will be that I don't think they had A4 paper in that time and place. So, unless you can show me some really good research . . . actually in a way, a lot of people will think that, so even if it's right, you have to make it wrong, don't you? In order to get the point across. Because that will feel more authentic. It's not about 'being' 'authentic'. It is about the audience's experience of this authenticity.

By using the framework and the language of this scenographic model, my own practice has been enhanced. This is a result of making explicit those things which had largely been driven by instinct before. This has had the dual effect of helping me diagnose scenographic issues and enabling me to communicate more effectively with the other artists collaborating on the production. I also believe my scenographic practice has become more engaging to audiences as my awareness of, and competency using, this model has grown. By rendering our scenographic decisions able to be described by three coordinates that can be defined in a non-technical, artistic language, it seems there is potential for us to collaborate more effectively with theatre artists outside of our own specialization, enabling us to find each other when we get lost.

The coordinates model is an attempt to respond to McAuley's call to arms and offers the potential to 'theorize with [slight but growing] confidence how spectators read performance'.[47] The framework seeks to simplify, generalize and examine the links between semiotics, phenomenology, performance studies and scenography. In doing so, I have sacrificed detail for the sake of simplicity. I hope this simplicity offers a useful tool to practitioners that may introduce them to, and excite them about the utility of, denser theoretical material. I also hope that this model suggests to theorists in other fields that scenographic practice, and stage management in particular, has much to offer them. I value this model's simplicity and the simplicity at the heart of semiotics and phenomenology. For it to be a useful representation of how audiences experience performance, this model must be based on constructs that we as humans use, without even being aware of them. This was brought home to me in my conversation with Passaro.

> Passaro: I think going to the theatre just feels more special now because there's just not anything like it in our daily lives anymore.
> Michael: Yeah, whereas it used to be part of our daily lives more.
> Passaro: Yeah. Even live television is not, doesn't, I don't know. I don't think there's anything like it in our entertainment sphere and our daily lives, so that when you actually do go and sit down it becomes something so magical and transporting. I'm not sure, audience members can necessarily – and I'm not doing a good job of it myself – put this in words, but I think they get that on a very primordial level.
> Michael: You want the audience to feel that, but you don't need an audience to come out being theatre scholars. That's not the point of the exercise.
> Passaro: That's a good point.

For me the point that Passaro was trying to put into words is called external topology in this framework. As pointed out earlier, it is the way the space is shared and used which distinguishes live performance. My confidence that this framework can help explain audience's experiences without them even being aware of it has grown as I have watched my daughter teach me about each aspect of it from the earliest age.

As she has grown to discover her place in the world, she has given me confidence in delving deeper into phenomenology, semiotics, theories of space and concordance, dissonance and topology as useful tools for analysing and creating scenography. From birth it seemed she was interested in getting mobile enough, and in control of her senses enough, to be able to have some impact on her environment. Her earliest moments where I could tell that she was trying to understand the world were all phenomenological. My earliest memory of this is her understanding that if she moved (not quite crawling, more wriggling) into the area that was brighter because the sunlight was streaming in she would be warmer – and boy was she happy when she could accomplish this! Once she had hit one dangly item and watched it swing, she believed that all dangly things could be batted and turned into a pendulum. It was through these sensory, embodied experiences that her first understandings of the world grew. In both of these examples can be seen the pattern recognition of concordance (all dangly things are potential pendulums), dissonance (it is brighter and warmer over there) and topology (there is this amount of space between me and there and if I do this for long enough I will get there). Her semiotic development started pre-language with indexes – mummy picking up the keys meant a journey in the car. Semiotic development exploded with language acquisition – recognizing categories of things and illustrations of them as icons. She also developed her own symbols based on what was important in her life – any collection of three objects of a similar nature, but in different sizes, was described symbolically as the dadda one, the mummy one and the baby one. Understanding all of these as signs relies on understanding patterns of similarity, difference and spatiotemporal relationships. With continued exposure to language, books, TV and theatre, and a desire to understand her own emotions, from the age of three she grew an understanding of audience and the beginnings of an understanding of external topology. From this age she understood that space can and does operate differently within the worlds of stories, and that she can't access their spaces in quite the same way the characters do no matter how much they break the 'fourth wall'. Tellingly, with live performance, this was more difficult for her to understand, at least physically. And, of course, many performances for children encourage audience interaction, perhaps precisely for this reason. So, when the theoretical material seems impenetrable at times, I always try to remember that at its heart scenography is child's play.

Conclusions

An artistic model of stage management then is a scenographic one. It advocates that a stage manager's artistry can be evaluated by their ability to manipulate and orchestrate performance environments in order to have an impact on the audience's experience. The analysis of this impact can be conducted through a wide range of critical lenses such as semiotics, phenomenology, performance studies and scenographic theory. By way of introduction to those fields stage managers could consider each of their decisions in terms of the relationships that decision forms with others being made about the performance environment in terms of concordance, dissonance or topology. Understanding that each decision scenographers make establishes relationships along all three coordinates and that audiences innately respond to these relationships are the hallmarks of a scenographic stage manager.

CHAPTER 7
OBJECTIVES OF STAGE MANAGEMENT

All the technical theatre arts, including stage management, can be analysed and evaluated in terms of their contribution to the audience experience as argued in the preceding chapter. However, each of these artforms set out to achieve different objectives in their contribution to manipulating and orchestrating the performance environment. Pilbrow outlines the objectives for lighting designers as being selective visibility, revelation of form, composition, mood or atmosphere and information.[1]

Pilbrow further suggests that there is a hierarchy to the order in which the objectives should be pursued by a technical theatre artist. This is not because those objectives listed later are any less significant, just that they are often a product of achieving the earlier objectives. For example, the combination of choices of which things to light (selective visibility) and which aspects of those things to feature more prominently than others (revelation of form) *is* the composition, so only minor changes to the properties of light may be needed to achieve the desired compositional balance. Often, having achieved this, no further changes need to be made to achieve the right mood or atmosphere.

The last objective listed, information, is a little different from the rest. Depending on the specificity of the information needed to be conveyed to an audience, sometimes this will require additional manipulation of lighting properties. For example, while lighting can suggest a general time of day, if it is important that the audience knows precisely what time things are happening, this can be achieved through adding a digital clock as a lighting source.

All these objectives have their equivalents in stage management. The objectives of stage management share this hierarchical nature. I propose the analogous objectives are selective information flow, targeted information flow, distributed cognition, mood or atmosphere and translation.

Selective information flow

The primary objective of stage management is *selective information flow*. Much of stage management involves creating systems to receive, filter and distribute information. This, of course, is also what effective administration also seeks to do. My argument is not that stage managers are not administrative, but that they use this knowledge of how to process and communicate information to influence the performance environment, rather than to create an efficient system. Often, of course, an efficient system helps create the desired audience experience, which is why the assumptions of administrative stage management persist. An artistic stage manager uses their knowledge about the production's scenographic needs to guide the selection of which information to pass on and where and when this information flows to.

Livoti described this information flow as the primary objective with the comment: 'for me it's about making sure what I'm putting out there is understandable for everybody. That's first and foremost.' The remainder of the *Phantom* stage management team agreed.

> Athens: If you're in production and putting the show together you need to have the latest information. It changes constantly when you're putting a show together.
>
> Michael: And that's what this job is really about, right? Sharing the information in a way that is for the good of the show. There's some information that you can't share, or can't share yet, or decide not to share but managing that process I think is what stage management is all about, really? Would you agree with that?
>
> Oliver: Yes!
>
> Fenton: I would. I mean yes, we do what's good for the show.

When focusing on what a stage manager does it is very easy to overlook that what they choose not to do is just as important. A critical part of the primary objective is in understanding this *selective* aspect. I contend most of the information a stage manager receives about a production they choose not to pass on. This is in stark contrast to the administrative model which implies that there is no judgement involved and all information should be passed on. This is the position Pallin takes in the quote 'to communicate effectively is to pass on all information as quickly and accurately as possible with the least amount of negative interaction' which may be recalled from the earlier discussion about communication design.[2] Of course, I don't think Pallin's comment is meant to be taken literally (unless a wide scope of what may constitute 'negative interaction' is given) because it is impossible to pass on all the information a stage manager has. From an administrative perspective, the focus is on the process of passing on the information, and a preference for passing on the information, rather than how to select which information to pass on in the first place. A scenographic approach takes the opposite stance.

Accepting the default position is for a stage manager not to pass on the information they have about the production is the equivalent of a lighting designer choosing to build a lighting state from a blackout. This is one source of the myth of stage management effectiveness being equated with invisibility. A lot of the information received by stage management is not useful to others involved. For example, if all departments needed to know everything that happened in a rehearsal they would attend themselves; instead they rely on stage management to communicate *only* that which is relevant to them. I call this *passive filtering* – the stage manager accomplishes this by 'doing nothing'. Of course, what they are actually doing is acutely attending to the rehearsal in order to ensure that they assess all information, evaluate what is relevant information to pass along and then how best to communicate this. What is relevant is summed up by Fenton's comment earlier about 'what is good for the show'. As already explained in Chapter 6, from an artistic perspective this notion relies on the stage manager understanding the scenographic implications of the information. If in doubt of its relevance, they should pass the information along because having a stage manager that does not reliably pass on the necessary information is worse for the production scenographically than having someone that passes on too much information. Thus, the result of the administrative and scenographic models is often the same information being passed along. This explains why the focus in training and the administrative paradigm of stage management rightly concentrates on capturing and passing on information rather than filtering it out.

Stage managers also employ *active filtering* by choosing not to pass on information which they have deemed relevant or by doing something to ensure information is not passed on. In the latter case, this is often due to issues of sensitivity or confidentiality which would be similarly dealt with in the administrative and management paradigms. In the former case, the reasoning is much more likely to be scenographic in nature. Here, the conversation with Hobden about the problems that may be caused by immediate communication technologies in Chapter 4 is pertinent again. Just because it is now possible for stage management to immediately ask for a newly added prop, for example, to be in the rehearsal room in a few hours doesn't mean they should. In choosing not to communicate this immediately, stage management can delay the request until more is known about the prop. This allows them to assess its relative importance and make the request, if needed, in a way and at a time that enhances the ability of the recipient of the request to maintain focus on the scenographic priorities of the production. According to Fenton sometimes when sharing information 'What you don't say is just as important as what you do say'. In choosing whether to communicate something a key factor seems to be regulating the levels of distraction and coordination across all members of the company.

Targeted information flow

Regulating distraction and coordination is also a key aspect of the second objective of stage management: *targeted information flow*. Targeting is choosing which aspects of the information being communicated are highlighted. This is similar to how the revelation of form objective of lighting design emphasizes different aspects of what is being lit. From an administrative perspective, the goal of targeting is to work towards reducing distraction and increasing coordination, because from an objective operational efficiency model this would be desirable. However, sometimes effective targeting of the information flow works in the opposite direction should the production's scenographic needs require it.

Targeting the information flow involves (after having chosen that this information does need to be communicated – the first objective) ensuring that the right parts of the message are communicated to the right recipients, at the right time, in the right way. As stage managers are in effect the communication designers for a production, they, more so than other members of the production team, need to ensure that the messages they are communicating are crafted with the recipients (and the production) in mind, rather than their own operational needs. Kincman points out this is a key distinction between self-expression and communication.[3] From a purely administrative viewpoint, a lot of the stage manager's work is redundant and wasteful, as it involves repackaging the same information in different ways and at different times for different users or making multiple copies of the same information available in many different places.

Livoti points out that stage management need to think through the implications of every decision, who that needs to be communicated to and why and how best to communicate that to them:

> Livoti: I've worked on shows where we've decided to switch somebody who entered stage left here may now be entering stage right, small stuff like that. But you think, 'Who do we have to tell?' Okay, the actors, great. Also the swings, oh also the vacation swings . . . We need to tell wardrobe their clothes are going to be in a different spot. Oh we need to tell hair, their hair changes might be in a different spot. Great. Oh, we need to tell the crew that somebody's going to be crossing backstage here while they're moving this piece that they have not had to worry about before. Oh, got to tell sound because now a microphone might need to be reprogrammed . . . So all of a sudden you realize you've got to tell the whole building when you think 'I'm just changing somebody's entrance.'
> Michael: And different people need to know for different reasons, and need to be told at different times and in different ways?
> Livoti: Right. So a blanket statement of, 'Michael will now be exiting the third scene from stage right', doesn't do it. You need to say, 'This is what it means for your department.'
>
> And you see the times where you feel great having successfully headed off a massive issue ahead of time because you have people talking to one another. You put a note in the report, and twenty minutes later you get responses from three different departments going, 'We need to talk about this right away.' Good, that's the point. That's the whole reason we write that report. If you don't put that in, and if you don't put it in three different sections of the report because they only read their section, and if you don't phrase it in three different ways, then you could be the reason why tech comes to a screeching halt.

From an administrative perspective, Livoti's suggestion of a blanket statement should be a sufficient delivery of the facts. It would also meet the first objective of stage management. By considering precisely who needs the information and tailoring the message differently according to their needs, Livoti is demonstrating how to meet this second objective. If only the first objective was met, all of those involved would have to consider whether such a change impacted them, how and what to do about it. This would mean that they would have less time and mental capacity to attend to their area of expertise and therefore could hinder their contribution to the performance environment.

Abel discussed how repetition of the same message in different media can be used to highlight different aspects of the message even when going to the same recipient.

> Michael: If you've got a piece of information to get out to the company, how do you go about tailoring that?
>
> Abel: I think it depends on what the information is. Of course, right? So, if it's a situation where I'm calling rehearsal, I'm going to do that via written communication, probably posted on the call board as well as emailing all of them. If it's a situation where I have to handle something that has gone amiss, I will usually do that in person. Because again, I sort of like to delineate between what the mass knows, and what the individual needs to know.
>
> Last evening, I spoke to the Associate Director and she said, 'Oh, I'd like to work with these people on Thursday.' I could have just emailed them, but I had already generated a schedule on Saturday night. So, I went to talk to them in person to say, 'Hey look, the AD wants to see you guys. I'll send it to you in an email as well. But I just wanted to let you know.' I did that because once that schedule comes out on Saturday, people set their lives. So, I thought, 'I wonder if they have a doctor's appointment or something else.' . . . I was with them right away . . . and they were both like, 'Okay.' I feel like there's certain ways to handle those situations in order to accomplish the goal.
>
> Michael: I find it interesting that you then followed up with an email. Can you unpack that for me?
>
> Abel: Simply because once it's in writing, then it's in stone.
>
> Michael: Excellent. My guess is that, as well as putting it in stone, you will have emphasized different bits of the information verbally and in writing? And they may have had a different tone?
>
> Abel: Correct. Exactly. Their names, the hours, and where they will be were bolded in the paperwork.
>
> Michael: Excellent. So, the same information is going out in two different ways, but different aspects of the information were highlighted.
>
> Abel: Correct.

Later in the conversation Abel also demonstrated how the choices of how to differentiate the aspects of the message followed the patterns of the coordinates model. I particularly like Abel's characterization that the paperwork is almost liquid. This is a very different approach from the prescriptive templates proffered by some stage management texts written from an administrative paradigm.

> Abel: When you come into a show, like I did with this one, things were set. And things were done in a certain way. So, the paperwork was not a big issue for me, because I was like, 'Okay. Well, they're all used to this. Let's do this.' Then

I discovered along the way, that somebody might not show up, and I'm like, 'Well, why didn't she show up?' Well, because she's generally never called on the schedule. Or the piano wouldn't be set in the house, and he was, 'Oh, I missed that on the schedule.' So, I went to the head of every department, and said, 'What would make this stand out for you?'

And so that then became part of what the look of the actual printed piece of paper would be. It's continuously changing. It's almost like the paperwork is liquid, is the way I look at it. Okay? Because the bottom line is that nothing is fixed. Even when I say it's set in stone, it can still change. . . .

The other trap you fall into is, you're sending out this weekly schedule and most people don't think to check because they're never called. . . . So, if I know the principals are going to be called to rehearsal, we will make a hard copy for those people and hand it directly to them. So now they'll get it via email, but they've also had one handed to them. And I say, 'You're on it.' You know, so that's one piece of information, given in several different ways . . .

Michael: It sounds like people get into the habit of, 'Oh, I'm never called, so I won't look at that. Oh, yeah, it's one of those things.'

Abel: Exactly. I'm never called. I won't even look at it. And so, when there's a change . . . you have to do something different, use dissonance, to highlight that.

Michael: And in this case part of that dissonance is caused by changing the space and the timing, or topology, by which they get their schedule? It's easy to ignore an email, but now you're in their space handing them an object which is a different relationship in space and time from how they usually get that information?

Abel: Correct again.

Livoti demonstrates how these two objectives go together, using the example of generating running sheets for different departments from the one master deck plot. In the master deck plot, the stage manager selects and records which information is needed to run a production in performance. By filtering and sorting this information by department in various ways before passing it on, they are targeting the information flow. In understanding that saving collaborators from having to deal with too much information enabled a better performance environment, Livoti shows the difference between an administrative and a scenographic approach.

Livoti: I think sometimes you need to tailor things specifically to whoever. Not everyone needs all the information.

I've become a big fan of having everything on one sheet and doing sortable tables. So, if I need to give a carpenter a run sheet. I have the master deck, but the carpenter does not need the prop moves and so on. I sort by carp and they just get that. That's something I learned, I used to give everybody everything. And say, 'They'll figure it out, they'll highlight it on their own.' A lot of people were having difficulty working with that much information, it was too much to look at. They just want to know what *their* job is, it's *my* job to know what everyone's doing.

This management of the information load for other collaborators is the next objective of stage management: *distributed cognition*.

Distributed cognition

Like composition in Pilbrow's model of lighting design objectives, the third objective of stage management, *distributed cognition*, is largely the result of the sum of all the choices made in achieving the first two objectives. That is, it naturally occurs from selecting and targeting the information flow. Tribble offers the best introduction to distributed cognition for theatre scholars and points out that it has been a part of theatre practice at least since the early modern theatre.[4] This interdisciplinary field comprises of disciplines including cognitive philosophy, artificial intelligence and anthropology which 'share a view of cognition that foregrounds its social and environmental nature.'[5] Tribble argues that in theatre practice 'cognition is distributed across the entire system. This is not in any way to suggest that individual agency has no place. On the contrary, an environment as cognitively rich as the early modern theatre is precisely calculated to maximize individual contributions.'[6] I believe this argument holds for all theatre since this time as well.

The goal of distributed cognition, as it pertains to contemporary stage management, is to enable all people involved in the creation of the performance for an audience to be able to focus as much of their attention on their contribution to this interaction as they possibly can. Sharing the terminology and concepts of distributed cognition to the stage managers interviewed evoked similar responses as when sharing the definition of scenography: many immediately resonated with the concept and were taken with the fact that in other fields it was deemed to be a worthy concept for academic study and having its own terminology.

> Michael: You've kind of neatly segued onto my next objective of stage management which is summarised by this term I've come across 'distributed cognition'. Which means spreading the thinking around, basically. When I came across the term, I'm like, 'Oh. That's what stage managers do.'
>
> Abel: Absolutely!
>
> Michael: We're doing some of the thinking for them and spreading it out. Not that we're doing their design. But we're their eyes, ears, and brains in the rehearsal room. So that they can focus on wherever they are in their process.
>
> McMillan: Absolutely. Distributed cognition? It's delightful that's got a name.
>
> Michael: The term I'm using for what you were just describing is one that I've stolen from cognitive philosophy of all places, which is called distributed cognition.

> Alexander: Ooh, I like that!

> Simpson: All of this makes so much sense to me and we've talked about this before. As soon you start discussing stage management in the performing arts in this way it becomes a valid and worthy field of study.

During many of the interviews distributed cognition became the motif by which we discussed many aspects of stage management. I think this is because it is at the fulcrum point of the objectives of stage management: selective information flow and targeted information flow contribute to distributed cognition, while how the cognition is distributed largely determines what is necessary to meet the remaining two objectives of stage management. Abel's and Freeburg's reactions regarding the centrality of distributed cognition to stage management serve as examples.

> Michael: And as soon as I read about distributed cognition, I'm like, 'I need this' because it's about making the space do the thinking for us. I was like 'That is props tables.'
> Abel: Absolutely. It's quick changes. It's *everything*. That's what we do.

> Freeburg: I think that's what, as stage management, that's what our job *is*. Our job is to help everyone else do their jobs without them having to think too much about how to do their jobs.

Distributed cognition is more than just facilitation: literally making things easier. It is making things easier for people in a particular way, using a skill set that involves understanding, creating and maintaining a system that works with regards to all of the competing needs of the various artists involved in making a theatrical production. If it was merely facilitation, the eternal debates over whether stage managers make coffee would have been settled long ago. From a facilitation viewpoint making someone coffee, or doing their dry-cleaning, or other menial tasks certainly makes their lives easier, but these tasks are not normally those which aid the distribution of cognition for the production the most, so stage management usually devotes their limited time elsewhere. These tasks are also generally seen as below the rank of management, so stage managers operating from a management paradigm will often flatly refuse to do them. This debate stems from the fact that Equity guidelines prohibit stage managers from participating in the ordering of food for the company, yet it still happens. The debate has come to stand for whether stage management is a menial service role or an artistic managerial one.

This is predicated on a false binary. From a scenographic perspective, stage management is both, because it is in service to the production and an artistic role. Stage managers do sometimes make coffee, order food, do the dry-cleaning and many other menial tasks but not because they are in servitude to the other theatre-makers. When they do these things, it is because doing so will help them reach the objectives of stage management. Typically, it is when these tasks have become important enough that they are the most important tasks to complete to distribute the cognition in the system better, or better serve to regulate the mood or atmosphere. In other words, when it is good for the production. This is plainly seen in smaller-scale companies when a member of the stage management team maintains costumes or makes consumable props. When such tasks are needed by a production they will be done without question. This debate cropped up a couple of times in the interviews with stage managers. Firstly, when Hawley brought it up (although, of course, being from the UK it was cups of tea):

> Hawley: But I think what I've noticed is that [student stage managers now are] not perhaps willing to . . . They say, 'Well, I'm not going to make cups of tea.' Okay, well, no, in the grand scheme of things, you shouldn't, you're not a catering assistant, and if somebody says to you 'Can you go and get ten cups of tea?' and then just dismisses you, then that's not right. But if somebody turns to you and says, 'Do you know what? Would you just mind making a cup of tea?' That's different and you need to be able to tell the difference between the two. It's a silly example.
>
> Michael: No, not at all. I think it's a perfect example for what I call 'putting the work first'. It doesn't matter whether you're the ASM, or the Company Stage Manager, our job is to put the work first.
>
> Hawley: Absolutely.
>
> Michael: Because we're all there to serve the work. And so sometimes, serving the work means making a cup of tea, regardless of whether our contract says in big bold letters '**WE ARE NOT HERE TO MAKE TEA**', because generations of stage managers have been exploited that way.
>
> Hawley: Yes, yes.
>
> Michael: But it's very different when a member of the company comes to you and says, 'This traumatic thing has happened to me . . . I need to leave early today' . . . and you're like, 'Well, of course. Let's talk about it. Can I make you a cup of tea?' So, you're doing something nice to help them. Firstly, because you're a nice person, but also, because that's going to help the whole process by allowing them to overcome the distraction caused by the trauma, or to improve the atmosphere in the room.
>
> Hawley: Yeah, absolutely.

By the time I discussed this later with Alexander I had internalized the same concept into my own vice of coffee.

> Michael: This ties into some of the stuff about pastoral care that some stage managers are somewhat resistant to is 'Well, it's not really my job to look after them. It's not my job to . . .' The classic is to make the coffee.
>
> Alexander: Actually, yes it is. Well, for me it's always been, I will do what is necessary so that you can do what you need to do to the best of your ability. So, I will support you in any way that makes your life easier because that's what I'm here for.

The concept of distributed cognition also captures how important the designing of workspaces is to a production better than the notion of facilitation. As Tribble points out, 'Distributed cognition emphasizes the effects of cognitively rich environments on the agent operating within that system. The design of a physical environment influences how agents behave within it.'[7] Norman gives the example of how a nuclear power plant control room is designed with controls that are much larger than they need to be mechanically depending on the importance of the operation.[8] These allow the employees within a space to know what the most important functions are and to find these critical controls in moments of stress easily because the system has done the thinking for them by clarifying and organizing the space.

As the job title suggests, for stage managers, the most important physical environment is where the performance happens. More specifically, stage managers organize spaces so that the cognition in the system is optimally distributed for what the audience experiences during a performance. This is why stage managers mark up the rehearsal room; are concerned with the masking and lighting of backstage areas, and the communication systems available within venues; and give much consideration to how backstage spaces, including dressing rooms, props tables and quick-change booths, are managed. It is why they organize all the spaces they manage in a manner that is sensitive to the needs of performers and other collaborators. Many examples of how stage managers distribute cognition in this way came up in the interviews, but McMillan's and Alexander's examples regarding props setting were perhaps the most pertinent.

> Michael: I think an awful lot of what we do, say, and write, has [distributed cognition] in mind. Would you agree with that?
> McMillan: I realize that that's what I do. It takes me back to thinking about things that I used to do with prop setting, like setting a match in a certain way, and doing it exactly the same every time, because you knew that an actor's muscle memory would go and pick it up and strike it like that . . . because if I do that, then Bob, who's coming on stage, can just be Bob. That's when I found out I was a stage manager. I started thinking like that all the time.

> Alexander: I recently had an ASM, just out of drama school, and she set up for the first act and kept all of Act Two underneath the props table. I asked, 'What are you doing?' and she went 'Well, I'll put that out at the interval.' I say, 'Well the problem is . . . any singer or actor worth their salt will be on this stage having a look for their things that they need, having a wander round. Big part of their process. And you've just taken away their Act Two. Can you please put act two on the tables?'
> Michael: 'We've got the space. Use another table.'
> Alexander: 'I can hang things from the ceiling if needs be. Let's just put Act Two out.' and her response was: 'But then I've got nothing to do in the interval.' Well, 'Have a look at my tiny violin!' No, we're not playing that game. You're going to leave that set up and then we all know it's there. Everyone knows where it is and it's done.

Michael: And you provide . . .
Alexander: The safety net.

This safety net, the reassurance offered by distributing cognition in a sensitive manner that supports the performance, is part of the next objective of stage management: regulating the mood and atmosphere of the work environment.

Controlling the mood and atmosphere

The stage management objective of controlling mood and atmosphere neatly corresponds with Pilbrow's mood and atmosphere objective of lighting design. Again, if care is taken to achieve those objectives listed earlier, then it arises that the later objectives are often achieved with little or no extra effort. It is common that collaborators will comment on and evaluate stage managers' work predominantly in terms of their atmospheric contribution because this is the aspect of a stage manager's work they most directly experience. This is often true of performers, directors and audiences when they discuss lighting design as well. Graham has discussed the slippages between mood and atmosphere and the fact that such terms 'often signal a lack of understanding about the precise nature of the contribution of the design', but 'there is a material and critical importance of scenographically constructed atmospheres in theatre practice'.[9] For this reason, it is tempting to make this objective the primary focus. Stage managers from the management paradigm are the most likely to do this. However, making this objective their primary concern is counterproductive. If the information is not flowing correctly and the cognition is not being distributed in a way that supports the production, then the mood of the workplace will be chaotic and unproductive, regardless of any steps the stage management team may make to improve morale. Whereas the lighting designer is chiefly concerned about mood as experienced by the audience, the stage manager is chiefly concerned about the mood experienced by all the theatre practitioners in all the spaces identified in McAuley's taxonomy,[10] especially in the practitioner spaces. This, in turn, enables all of those working on the production (stage managers included) to effectively create the desired mood for the audience's experience.

Concentrating on the earlier objectives first also helps to establish the stage management team as trustworthy and professional which the interviewees suggested were key elements of how both the stage management team and the workplace should be perceived. Studham suggests this starts with consistency.

> Studham: And I think that consistency not only supports other people and their processes, but as a stage manager, if you are always consistent, it also builds trust. So that when it comes right down to it, that people on stage will trust that if something does happen, if something out of the ordinary happens in a show, you have their back. You have consistently supported them; you will continue to do that should anything happen in performance or any time.

Stage Management

> Michael: Yeah, so that's another objective of stage management in my opinion is establishing a rapport and keeping things professional so that there is that level of trust.
>
> Studham: Absolutely. Well, you're setting the tone . . . So, yes, always start with a professional attitude, approachable, and warm.

The *Phantom* team points out how stage management can use this trust to resolve problems quickly by taking the cognitive load off their collaborators early, which can stop a problem from ruining the workplace's atmosphere.

> Fenton: There is a little bit of deception involved sometimes when you're talking to people – actually a lot sometimes. You let them hear what they want to hear. You know that you can solve the problem but you don't have to necessarily tell them what the solution is . . . You can alleviate a problem or an issue very quickly by – it's not lying, really, it's just . . .
>
> Athens: Dancing around it.
>
> Fenton: Dancing around a few things to make it easier for you to solve the problem without them getting involved. Somebody comes in and says, 'This is an issue.' I might say, 'Yeah I know, I'm dealing with it' even if it's the first time I've heard of it. I just know what that issue is and how to solve it without them having to get even more worked up about it.
>
> Michael: You're just reassuring them that you've got the issue in hand?
>
> Fenton: Yeah.
>
> Michael: One of the other reasons why we tailor our communication is to set the tone and it needs to be a confident, reassuring kind of space, I think.
>
> Fenton: There's a big difference between doing that and then not doing anything.
>
> Michael: That would undermine trust kind of quickly.
>
> Athens: If you're going to use that deception, you have to come through.
>
> Oliver: Yes.
>
> Michael: It kind of defeats the point if people just go, 'oh, you're patronising me'?
>
> Fenton: They no longer trust you, so what's the point?

Passaro and McMillan point out that gaining trust is done in different ways by different stage managers as it relies on being true to your own personality. For Passaro starting early and maintaining regular contact are key.

> Passaro: I think you can only really [know the source of people's problems] by building up an incredible amount of trust from day one. Stage managers have different ways of doing that. One of my things is that I try to make it around to every single department in some way [daily] . . . because usually it's at that moment that people will say, 'Oh by the way, what do you know about this?' . . . So instead of people coming to you with problems after the fact, you're helping to sort of solve things before they become problems. And that's true whatever the

department is, coming by to say hello usually means you're going to find out more than just how people are. I call this MBWA: Management By Walking Around.

McMillan emphasizes the need to maintain a professional tone in her practice.

> McMillan: The way I work is that there's my professional life and my personal life . . . and they have always been quite separate. Maybe go for the first night drink and then that's it, there isn't any other kind of socializing that I will do with the company. I keep that separate.
> Michael: That's part of your communication strategy. To make sure that the tone and the atmosphere of the workspace is . . .
> McMillan: Professional.
> Michael: Yes. So that you've got the respect and the authority that you need to have. And different stage managers do it differently.
> McMillan: Of course they do, and I wouldn't look down on anyone who has a different way of working. It's what works for them.

The other key point the interviewees made about regulating the tone of the workplace is that it relies on the stage management team's ability to adapt their communication, even when the desired tone remains the same. It is not a matter of 'set and forget', because while stage managers may be responsible for regulating it, they are not the only factor that contributes to the overall atmosphere.

The first step of effectively regulating the mood is being able to successfully monitor it. Freeburg talks about some of the factors that change the atmosphere in the room and some general guidelines for how the room should feel.

> Michael: One thing I'd like to talk about it is setting the mood and the atmosphere, which different stage managers call different things. 'Reading a room' is a common way of expressing it. Is that another one of our objectives in adapting our communication?
> Freeburg: Absolutely.
> Michael: Like most things in stage management, it's not like there's one ideal way a room needs to be run. That changes.
> Freeburg: Every director, every process, every group of people, on a day-to-day basis it can change . . . There's a basic way I like to have my room feel, but it depends on who the director is, and who's in the cast, and what the time commitment is, and how emotionally heavy the show is. All of those factors come into the room every day.
> Michael: Yeah. Generally speaking, there's a couple of guidelines. We need to keep spaces safe for a start, that's not negotiable. But even that term, a 'safe space', means different things depending on the content of the show that you're working on and how to keep that space safe might change.
> Freeburg: Exactly, yeah.

> Michael: You want to keep it professional. You want to keep it creative. Again, these are vague terms, which shift. They're generally good things to be aiming for? I like to think that usually we want to keep it fun in some way.
>
> Freeburg: The job is so hard that if you aren't having fun, something's wrong. You might not be having fun in the moment, because you're doing something really challenging, but you want to be able to step out of that and be able to turn and crack a joke with someone, and all leave the room happy.
>
> Michael: That's part of the artistry of reading the room, and going, okay, now is not the time to crack the joke.
>
> Freeburg: Right, exactly, yes. That's the reward for making it over this emotional hump right here, yeah. Or that can be bringing in chocolates for everybody, or taking a break, or everyone going to have a cup of tea.

Scribner believes it is stage management's job to adapt based on the other factors, but overall a warm, caring atmosphere is the goal.

> Michael: You keep talking of a warm feeling. Is that something that you bring to every show, and every stage management team?
>
> Scribner: So, this is twofold for me. What I bring myself to the first rehearsal, and every first design meeting, and then I have to see how to adapt to what the other people are bringing. Really, it's my job to be the one that adapts. So, I can play good cop, and I can play bad cop, and depending on the director, I will adjust accordingly. The choreographer, the producer, the general manager, all of these people have a hand in the temperature, the balance, and the tone, but I think it's vital to set a tone from the beginning of honesty and respect. Warmth, I think is a great word to use, and it is important to me. To feel like it's a safe space, and to create what we all want, which is a piece of meaningful theatre in some way.
>
> Michael: You think that's part of stage management's job, is to set, monitor, and maintain the right tone, atmosphere?
>
> Scribner: That's right. I feel like the stage managers have the power to make or break the tone of a room. It's very possible that that tone can be set by the production, by the content, the material that you're working on, the director's vision, the way that the producer provides for the space, the theatre itself. So, you can be working with, or against, all of those factors as a stage manager, but it's an unspoken duty that the stage manager provides what is necessary to create a safe, comfortable environment. That's both what you physically see, and also what you feel in the theatre. It's that unspoken warmth that I think is vital.

Abel points out that sometimes stage managers need to adapt to change the atmosphere away from that which is generally desirable for specific purposes and that the tone of the backstage workspace has a direct impact on the audience's experience.

> Abel: Or even *how* you do it, right? The attitude that you have towards that communication.

Michael: [Well that leads into] . . . the next thing I wanted to talk about, is setting the right mood, tone, or atmosphere. And that's precisely to do with how you communicate.

Abel: Absolutely. Absolutely, Yeah! And it's interesting that you say that, too, because even in terms of the dressing room itself, you can get different personalities. You can see that some stations are highly organized and others are an absolute mess. So that also determines how I communicate with these people. I can say one thing to you knowing the type of individual that I perceive you to be. And I can say the exact same thing to someone else in a totally different tone because I've perceived them to be different. And then of course, as you run along, you find out really what kind of personality each person has and we'll play that psychological game of how can I manipulate this person into doing what I need them to do, while allowing them to think that they've done it.

Michael: Yeah. And that I'm a nice person?

Abel: And that I'm a nice person. This is a pleasant atmosphere to work in. Exactly. But then of course, you also have those times when, you know what? It's not going to be a pleasant conversation. It's not going to be a pleasant atmosphere.

Michael: Yep. And you have to be in control of that. And you also have to be receiving the feedback –

Abel: And be willing to also say, 'I didn't understand it that way. I apologize for approaching you that way.' Or, 'No, you're not hearing what I'm saying to you right now.' You know?

Michael: Yeah. Sometimes you get the person who isn't getting the serious tone. Because they're used to dealing with you as a fun, friendly, 'Let's keep company morale up' kind of person. And so they think, 'Oh you're just joking around'. And so you have to . . .

Abel: . . . approach it again. Yeah, maybe in another way. And maybe just in terms of, 'Oh, no. I'm not joking. Here it is again. You can tell by the fact that I'm giving it to you again, and nothing has changed, that you haven't received this information correctly. Not quite the way that I wanted you to.'

Michael: Yeah. Like everything, it depends on the show. And there's no one kind of atmosphere that you're trying to go for in a room, necessarily. But are there some guiding principles?

Abel: This is the thing. I'm a real firm believer in like, whatever the temperament is backstage, is what the audience is going to get. So, if we're doing a serious show, the temperament backstage is a totally different thing from doing like a big musical theatre piece. And I think that that tone has to be set by the stage manager. That's not to say that you cannot have fun. But it also means that you don't want to be telling a joke before somebody has to go do like a monologue about them dying.

One of the things that has the potential to disrupt the desired working atmosphere is if there are misunderstandings between collaborators on a production. This is when stage management needs to focus on their final objective of *translation*.

Stage Management

Translation

The *translation* objective of stage management is similar to Pilbrow's information objective of lighting design, in that, whether or not achieving this objective requires additional effort depends on how specific the needs for this objective are. Translation here is broadly defined to mean either transposing from one *mode* of communication to another and/or from one *'language'* to another. By language I am referring to the particular vocabularies, informed by a knowledge of the tools, techniques and processes, of each distinct discipline involved in the production.

Scribner eloquently described the importance of translation to stage management:

> Scribner: As a stage manager you need to understand how the process unfolds for each person and speak their language. To be able to hear, and assess what is going on for each person, and then be able to communicate other people's needs back to them. You have to listen to one another, and as detectives suss out where we are with each department and what their needs are, and then translate that into other people's language. So, I like to think that it looks very simple from the outside, but it has a lot of layers from the inside, and there is an art to communicating.

A common act of translating between *modes* is the stage manager's recording of blocking notation in the prompt copy: translating a spatial experiential mode into a written mode of expression. The danger for an administrative stage manager in trying to translate between these different modes is that an overly *literal* translation is possible. This is more likely to happen when stage managers are learning how to take blocking notation and they have been instructed to give blocking notes to actors. Stage managers then try to capture and regulate every move that the actors make and this can interrupt the flow of the rehearsal process. If the stage managers' understanding of the scenography of the production informs this style of translation it allows the stage manager to appreciate and record only those movements of the actors which are significant (which is dependent on the production and its desired impact on the audience). This selection of which information to capture, of course, is a return to the primary objective of stage management.

Thus, most stage management translation occurs as a by-product of achieving the earlier objectives. Because this style of translation is reflexively embedded within, and a result of, a wide variety of stage management practice, many examples from the interviews can already be found throughout this book. Rehearsal reports (which have featured in many of the interview extracts), for example, involve translating the embodied experience of people in the rehearsal room into a written mode of communication. Understanding the scenographic needs of a production to inform the selection of which information to report; which aspects of that information is targeted; how to report it so that the cognition is effectively distributed; and the correct tone to be conveyed is what separates a scenographic report from an administrative one. There is not much to add conceptually about translations of this sort. No extra effort is required by stage management to achieve this objective because once you have achieved the other objectives in your completion of the task, the task's completion is itself the translation.

There is one act of translation between modes which deserves a separate mention. The stage manager's most direct contribution to the performance environment as experienced by an audience is an act of translation: from an informational mode to an experiential mode. During the act of performance, the stage management team's function is precisely to manipulate the performance environment to have an impact on the audience whether that be through managing or completing set, props or costume changes or through the calling or operation of technical cues. Even Fazio's first edition concedes[11] that there is an artistic element to the translation of the director's and designers' decisions into a cue calling script and then timing the calling of these cues precisely in order that they have the desired impact on the audience.

At different points throughout this book there have been discussions about the difference between calling a show cleanly and calling it well. Calling a show cleanly can result when stage management translates this information too literally (as in the administrative paradigm) without understanding the scenographic intention of each of these transitions and the nature of liveness in live performance. A clean performance is one which is regarded as error-free such that any unintentional dissonance between the technical apparatus of the performance and the performers was not perceived to be significant by the audience. The scenographic approach, on the other hand, attempts to achieve such alignment between the technical apparatus and the performers in their concordance and use of topology, that every cue 'lands' perfectly, enhancing their significative potential for the audience. This distinction can be used to summarize the key distinctions between the two models. Administrative stage management focuses on error-free productions; scenographic stage management seeks to enhance the audience's experience.

The other style of translation from one 'language' to another often does require extra attention from stage management. When it is done asynchronously, it usually is part of the first kind of translation, because it usually also involves a change in mode as the stage manager is passing on information in a different forum later. Again, this is simply achieving the earlier objectives of stage management. To achieve these earlier objectives effectively, stage management needs to understand the different 'languages' of the different collaborators. Maccoy illustrated this with regards to the different languages used to discuss safety in productions.

> Maccoy: There are four words that you don't mention in front of a Director and they are 'health', 'safety' and 'risk assessment' because you are waving a red flag at a bull . . . Instead, you say 'I'm worried that this might be dangerous and that somebody might get hurt'.
> Michael: Exactly. One of the objectives that I think we have in designing our communication is 'translation' and making sure that you're using the right language, if you will, to different people. So yes, if you're talking to the

> Production Manager, you'll be saying 'yes I've done the risk assessment for this' but you don't use the same language about the same thing to the Director because that just kills the creative atmosphere in the rehearsal room.
>
> Maccoy: But if you're talking in terms of danger and making sure people aren't getting hurt that is actually maintaining that creative atmosphere.

Extra effort is usually required by stage management on translation when the need for it is so pronounced, precise or unusual that it needs to happen synchronously. That is, translating between people in the same time and using the same mode of communication. This synchronous translation often occurs during production meetings or technical rehearsals. In trivial cases it may be simple substitution or explanation of terminology. For example, a lighting designer may refer to a specific kind of lighting instrument, whereas the director wants to know that it has a hard edge; or, conversely, the director may refer to something by a name it has acquired during the rehearsal period that may not make sense to people who weren't in the room. However, the need is sometimes a result of an earlier misunderstanding which could have been dealt with asynchronously earlier if detected.

Translation only helps in this case if the stage manager's understanding of the scenography of the production can aid the two people who are talking at cross-purposes by using scenography as the lingua franca between the collaborators. These misunderstandings are usually revealed at stressful times, can be frustrating and can often feel to one or more of the collaborators that their agency for their department is being threatened. For these reasons, the way that stage management offers translation in these moments needs to be nuanced, respectful and conducive to helping regulate the tone of the workplace as much as is possible. Freeburg suggested that this could be achieved by offering a scenographic explanation between the two positions that centres the audience, while centring yourself as the stage manager as the cause of any misunderstanding.

> Michael: There's different languages, if you like, that a director uses, from a lighting designer, from the actors, from wardrobe and so on. Sometimes the artistry is in . . .
>
> Freeburg: . . . getting the director and the lighting designer to understand each other.
>
> Michael: Is that a skill that you think you need?
>
> Freeburg: Absolutely. We've all been in the room in tech, where you know that the director and the lighting designer are not talking the same language. They say one thing, and the other hears something else, and so you say 'I think what she means to say is she wants it to feel like this, and I think what he's trying to say is, if it feels like this, then this is why it feels like that. Is that what we're talking about? I just want to make sure that I understand what you both want.' Then, that opens it up to make them both explain it in a different way.
>
> Michael: I love the way that you expressed it, how when you're using that skill of translation, you're like, *I* don't understand. 'Please can someone explain this to *me*?' When we're doing that style of translation, we do it more subtly than an

interpreter. We don't say, 'Here is what you are saying.' We say, '*I think* you're saying these things. Is everyone comfortable with that?' We offer our solution while putting ourselves as the source of the problem: '*I'm* not understanding what's going on here. I thought we were trying to do this. Is that what everybody else thinks? Okay, then if that's what we're trying to do, then I don't understand why this is happening.' The lack of understanding . . .

Freeburg: Right, 'The lack of understanding is on *my* part.' Exactly.

Because translation is actually implied in each of the other objectives, often stage managers do not need to worry about this objective directly. This requires, of course, that they are mindful of the need for information to be captured, understood, retrieved and shared in different modes and in different languages when they are focused on the other objectives. Conversely, when encountering those few things in any production which have been 'lost in translation' earlier so that stage management must focus specifically on meeting this objective, great care must be taken to not sacrifice the earlier objectives in these moments. These moments can be stressful, so attention on maintaining the appropriate mood and atmosphere, in particular, is advised.

Conclusions

The objectives of stage management then are selective information flow, targeted information flow, distributed cognition, controlling the mood and atmosphere and translation. An understanding of the scenographic needs of the production provides the rationale for what constitutes the successful achievement of these objectives. For example, the information selected to be passed on is that which is scenographically significant for this production. Stage management should attend to these objectives in this order because the later objectives are often achieved as a consequence of achieving the earlier ones. That strict hierarchy does need to be problematized, however, as all the objectives are, in fact, reflexive. The correct selection and targeting of information relies on knowing the likely consequences of how cognition will be distributed, how the tone of the workplace will be impacted and in which 'languages' the information needs to be understood. Understanding the scenographic intentions of a production enables stage management to achieve these objectives, as Maccoy writes, 'an understanding of "why" that will lead to "how".[12] In turn, understanding these objectives enables stage management to determine what to do when they manipulate the properties of communication.

CHAPTER 8
THE PROPERTIES OF COMMUNICATION

So far we have looked at the why (including the central issues of scenography to which all technical theatre artists contribute) and the how (by achieving the objectives outlined in the last chapter) of stage management practice. It may seem strange but now in the second last chapter of the book I will finally consider *what* stage managers do. Even here, though, I am interested in the artistry of what stage managers do rather than cataloguing the tools and processes they use. From an artistic standpoint what stage managers do is design the communication for a production.

Like the other theories introduced in this book as sites for further interdisciplinary research, I do not intend to offer a fulsome description of communication theory, but I do recommend it as a source of inspiration for those wishing to learn more about their stage management practice. This is partly because, similar to other areas of scholarship that stage management intersects with, communication is a diverse and contested academic field in its own right. To approach the discipline, the overview of many diverse theories provided by Littlejohn et al. is a good place to start.[1] For the purposes of the discussion in this book, in the interest of simplicity, a transmission model of communication where a message is sent to one or more recipients is explored in the context of stage management processes. The aspects of this transmission which constitute the properties of communication that stage managers design are explored in this chapter.

This implies the medium of stage management is communication. Part of the reason why stage management appears superficially different from the artistry of other technical theatre disciplines is in its intangibility and unclear association with its medium. It is apparent even to people who have never been to the theatre that a lighting designer produces a part of the experience and has some artistic control over a specific medium. It is not clear from the term stage manager that they are, in effect, the communication designer for the production. For many of the stage managers interviewed, however, this was clear. These statements from Abel and McMillan serve as examples.

> Michael: When you say a lighting designer is an artist you know that the medium of their artform is light. And it's not as obvious with stage management but my argument is that the medium of our artform, if it is an artform, is communication.
> Abel: Totally agree with you 100%. Absolutely . . . I really feel like absolutely communication is utmost.

Michael: A painter uses the medium of paint. As stage managers, our medium is communication, if we are artists and if we have a medium. Is that something you agree with?

McMillan: Yeah, absolutely. Yeah. . . . Being able to manage other team members, people's personalities, to be able to work with different personalities and, 100% of the job, I would say is communication.

Michael: Yeah. That's the other important thing: the flexibility involved in the communication. To maintain the goals you were talking about of the good working relationship, or building rapport or setting the tone in the rehearsal room, sometimes your communication has to adapt, to be designed, to achieve the same goal.

McMillan: I think it always does. Not sometimes. I think probably it always has to.

I am not arguing that stage management teams should change their titles to communication designers. I think their central objective as prime distributors of cognition for performance spaces and the current title of stage manager are very well suited. I do think, however, if all theatre-makers and researchers (including stage managers themselves) understood the role of stage management as communication design then the similarities between their practice and that of other technical theatre artists would become more apparent.

Both administrative and scenographic views of stage management – as well as the managerial conception and I imagine any other – understand communication is central to the practice. Where they differ is how much agency stage management is given in designing this communication. If we were to take both conceptions of stage management to their extremes, administrative stage management would consider stage management to be effective if all of the prescribed communication tools and techniques were applied by rote to every production so that all of the customary processes were completed in order, on time and within budget. Scenographic stage management, on the other hand, would eschew any customary communication tools and would design each piece of communication from the ground up with the audience's experience in mind. Neither of these extremes represents effective stage management. The former would perhaps do less harm to the production overall which is another reason why administrative thinking predominates. A sensible compromise may be reached if the customary communication tools (by which I mean things such as rehearsal reports, prompt copies, running sheets and tasks stage managers customarily do) are seen as a guide to a particular way of manipulating the properties of communication that have proven to be effective in the past and which are in common usage in the industry. Each of the tools allows for a certain flexibility in how and why they can be applied, but by virtue of their familiarity they offer expediency and a great deal of distributed cognition immediately.

This is, unsurprisingly, remarkably similar to the designing of other technical theatre artists. To continue the comparison of lighting design with stage management, the extremes of an administrative lighting design (which seems a strange contradiction in terms already because of the presence of the word 'design') could be turning the stage workers on and the house lights off at the beginning of the show and reversing this at the end of the show. The extreme scenographic lighting design would eschew all usual theatrical lighting technology and develop the required lighting sources for each different lighting state required for the desired audience's experience. In actuality, most lighting designers use standard procedures, software, tools and techniques to create their design for most of their productions. They choose specific lighting tools knowing the constraints of those tools and with their desired manipulation of the properties of light in mind.

Some of the resistance to regarding stage management as artistry (including from stage managers themselves) stems from how unconsciously it is done. Alexander and Franklin described the artistry with which they send messages, respectively, as routine or natural.

> Michael: [We adapt our communication according to] who needs to know that information, and when they need to know that information, and how they need to receive that information. All of that we do –
>
> Alexander: Without really thinking about it most of the time. Thankfully these processes have been put in place for years, so a lot of us just follow the same routine of 'Well, it's the end of the day of rehearsals, what's happened today? Who needs to know about what's happened today?'
>
> Franklin: Again, I don't even think about it, because I've done it for such a long time. It's like a natural process. It's getting all that information, and then working out how to send it out again and give it to the right people in the right formats that they can use.

To me, though, this highlights the artistry involved. That such complicated determinations about which messages to send (and how to send them so that ultimately the performance environment is continuously orchestrated and manipulated in the desired way) can become instinctive over time demonstrates a level of facility with communication design and scenography. The fact that various aspects of a lighting designer's work are done instinctively does not lessen the general view of their practice as technical or artistic.

Stage management is also sometimes dismissed as non-technical and non-artistic because the tools and processes by which messages are sent out are understood as 'natural'. This argument contends that all people send messages by communicating, and that all collaborators have as their goal effective communication and collaboration, so there is no specific artistry to stage management. This has more to do with the myth of the invisible stage manager than reality. One source of this myth is because one of the ways stage managers try not to impede others' communication is by trying hard not to demonstrate the effort and labours involved in their work. To the extent that it is true that we all naturally communicate, we all naturally adjust the spatial, illuminative and sonic aspects of our environment as well, but that does not make us as knowledgeable, technical or artistic as professional set, lighting or sound designers. The processes involved in the selection of appropriate lighting instruments, focusing them or programming them are much more technically and artistically precise than adjusting the gooseneck lamp to the proper place on the production desk or turning off the lights to go to sleep at night. In much the same way, the detailed consideration of how to manipulate the properties of communication in stage management is much more technically and artistically precise than just talking to people or writing something down.

The properties of a medium of an artform are those characteristics that each instance of the medium must have which can be controlled by the artist. Pilbrow's properties of light are intensity, colour, distribution and movement.[2] These properties are hierarchical because although each instance of light has these properties, perception of those properties listed later relies on perceiving the earlier ones first. That is, a light needs to be of a certain intensity before its colour is apparent to us, its colour becomes apparent before its distribution (by which Pilbrow means properties associated with what is producing the light, for example, whether the beam has a hard or soft edge, is flat or textured or the angle it is coming from). The final property listed (movement) is a change in any of the other properties of the medium. Such changes occur over time, and the transitions can be seen or unseen. This change must be large enough for it to be perceived as movement.

It is important to understand these nuances of these relationships between the properties of light because they all have their analogues in stage management. For stage management, I term the hierarchy of the properties of communication as the message, mode, distribution and updates. Many times in the examples that follow earlier interview excerpts will be referred to rather than new ones because it is hard to talk about how or why to do something without some mention of what that thing is, so many of the examples of stage management practice already discussed demonstrate the manipulation of the properties of communication.

Message

The first property of communication is the *message*. This is the information that has been communicated. In this case in a controlled way by the stage manager, in much the same way that a lighting designer controls the intensity of the light. This message may be very explicit or extremely subtle. At one extreme, giving a direct instruction is clearly communicating a message and, at the other, choosing to not communicate anything can be a significant and potent choice. This is the equivalent of a black out being a potent lighting choice for a lighting designer.

This concept of giving out no messages is interesting for two reasons. Firstly, it is impossible. This is the myth of the invisible stage manager again. For stage management, what is meant by this desired notion of invisibility and lack of communication is the desirability for stage management to not be sending undesired messages or impede others' ability to communicate. By their very presence, or absence, a stage manager is communicating something. Take the example of a stage manager in the rehearsal room. It is generally desirable for them to be 'invisible' to the director and the actors. The best way to do that is for the stage manager to be seen to be attending to the rehearsal in a way that meets all the objectives of their communication. Recall in Chapter 4 there was discussion about to what extent a rehearsal room stage manager using a laptop disturbs the rehearsal process. Maccoy pointed out that this could be distracting because it gives others in the room the suspicion that they may not be attending fully to the rehearsal. The presence of the laptop, especially when it is the only one in the room, sends out messages that the stage manager is not in control of, thus making them more visible in the room.

Paradoxically, the only way for stage management to be unseen is by being seen to be selecting appropriate information, targeting the information flow, distributing cognition, regulating the mood and atmosphere and translating where appropriate. Their general demeanour in the rehearsal room, when they are not trying to transmit any particular new piece of information, must be sending these messages to provide the trust and reassurance needed to regulate the tone of the rehearsal room as was discussed in the last chapter. If stage managers *try* to be invisible and regard this as their objective, their attempts to remain hidden can make them obvious which makes achieving their other objectives more difficult. I have most often seen this with beginning stage managers. Especially when they must enter a workplace – especially rehearsal rooms – during a working session. Those that enter trying desperately not to interrupt often end up being the very distraction they are trying to avoid, while those entering in 'stage management mode' are barely noticed because they are attending to the production's needs rather than their desire to not be seen.

The second reason this concept of 'no messages' is interesting is a consequence of this fact that it is impossible to actually be sending no messages. Therefore, if you want to actually send the message 'there is an absence of messages' then you must be explicit about it, as Alexander points out.

> Alexander: So we think, 'Ooh, I haven't got anything [for that department for the rehearsal report today]. Shall I just tell them what a great day we had? Yeah, let's just do that. Keep everyone involved and feel like they're part of something.'
> Michael: Yes, that's important. And I would go so far as to say it's really important to let the sound department know that there are –
> Alexander: no notes for them today. So that they don't think that you've missed something.

As this excerpt demonstrates being explicit about the absence of messages can help regulate the mood ('keep everyone involved') and distribute the cognition effectively (the department is not worried that something has been missed).

Mode

The more explicit the message is, the easier it is for someone to determine the *mode* of the message which refers to how the message is expressed. Examples include verbally, in a written format, experientially, by manipulating the space or through body language. This second property of stage management communication is analogous to colour in Pilbrow's properties of lighting. For colour to be perceived, the illumination must be sufficiently bright. Further, by using unsaturated colours that may be perceived as neutral or having no colour, or being warmer or cooler, quite bright lighting can be used without the perception of colour. In stage management terms, this suggests that a message must be minimally explicit for the mode to be discerned. Sometimes stage managers want to convey a message very subtly without the recipient discerning the mode. Further, sometimes the mode is hard to determine even when the message is quite explicit. Obscuring the mode of the message is often helpful when trying to achieve the latter objectives of distributing the cognition and regulating the mood of the workplace as these objectives tend to be supported by buy-in from all collaborators rather than a one-way method of information flowing from a sender to a receiver. The mode chosen by stage managers is dependent on the available communication technologies and the needs of the recipients.

The reason why many stage managers mentioned the advances in communication technologies in Chapter 4 when asked for examples of what had changed in the field recently is because it has meant that new modes of communication are available to them. While the influences of the ubiquity of smartphones, email, the internet and portable computers can be felt in many fields, for stage managers this is more fundamental because it represents a whole new set of tools with which they can practice their art. Continuing our comparison with lighting design, this explosion of communication technologies is akin to the advent of moving and intelligent lights which I discussed with Abel.

> Michael: And the art is in knowing what's appropriate to email or text. Or needs . . .
> Abel: . . . an actual face-to-face conversation.
> Michael: And knowing which messages that you're sending out will be received well by which tool you're using.
> Abel: Exactly. Yeah.
> Michael: To compare it to lighting, because that's my other gig. Do I choose this lighting instrument or that lighting instrument? It's still light. With us it's still communication. But you use different ones for different reasons. And that's part of the art of communication is using the different tools available.
> Abel: Yes. Yeah. Absolutely.
> Michael: And sometimes, just like when moving lights came out, it seemed for like years the shows were all about the moving lights.
> Abel: Oh my god, yes.
> Michael: Now, thankfully, it's not about the technology.
> Abel: Do you remember that? You're absolutely right. Nobody even watched the show we were watching the lights.
> Michael: Now, they're being used as a tool for the art. For a while technology takes over and then it . . .
> Abel: It can be detrimental, right?

> Michael: . . . Is detrimental to the artform. Exactly.
> Abel: Yeah, yeah. When it becomes about the tool rather than supporting the art. Fascinating, yeah.

This pattern can be seen in some of the complaints about these new technologies discussed in Chapter 4. Using these tools of 'immediacy' simply because they are available can harm achieving the objectives of communication and, ultimately, the audience's experience.

With many more methods of communication available Scribner points out that the recipient's needs or desires are important considerations when deciding which method to choose.

> Scribner: So, we have some people who like to group text, there's individual texting, there's emailing, there are people who only want to be spoken to in person. There are people who leave voicemails and make phone calls on the show. So, I can't say I have a style of communication, because ultimately I'm adapting to every single person's needs, and I have a menu of options to choose from.

Understanding the communication needs and preferences of the collaborators is important if stage managers are to design communication that meets the objectives, especially of distributing cognition effectively and of regulating the mood of the workplace. This is because messages sent using the wrong mode or method may be missed or ignored or frustrating and off-putting to the recipients. This, in turn, will have an impact on the performance environment and the audience's experience. Even if stage management knows little else about the specifics of a certain department's or collaborator's process, understanding their communication needs is paramount as Hobden outlines.

> Hobden: I don't know very much about sound, but I appreciate what they're doing. I know that I'm not going to flash the sound operator to have a conversation about something, unless it's vital.
> Michael: Because they don't want to be listening to you. Especially in a musical.
> Hobden: Unless I'm telling them that the violinist is sick and kill the mic, but even then there's even a better way to do that, because you go through the Sound Number Two and they type the message. It's just knowing that they have that facility. Just having an appreciation of the departments around you.
> Michael: That's a great example. Different departments have different ways of working, and it's our job to know those different ways of working and to adapt our communication to fit in with them, not the other way around. Stage management doesn't work if we all say 'No, no, this is how I'm calling the show. You adapt to me.'

Hobden also discusses the differing and competing needs of communication during the running of a performance and the process by which that is tailored in response to the specific needs of the performance environment. Here she problematizes the need for the stage manager to be the one who always adapts. If the needs of the performance are such that, for given moments, some department needs to adapt to stage management then that process is negotiated. Note that this isn't done for the convenience of stage management but only when the audience's experience is enhanced by such an approach.

> Hobden: There's a certain amount of 'This is how I do it', but I would always say, to like the lighting operator on this show, 'Okay Act One at the end, it's really busy, I'm just going stand you by for the whole act. Is that okay? Or, as we go through, let me know if there's a point where, "actually can you just stand me by?"' 'And I'll do that.' Again to sound, I'll say to them, 'I need to cue you for these two because they go with LX cues.'
> They go with lighting or they start a scene change. It's like the MD, most of the time, I'm responding to him, but there are a few times where I have to give him a 'clear' to come out of the hold bar, that we've achieved something, or to start the act. Again it's all communication. And again, with the MD, occasionally, I might say 'Actually, I can't see that cut-off, can you show me what you're going to do?' Nine times out of ten, they're more than happy to just go 'Oh, would it be easier if I did this instead' 'Brilliant! Thank you very much!' instead of struggling and getting it wrong all the time.

Here Hobden talks about the need to record even those cues that aren't called by stage management.

> Hobden: 'Do you want me to cue you for these other ones? I know you take them yourself and if it's not necessary, I'll just have a note of where it goes in the book, but I won't waste that time giving you a cue and you ignore it.'
> Michael: I keep them in my book, but in brackets and with the note 'don't call this one'.
> Hobden: I colour code, so if they're in blue, it means it is information and I know it's there. But I know that when I'm calling I don't have to. I'll be listening out for it, but I won't call it.
> Michael: Because if it's not in the book at all, then sometimes you get surprised by it. 'What's the sound operator doing?' You need to know that it's coming up, even if you're not calling it.

An important aspect of this extract is the reminder that important recipients of communication to consider are the stage management team themselves. This can often be overlooked in our quest to distribute cognition for others. When I suggested that stage managers always need to adapt their communication based on the needs of the other people, Hobden countered, quite rightly, with the point that there are times when the collaborators need to adapt to stage management needs. These aren't just stage management whims or preferences but are driven by the needs of the performance.

Stage Management

Examples are deviating from normal stand-by procedures because the cue sequence is too busy; specifying which cues must be given to the sound department even if their preference is not to be cued; distributing the cognition for stage management itself in the prompt copy for cues which exist but aren't called; and asking the MD either to practice or change their conducting at certain points to enable clearer communication for stage management. The goal in tailoring communication for the recipients' needs therefore relies on a scenographic understanding of the performance environment to understand which recipients' needs to prioritize.

Distribution

The third property of stage management communication has so much in common with Pilbrow's third property of light that it even shares the same term: *distribution*. Just as with lighting, the properties of the communication associated with its source can be significant. In both lighting and stage management, distribution captures a collection of properties together. For communication, the distribution includes such things as the source, tone, the recipients and the timing of the message. The source of the message is where the recipient perceives the message has come from. Sometimes stage managers will ask the director or designer to pass on a message, sometimes they will be asked to pass on a message on someone else's behalf and sometimes stage managers will arrange spaces so that the message is perceived to come from the space itself. Tone exists in all modes of communication, not just verbal. Recipients may respond very differently if they are the only recipient of the message from if they are one of many to receive the same communication. Recipients will also respond very differently to messages depending on the time at which they receive them.

Like many aspects in this chapter, there are many examples from earlier chapters which demonstrate the commitment stage managers have in manipulating the distribution of their messages. Of course, because each instance of communication has all the properties of communication, these properties are reflexive so that even in the preceding section on the mode of the communication, much consideration was given to the recipients. As discussed in Chapter 4, stage managers must remember it is the timing of the *receiving* of the message which is important, which may be very different from the time it was sent. Because of the speed of the act of distribution via email or text, rather than the laborious task of printing and placing the rehearsal notes in pigeonholes, this is now easier to forget than it once was. The *Phantom* stage management team emphasized the importance of the timing of the message.

This was reinforced in my individual conversation with Livoti.

> Livoti: And I find that even if you're relaying really bad news, if you're really ahead of time rather than the day that they have to deal with it, it's a much better conversation. 'Look, I know this makes your life harder. This is what the director wants, this is what the choreographer wants. This is what I need in the wings

here to make this quick-change happen. Solve for X, but I'm giving you a week to solve for X. Or if you're in tech, I'm giving you a day-and-a-half to solve for X, because we're going to get there in two days.' So, the more time that you can let people have, that way they can have their initial emotional response, and then half-an-hour later go, 'Okay this isn't actually that bad. Let me just figure this out.' It makes for a much easier process, and I think the people who are better communicators . . . Look I'm not perfect, I miss stuff, I think we all do.

Michael: Everyone does.

Livoti: But the people who are better communicators make for smoother processes because people know what to expect, and they can solve problems ahead of time.

Michael: So, timing of the communication is really important?

Livoti: For me it is.

It also came up in the group conversation with the rest of the *Phantom* team.

Michael: In addition to what you do and don't say, there's this issue of timing. When you choose to say it.

Athens: Yes.

Fenton: Oh yeah, yeah. Timing is very important.

Oliver: Everything one could say.

Michael: Ha Ha! Timing is everything. Love it.

Fenton: Well, it is. One of my things is the psychology of the timing thing. Two days ago, on Tuesday, I put up, the new schedule because we are changing it next week. I was going to put it up on Saturday but I thought, don't put it up on Saturday, because it's the end of the week and then for those two shows on Saturday everyone's going to be, 'Oh for goodness sake we're changing schedule again!' You put it out on the Tuesday, people go, 'Oh no!' but by the end of the week they've forgotten about it. People have a very short memory. If you can get through two or three days with something, you're fine. I find.

Athens: That happens, with note giving and taking too.

Oliver: Yes.

In these examples all the stage managers are demonstrating that they manipulate the timing of messages to meet the objective of, in these cases, controlling the mood and atmosphere.

Updates

The final property of stage management communication I will call *updates*. This is analogous to movement in Pilbrow's properties of lighting design as it expresses a change in any of the other properties of communication. Updates are required either when a previous message has changed or when the message is the same but it has not been received or acted upon in the desired manner. In this case, the message is repeated with a change in properties. This change in properties could be minimal. That is, the message could be communicated in exactly the same way, but because it is being repeated, the timing has changed. Usually when repeating a message, more properties are changed, and sometimes it is appropriate to call attention to the fact that it is a repeated message not a new message being communicated. For example, Abel explains how she draws attention to revisions when distributing paperwork. 'Anytime anything is revised, it's in red. So, if it's generated and then it goes out, and then I have to adjust it... everyone looks at the red, and they see their name, they know they're called.' This also demonstrates her use of semiotics to update the properties of communication to meet the objective of targeting the information.

Here is an example of the other need for updates, where the message remains the same, outlined in Livoti's polite, understated manner.

> Livoti: There's the 'This is the first time I'm giving this note' way. There's 'This is the second time I'm giving this note' way. And there are the third, fourth, and fifth time we're talking about this ways. And those all have different conversations associated with them.

Sometimes a message is so important that stage management repeats it immediately to signify emphasis and enhance clarity of the message, rather than it being an update. The classic example is a pre-show call such as 'Esteemed colleagues of the... company, this is your fifteen-minute call. Fifteen minutes, please.' The most important aspect (how much time) is repeated after the attention-getting and tone-setting phrase at the beginning. The 'please' at the end has the same function as 'over' on walkie-talkies but again with a tone that regulates the mood. This level of precision is the goal for every piece of communication that stage management designs.

Conclusions

Outlining these properties completes our reverse engineering process. The results of this process demonstrate the relationships between the medium, properties and objectives of stage management as an artistic practice and can be seen in Figure 3. The precise manipulation of the properties of communication is what constitutes the technique of stage management. Designing this manipulation to meet the objectives outlined in the previous chapter is the artistry of stage management. Setting these objectives with a view to how they enhance the performance environment for the audience's experience is the scenography of stage management.

The properties of communication which can be controlled by stage management can be thought of as a hierarchy from message, through mode, distribution and updates. This implies that while each instance of communication has all these properties each former property needs to be sufficiently explicit before the next can be discerned. Just as with the hierarchy of objectives, the structure is problematized because it is reflexive in nature. This means in choosing a piece of information to send out, stage management

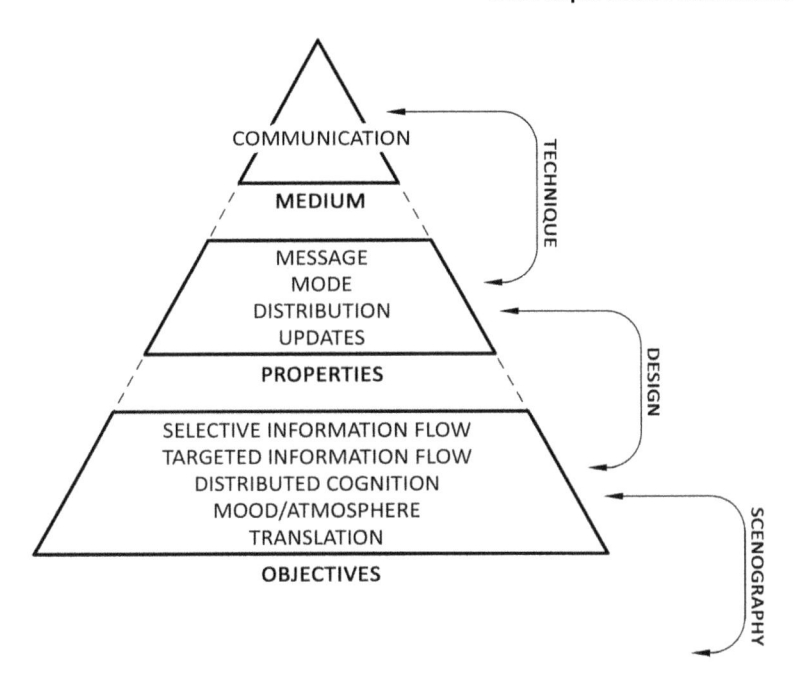

Figure 3 Stage management: medium, properties and objectives. Graphic design by Eduardo Canalejo.

should design all its properties at once. This design should be based on what is most effective in achieving the objectives of their communication and, ultimately, what best serves the production's performance environment. Frequently, this will overlap with the administrative approach of following the most efficient way of transmitting the information, but not always. This is the defining difference between administrative and scenographic stage management.

CHAPTER 9
RATIONALES, IMPLICATIONS AND CONCLUSIONS

This book was conceived as a way of understanding if there was any commonality to why stage managers do what they do. This is a worthwhile exercise in any field but is perhaps more urgently needed in a field which valorizes invisibility and whose literature consists largely of instruction manuals written from one individual's perspective. From the variety of factors identified that necessitate varying approaches to stage management three overarching perspectives emerged. These perspectives of administrative, managerial and scenographic stage management have been outlined to explain what stage management offers to the process of mounting productions.

In this chapter I want to examine these perspectives from other angles. Firstly, how do these approaches inform the rationale of stage managers? Secondly, what can broadening the conception of stage management mean for others? Specifically, what are some of the implications for the training of stage management, for researchers in other fields and for the professional practice of other performance makers? Even less so than the rest of the book, this chapter does not seek to provide complete answers to these questions. Instead, it hopes to be a provocation for further contemplation and research. The final section offers a summation of the book and some hopes for where these conversations may lead in the future.

Rationales

What does stage management offer to stage managers themselves? As a group, when asked 'why do we do what we do as stage managers?' the natural tendency is to interpret the question as why stage management is important for productions, rather than reflecting on the personal benefits we derive from being stage managers. In other words, we concentrate on the rationale for the doing, rather than the personal motivation for the work. In shifting the focus of the question, I have found three personal drivers within the stage managers interviewed. One is a sense of *artistry* and a desire to create experiences for an audience. One is a passion for teamwork and the intensity of the *collaboration* and relationships forged in mounting a production. The other is a sense of *professionalism* with a commitment to building a career and mastering the production process and an identity as a stage manager. While it is tempting to correlate an artistic drive with a scenographic approach, a collaborative drive with a managerial approach and a professional drive with an administrative approach, there are many reasons to avoid this temptation.

Firstly, there is not enough evidence within the research done to date to support this claim. Should people find this an important point to resolve further research must be done. Secondly, I suspect that the divisions between the drives and the approaches to stage management are not that neat and that most practicing stage managers are a blend of all six. Personally, as is probably plain from this book, my own bias is towards a scenographic approach because I have an artistic drive, but I recognize the other elements play a part as well. Finally, and most importantly, these categories, as with most such attempts at categorizing things, provide useful simplifications but do not capture the richness and diversity of the personal drives and philosophies of stage managers.

In order to demonstrate this richness, diversity and blend of personal drives that inform stage management practice I will present my interpretation of the rationale of each of the stage managers interviewed. I also offer these extracts to acknowledge each of the stage managers who took the time to talk to me about their practice. Like the introductions to them in the first chapter, these few words are overly reductive. As noted earlier, as stage managers we tend to discuss our outward rationale more than our inner one, so sometimes the inner drive of the stage manager must be inferred through thoughts and perceptions about the purpose of stage management. This is partly because as a stage manager myself, the interviews largely concentrated on how we contribute to performances and I did not usually specifically ask for their own personal motivations. Thus, often the words that I've selected to sum up their approaches to, and relationships with, stage management come from answers to questions regarding how the stage manager got involved with this profession in the first place or asking them how they make decisions about stage management.

In this sense, I pre-empted the responses by grounding the inquiry within the scope of these prior discussions. If I had have asked them directly about their personal motivations, undoubtedly, their answers would have been different. It transpires that these responses may say as much, or more, about myself than the individuals concerned. Unlike the other interview extracts in the book I offer these without much commentary of my own, except to say that I think in total they offer a good mix of the artistic, collaborative and professional drives for, and of the administrative, managerial and scenographic approaches of, stage managers. Sometimes all of these can be found within the one response.

> Abel: And we're problem solvers. That's our job. And so therefore the problem needs to be addressed, communicated, and solved in order for the show to be artistically maintained and have the integrity that the creatives want it to have for the paying audience.
> Alexander: I think the best stage managers care about people. It's a very people person job. And I think that's why people are drawn to it as well. Because you are part of something that's slightly bigger than you. It's that being a part of that team

and to me my team is not only my stage management team, but also my cast, the producers. We're all part of the team that puts this show own.

Athens: It's all in the timing and tailoring to each person. [If something comes up, I will be] thinking about, here's who it involves, A, B, C, I know how C will react, B, okay yeah, I'm thinking this through and you know, we'll take it from there and see how this goes. Obviously each person is different.

Dyer: I still think best practice is to respond to a room. But how do you? How do you, when there are a million, there's infinite, kind of, rooms and there's infinite responses. But it's actually not about what I think stage management is. I think it's a collective, personal, what is my management style? And how do I bring that to the table? And bring that to a rehearsal room? And bring that to a show? And how do I make sure that my stage management style, you know, is actually not a hindrance but a support.

Evans: Making theatre is teamwork. You have to work together to produce that final thing. That means that even if you've got everybody with their jobs and segregation in that way, you still have a connection and a communication between all of the departments, which allows input to the final product.

Fenton: Basically it's how you communicate certain things to certain people and it has to be phrased in a way so that the information comes through and they get it.

Franklin: Being a stage manager is who you are, it's just a part of you. I am a stage manager, that's just what I am, and I'd probably say I am that first, before academic, or teacher, or mother. That's terrible really, isn't it?

Freeburg: Why do we do theatre if we're not doing it for the audience's experience?

Hawley: I was actually thinking about this the other day about my career and why I actually am still doing it. I actually have no idea, because it is hard work, it is long hours, but clearly there was something about it that just grabbed me. And certainly when I first started, I remember walking into the professional theatre I worked in when I was 17 and 18, and the feeling of excitement! Sometimes now when you work with the kids on summer schools, you get that palpable feeling back again, and that's why I did it in the first place.

Hobden: Ninety per cent is the communication and the encouragement of everybody . . . I very much come from a sort of school of thought, where it has to be collaborative. Because if people feel . . . they have an ownership of part of it, or that the bit they are doing is valued, then people are going to be more invested in doing that correctly in three months' time.

Lawrence: As you well know, it's mostly about making it up as you go along. It's responding to what's in front of you. If you're hide-bound and you have a fixed way of doing it, you're fucked.

Legah: I always say, 'The moment you don't like coming in to work, is the moment you need to start looking for other work.' You have to feel like it belongs to you, because you have to have that connection with the people that you work with and the audience.

Rationales, Implications and Conclusions

Livoti: I know some PSMs who say, 'I'm PSM and these are my assistants.' And to me, that is the opposite way to think about the show, or the team structure. For me, it is a team. I am the captain of the team, right? But it's a team. And on that team is a first assistant stage manager, and a second assistant stage manager, and however many PAs we have on the team. That is the team. They are not there to assist me, they're there to stage manage the show.

Loth: So I remember the first show that I went and saw. I was 13 and my mum took me to see *Fame*. And I remember sitting in the theatre and just going, 'I want to do that. I don't care what I'm doing, but I want to make people feel like I'm feeling now.' And as I've learned more and more about what a stage manager is and what a stage manager does, it becomes apparent that the stage manager and the stage management team tends to be the glue, particularly once the show is up and running.

Maccoy: For me that's the really interesting bit: it's the fascination of different people who you work with and how you manage them and how you have to approach people differently and things like that. We were talking about communication but I think in terms of actually managing and how you're finding your way around it.

Marich: And I realised, 'This is why we do this. This is why we do this. We are gifting. We are gifting ourselves.' And that one audience person will remember the experience of that performance for the rest of their lives.

McMillan: The stage management team are the lynch pin for the whole production. It doesn't matter if you're talking about the DSM, Stage Manager, or the Assistant Stage Manager. I look at them as like one thing. I hate the hierarchy between DSM, SM, and ASM. I think that it's not good for people. You might be all different pay grades, but I think you all need to work as a cohesive team and you treat each other with the same respect as you would anybody. I think that team needs to be able to communicate and then be able to mould themselves to the project to make it work.

Mont: I really believe that a good stage manager does what is best for the show. Doing what's best for the show is the key and that is a simple statement that I think is quite easy to understand even though it's going to have different definitions in almost every case.

Oliver: So what's my guiding principle when I'm trying to make decisions? The most people happy.

Passaro: So that's the view from 35,000 feet, you know, in terms of developing my own philosophy not only as a stage manager but as someone who now teaches stage management. And it continues to deepen that fundamental belief that 'the people are your most important resource. It's the *human resource* that is most valuable.' I think that anybody who's spent a lot of time around the theatre will know that inherently, or I hope they do anyway.

Rawlinson: We are the communicators but, also, we are managers. These things go hand in hand. Stage managers lead the team, we're not passive.

> Scribner: Understanding the endgame. When it comes to art, when it comes to theatre, the endgame is not always obvious. So, you need to read into the layers of the author's vision, the director's vision, the producer's vision, the actor's vision, and understand where you fall in with that, and how you can help implement the vision, and facilitate as many people's visions coming together: unified.
>
> Simpson: In that way I'm a great believer in that stage management in our industries are there to create a space in which others can then do their own creative work and in that respect you maintain and you hold onto that creativity even once you've created the space. You're also maintaining that creativity within the space. For me there's a sequence there which it's our job to support it, maintain it, but equally be part of it. So we're not just without it, we are within it.
>
> Studham: We are the organizers. However, you can creatively organize. There is a lot of creativity that goes into how you're going to schedule, how you are going to make everything work, how you are problem-solving to support the production itself. So what we're doing is supporting the production in different ways.
>
> Trott: It's doing your job to make sure all the things and the people are in the right place at the right time. And if you get run over by a bus, you need to make sure someone else will be able to know where the things and people need to be.

This interplay between a stage manager's motivations for doing stage management and their personal blend of approaches to the practice of stage management informs their decision-making processes. To ascertain this process, I tended to end the interviews with the same question: 'when you have to make a decision as a stage manager and you are faced with two options, A or B, how do you go about deciding which is better?' Almost universally, and quite rightly, the initial response was to point out how vague the question was. For those who pushed for more details, I repeated the question but prefaced it with 'In the rehearsal room'. In fact, I was pushed for more parameters so often that in some interviews I offered up that constraint in the initial question.

For many who latched onto the rehearsal room aspect of the question, like Livoti and Oliver, the answer tended to revolve around scheduling.

> Livoti: In the rehearsal room, it's entirely schedule driven. All things being equal, what makes it easier to get every department's wish list accomplished?
>
> Oliver: I don't know why, even though you were vague, intentionally, the scenario that instantly popped into my head was scheduling. That's what led me to think, well, if we have to change a schedule and there's going to be 16 people who are upset because now they have to come in an hour early as opposed to if we do B and two people have to adjust their day by 10 minutes, I'm going B. Of course, all other things being equal.

This demonstrates the stage management tendency to concentrate on others and the concrete even when encouraged to be vague and conceptual.

Rationales, Implications and Conclusions

Hawley and Lawrence pointed out that often the most important thing is that the decision gets made.

> Hawley: Importantly, you've got to have the confidence to make a decision, either A or B, and get on with it. That's the first thing, and that's a thing you've got to learn. How to choose A or B, I would say, again, it's being able to see what's coming. When I was a younger stage manager, I thought . . . 'Okay, I'm making this decision, I'm not quite sure whether it's right or not, but I'm going to go with it, and then if it's wrong, then we'll just work that out once we get to it.'
> Older me knows what's coming. I've seen both options, I know they're the only two options, know that if I take that one, it can go to the dungeon of hell, or if I take this path, it will be the path of salvation, and it might be halfway down, both paths, it swaps, and you need to be able to then change it midstream, but that does come from [experience].

> Lawrence: I'm going to illustrate this with a story. Mike Nichols directed his first movie which was, *Who's Afraid of Virginia Wolf?* with Richard Burton and Elizabeth Taylor. Which was shot in black and white if you remember. The first day, Elizabeth Taylor came up to Mike. They had barely met and she had each fingernail painted a different color. She went, 'Which one?' Mike goes, 'That one.' I said, 'How did you make that decision?' 'It doesn't matter what decision it is. Just fuckin' make it. It doesn't matter.' If you make the wrong decision about something, you can always change your mind.
> I think that one of the keys to Stage Management and the reason people either trust you or don't, is you're not buffering around all the time. You're capable of making a decision on the spot.
> By me, A or B, most of the time doesn't matter. Look, if it's a safety issue, if it's a legal issue, those things take care of themselves. But if they're similar options, who gives a shit?

> Michael: Right. Make the decision and move along?

> Lawrence: That's exactly right. It doesn't matter which decision. There you go. That's my take.

Making decisions quickly stops others from worrying about the lack of a decision or from trying to make the decision themselves and, therefore, is part of the stage management objective of distributed cognition.

Franklin and Dyer suggest stage managers need to rely on their instincts when making decisions. This is closely aligned with the need for decisions to be made and made quickly.

> Franklin: My first reaction is to say, 'I go with gut feeling first.' I've discovered in the last few years that you should trust your gut feeling. I mean obviously there are some things that you have to think through.

As a stage manager, you have to get used to making a quick decision, because you have to in a show. You've got to decide straight away, what you are going to do. You haven't got time to spend ages researching. You've just got to decide.

Dyer: I'd say, 'What does your gut tell you?' . . . So, I always try to trust my gut. I trust my intuition and so I highly encourage my students to do the same thing. Right or wrong, that's fine, that's a learning thing for them. And if they follow their gut and go, 'I'm going to go with option A', and it turns out that B was best all along, well, then at least they've learnt something from it. So, I always just say, 'Trust your gut.'

It is interesting to note that these suggestions of making the decision and relying on instincts come from very experienced stage managers who also have experience training stage managers. As Dyer points out, though, this is something that beginning stage managers need to learn and practice, so even inexperienced stage managers should practice making quick decisions and trusting their instincts.

Ultimately, though, all the responses from the stage managers were a variation of what the stage manager thought was best for the production. Sometimes those interviewed would state that immediately. As examples Athens said, 'My mind goes to, what's best for the show and for the team and for the people', and Alexander responded:

Alexander: There are so many variables. What are those things? What's happened? What goes through your head? You have to decide what's best for the show. What is immediately available, what's the time frame, what staffing does anything require? If it's an immediate thing that has to happen now, what have I got here now? What can I make something of? What can I repurpose? Who else needs to know?

For others, analysing their responses would lead them to that conclusion.

Maccoy: I think you write out pros and cons and you look at what the constraints are. So, if it's a time thing then you must be going for the quickest. You might look at which is going to satisfy the creative side. I probably wouldn't do it alone; I would discuss it and I would put forward the different constraints and what those options were and I would probably suggest the one that I felt was the most appropriate.

Michael: And by the 'most appropriate' if I can put words in your mouth it sounds like ultimately you're weighing up all the resources and deciding what is best for that production?

Maccoy: Yes.

Trott and Studham emphasized that looking after everyone's health and safety first was what was best for the production.

Trott: I'd be interested in maintaining the artistic vision of the production. But within that artistic vision of the production is the well-being of everybody in the room. Both in a physical and an emotional sense. I would compromise the artistic vision if it meant that someone was going to be hurt, in an emotional or physical sense. But I think that the artistic vision is the priority.

Studham: Okay, so I'm in a rehearsal room and I have to make a decision. . . . Whatever it is, as long as everyone is safe, it is preferencing the production. So, it's what the production needs. I think that it's not cut and dried.

This notion of what was best for the production was sometimes expressed in terms of being best for the production's administration or the management of the people involved. As we have seen, stage managers carry a lot of responsibility in these areas. But the production exists for the audience, so, as other stage managers suggested, what is best for the production relies on a stage manager's sense of what is best for the audience. Often, as can be seen in the earlier responses, there is conflict between these three approaches in making the decision. If generalizations can be made from these and the responses from the other interviewees, they would suggest that managing people's health and safety is the first way to ensure what is best for the production, then attending to artistic concerns, then attending to other managerial and administrative needs.

Stage managers may be personally motivated by the professionalism, identity and unique career offered; the intense collaboration and relationships which are formed and need to be managed in the performing arts; the desire to help shape experiences for audiences; or some combination of the three. These personal motivations may be related to the blend of administrative, managerial and scenographic approaches to stage management a particular stage manager adopts. Regardless of their personal motivation and approach, a stage manager operates with a keen sense of what is best for the production. As productions are ultimately for audiences, understanding what is best for the production involves understanding the production's artistic goals. All stage management teams need to strive to fulfil the administrative, managerial and scenographic objectives of the production.

Implications

There are some profound implications in adopting this more holistic view of stage management which includes their scenographic contribution. These implications can be found most keenly in the training of stage managers, how this view of stage management opens the field to cross-disciplinary research and in aspects of the professional practice of stage management.

As we saw in Chapter 5, for many training institutions and much of the literature, the administrative approach remains predominant. Where this dominance crowds out other approaches this can lead to problems. McMillan points out that in Scotland, while it is changing, there is still overly prescriptive training.

McMillan: Back to the stage management training . . . it does need to be updated or refreshed . . . I think [in] Scottish stage management I would say there is still a bit of prescriptive training. I think that always has to be there, because there always has to be a formula, I suppose, to work from, because otherwise it would be chaos . . . To begin with.

Michael: Yeah. Like I said, it's not that the [administrative stage management] books are wrong. It's just that, some of them, present it as that is the whole job, rather than the tools with which to do the bigger job. They don't say explicitly enough 'These are some tools but they're not the only ones. You can design your own and you will need to because each production is different.' They don't say, like you just did, that each time that you start a project you need to sit down with the director and start from there and ask, 'What is this production about?'

McMillan: 'What do you need me to do?'

Michael: 'Who are you?' and 'How do I relate to you?'

McMillan: Absolutely!

Perhaps the framework offered in this book could offer enough of a 'formula' to prevent the 'chaos' which I agree would result from just telling stage managers they are artists and they could do whatever they wanted. Of course, ideally it should be presented to students along with the administrative and managerial frameworks as well.

Franklin and Scribner point out training that only values the administrative perspective of stage management can lead to the misunderstanding that stage management departments and their students are there to service other departments rather than sharing the common goal of servicing productions, which reminds me of the 'stage managers don't make coffee' debates discussed in Chapter 7.

Franklin: [Stage management students] do a lot of unpaid labour in any drama school. Things like moving chairs around from one rehearsal studio to another. Just keeping communication lines open that don't necessarily work through university systems. I don't think people realize that.

Michael: They don't. And we're our own worst enemies in some respects. Because we don't want people to realize that. Because we don't want the effort that we put in, and the work that it takes to do stage management, to detract from other people's work during productions. That would go against the objective of distributed cognition. And so, it's actually counterproductive, in production, for us to make a big song and dance about it, about us doing all of this extra work, you know?

Franklin: Yeah. Except how it goes wrong for us is then that's just expected that you do the extra work. There's the danger of becoming what I call 'servant class', within drama schools. People who are actors, directors, they're always in danger of thinking, 'Okay, there's the stage manager. They're nice people, but they're there to do something for me.' Especially, in a higher education situation, we're not necessarily connected. I'm not there to do stuff for them. I think I've tried quite hard over the last few years to push back against that, and not be the person that just resolves everything.

> When I first got this job, we would move people's office furniture for them. Then I was like, 'Why are we doing this? No other academic would be expected to move another academic's office furniture.'
>
> Michael: Yeah. There is a fine line between servicing the production, and becoming a servant, becoming that 'servant class'.

> Scribner: I realized very early on in my schooling that what I really wanted to be doing was doing the work because, although I had great teachers, I wanted to get out and get mentored and actually get paid to do it instead of paying to do it. Not to mention that there's something I'm sure stage management students around the world can relate to, that we get drawn in to help facilitate the department's needs. So, I felt like I was already working for the school in a way.

Many of the stage managers interviewed have been heavily involved in training other stage managers. Many reflected that stage management training is shifting away from an administrative model. In the following example, Franklin explains that this shift is partly a result of stage management academics thinking critically about their own practice as they transitioned into an academic role. Franklin discusses this in terms of stage management filling in the scenographic gaps between others in the production team and suggests explicitly teaching stage managers to think artistically about their practice can develop their instincts and professionalism faster than relying on experience gained through an administrative-only paradigm.

> Michael: What do you understand about stage management now because you are a teacher of it, that you didn't realize when you were doing it?
>
> Franklin: That it's actually a lot harder than it looks. I think when you start off as an ASM, it seems quite straightforward. You are just going to do this stuff and get the show on. You pick it up without even thinking about it. Now, I encourage my students to think about it. But when I was their age, it wasn't like that. We didn't think about it, we just did it. I would have said 20 years ago, 'Just do it. It's just a set of skills that you have, and you just learn. It's just common sense.'
>
> I would never say that now, because it's so much more ... It's how you do it, it's your interactions, it's the filling in of the gaps. I was telling my colleague about your concept of stage management being a scenographic practice. She said, 'Of course it has to be, because we fill in the gaps for everybody else.' Think about masking. You don't even think about it. You put masking where you think it is going to look good. What you're doing is you're filling the scenographic gaps for everybody else.
>
> All of that stuff becomes innate. What I try to do is get students to start thinking about that at an early stage now. Out of the people I've spoken to, in other institutions, I'm fairly confident that quite a lot of them have come to similar

realizations, and their teaching practices are informed by that. You don't need to have long years of experience. We only needed to have long years of experience because when we were stage managers, these things weren't talked about. Maybe the young people now will have that understanding, and knowledge, because they are talking about it all the time.

Part of this shift involves achieving a balance between theoretical and practical training. A theory-laden approach to training values thinking critically about the processes involved and placing them within broader contexts. Such approaches can often be found in theatre departments in research-driven institutions (often called drama or performance studies as further evidence of their distance from the concerns of actually mounting productions for audiences). On the other hand, the practical approach – often found in an administratively focused conservatoire – values the techniques required for mounting productions and values learning-by-doing above other pedagogical styles. Franklin and Trott both discussed this divide and conclude that both approaches have their merits, but at the extremes they can become problematic, and both could benefit from learning from the other side of the divide.

> Trott: So, I'm doing a Ph.D., not in anything to do with stage management, but I am using stage management reports as one of my data sources. I would like to teach into technical theatre programs and drama and theatre studies. I think because I also like the theatre studies part of it and there's really cool work on theatre as an artform. I want to be able to do both.
>
> Michael: I am interested in moving stage management training out of the conservatoire mode and get the balance right between more critical approaches to thinking about theatre and bringing that in to technical theatre and vice versa. So, what I'm really interested in in your Ph.D. research is using the stuff that stage managers produce and using them as research material for the broader field. I think stage management practices offer rich fodder for all kinds of research.
>
> Trott: Yes. I also think that the divide between the conservatoire and the academic model needs to break down because people have so much to gain . . . it goes both ways. You're a better technician if you can analyse what you're doing, and you're a better theatre researcher if you know what happens behind the scenes. And yeah, there's rich fodder there.
>
> Michael: I trained in a conservatoire and I actually got through my undergraduate degree learning much more about the different kinds of screws needed to put together a flat than different theatre practitioners.
>
> Franklin: I have to say having done a normal undergraduate drama degree first is another thing that's been advantageous to me. Because I've got more theoretical knowledge than most other stage managers. That's been incredibly useful to me. At least I've got some base knowledge of who Stanislavski was, you know?

Michael: Yeah. And I think, in your writing you talk about this kind of hybrid institution that's not a university, and not a conservatoire, but brings together the best of both worlds. I think that's what I think we still need to search for. I think the conservatoires need to understand theory. Not teaching their students necessarily to analyse the performance of brushing one's teeth, or an Occupy Wall Street protest or whatever, but having more of that theoretical grounding you get from a normal drama degree and vice versa.

I also think the research-intensive universities need to understand practice more. When I first went to university, I did a year and a half at a research-intensive university. I was doing a degree in psychology, but picking up some drama electives. I was struggling with the drama courses, which I was taking because I thought it would be really easy, because I've been involved in the theatre all my life. But, they were talking about things that had nothing to do with audiences. Now, looking back, I can see why some of those things that they were trying to introduce me to are important to audiences. But no one ever actually bothered to explain that, because that's not what the drama researchers were interested in. It's kind of assumed that audiences happen, or performances happen, but I'm going to be researching this esoteric aspect of it, you know?

Franklin: Yeah, I know!

Achieving this balance seems to be a journey for all stage managers transitioning to an academic role as Franklin suggested earlier. As this has been part of my journey, I often disclosed even more of my personal beliefs and struggles to fellow academics when the discussions turned towards training than in the other parts of the interview. This can be seen in this part of my conversation with Legah.

Legah: I want to do a Ph.D. Because the one thing I haven't done is, I still don't feel like an academic. I still feel like a practitioner. I almost feel like I'm a little bit of a charlatan by coming into the world of academia to impart this knowledge.

Michael: Well, I've often found that's really hard in the technical theatre world. Because it is such a practical course.

Legah: Absolutely.

Michael: The more I tried to teach it, the more I found I didn't have the right language for any of the bits that weren't practical. Those parts which people kept saying, 'You can't train that part of the job.' I'm like, 'Why not?' If I'm putting out my shingle and saying, 'Here, come and learn how to be a stage manager.' I felt like a charlatan too, going, 'Oh, well I can't teach you that bit of the job.'

Well, why do a degree then? Go knock on the doors of the theatre and follow another stage manager around if on-the-job training is the best kind of training there is. I felt a bit let down by my undergraduate degree, because we didn't really talk about the audience, or our function in terms of telling a story. It was very much, 'These are the processes.'

Legah: You do A, B, C . . . absolutely.

Michael: And, if you happen to work out that the reason *why* you do that is so that you've got a better show at the end of it, that's the bit they didn't teach. So that's how I went down the rabbit hole of doing more research. Especially when I was teaching stage management to not just people who wanted to be stage managers, but also to actors, directors, playwrights and so on. They don't care how to write a rehearsal report, but they do need to know what a stage manager can do for them, and how stage management can support the production process.

Legah: Absolutely.

Michael: And so, it's that common ground about what it is to do theatre and what it is to have an audience. And, understanding that the common ground *is* that all of our work is for the audience.

Legah: Which, actually, that's interesting. I like how you said that. I want to nick that.

Reflecting on the why was also critical in Franklin's development as an academic. Centring the why and the common ground of the audience is the key distinction between the scenographic and administrative approaches to stage management.

Franklin: That was a really useful exercise in making you think, 'Why am I teaching like I'm teaching?' And if you can work out why, 'the why leads to the how,' and that's a quote from Maccoy. 'The why leads to the how,' which I use quite a lot.

Michael: Yeah, and we don't spend enough time talking about or thinking about the why. What I was taught was fantastic, and vital, and important, but I was kind of left to work out the 'why' by myself. Whereas when I came to teach it, I'm like, 'Well, the why is the most important bit.'

Franklin: I never thought about the why until I started teaching.

The 'why leading to the how' suggests adopting a scenographic bias in the training can lead to the managerial and administrative perspectives and may solve the problem of much of what constitutes stage management being regarded as 'unteachable' as alluded to earlier.

Changing the signature pedagogy[1] of stage management from an administrative-based apprentice-like system to a scenographic-based critical enquiry system like the one presented in Chapter 6 would open the connections stage management has with other fields. A holistic approach to stage management training would still be vocational in its orientation. Vocational training and critical pedagogy[2] can be aligned through the scenographic perspective, becoming reflexively beneficial rather than mutually exclusive. Trott alluded to some of the possibilities in the earlier extract. Franklin and I expressed enthusiasm about the potential.

Franklin: That's what's so great about our degrees, you are getting the opportunity to actually be a stage manager on a show. You actually get to do the thing you're studying. You know, I think that's absolutely brilliant. So few higher education contexts enable that engagement with the real thing, you are really going to do this, because people are really going to buy tickets, and sit down and watch it.

Michael: That's right. Some of what we do as vocational theatre academics, other academics in the university would love to be able to do that.

Franklin: I know, yeah.

Michael: Because it's all project-based learning. And I think all of the theatrical activity that's undertaken in higher education, in general, but stage management in particular, is an underdeveloped source for studying all kinds of things like critical pedagogy, organizational psychology, human resource management, cognitive science, ethnography, phenomenology, semiotics, all of that. Because we do it. We don't just teach it, we teach it by doing it.

Franklin: Yeah!

An administrative-based pedagogy does stage managers a disservice if it only teaches them systems and processes. From an administrative perspective, many of the objectives of stage management explored earlier are unteachable because they do not lead to increased efficiency. Instead, stage management training should acknowledge that systems, processes, paperwork and efficiency of communication are all important. However, these are tools which allow you to work with the other people involved including, importantly, the audience. Indeed, I argue the audience is who we are working for. Therefore, learning how theatre communicates to an audience should be the central aspect of the training. The particulars regarding stage management practice are in service of this, not separate from it. The impact on the audience is how to make decisions about whether to include something in the rehearsal report, or how and when to give that prop to the actor, or any of the other decisions stage managers make. The training needs to encourage stage managers to think through the implications of every decision, build their sense of priorities and adapt their communication based on their eventual contribution to the audience's experience.

Adaptability is not of value only when things go 'wrong' in live performance as the quotes from the administrative stage management literature presented in Chapter 5 suggest. Adaptability is essential for stage managers for it to go 'right' in the first place. This is because live performance happens differently all the time. It is supposed to. If stage managers do not adapt based on the audience's experience they risk strangling the life out of the performance.

Including these broader perspectives of stage management means that a university degree could consist solely of stage management courses. It need not consist of practical training in the theatre components and additional courses from other fields that are more academic to justify the degree to the university. Of course, additional courses can contribute to a well-rounded education and may enhance a stage manager's ability to understand and communicate with audiences. But the two modes of thinking need not be completely separate, and indeed should not be, because there is a level of conceptual thinking that can be applied to, and can enhance, the field of stage management.

Stage Management

Reframing the training of stage managers in this way seems to have been of interest to both Franklin and Simpson.

> Franklin: I do think we need to get this [way of thinking about stage management] out there. I think we have come a long way from the days where the attitude was, 'Well, just sort them out,' and 'that's stage management, it's done'.

> Simpson: The problem I think with stage management is it is currently thought of as purely a facilitation exercise. These are the tools we use and this is how you do it. And there is so much more to it than that. It's about the breadth of thinking. It is about the creative problem-solving, it's about the psychology of the environment and the people involved. It's about the environment that you create and the effectiveness of that. It's about where your studies are taking you into distributed cognition and the concept of the communication designer which I think are all what makes this worthy of study. In some ways it's something that we already teach within management classes. But where it's so valuable and so useful is that you are now developing terms and concepts, which we can hang all of this thinking off.
> Michael: Well I'm stealing these terms from other places of course.
> Simpson: But they are fields of study which are directly applicable. And that's where I think this is so interesting. For me, where in class I'm always banging on about the sequence of creativity for example and understanding how people are using the rehearsal space. This is what you are able to contextualize within the field of study of distributed cognition. And that for me is what we need.

Adopting a holistic perspective of stage management, with the scenographic approach at the centre, also has profound implications for professional practice. Firstly, it could foster greater understanding of, and enhance collaboration with, stage management amongst other theatre-makers. Secondly, it challenges stage managers to evaluate their contributions to productions differently.

If stage managers have traditionally viewed themselves as administrators of productions and devalued their artistic contribution, it is hardly surprising that others in the theatre industry do not recognize this aspect of the role. Marich suggests that stage management is poorly understood amongst even seasoned fellow collaborators.

> Marich: The thing is, what I've very, very slowly come to realize is, that it doesn't matter how experienced an actor or a technician or a touring staff person might be, the understanding of the scope and depth of the role of a stage manager is poorly understood or underappreciated.

Dyer notes that the shifts in training discussed earlier have already started to shift the perception of stage management within the industry.

> Dyer: When I first graduated it was all about, 'Just do what you're told. Keep your head down. Do your paperwork.' But I do think the more we can instigate [a more artistic approach to stage management] here, within education, then as the students move into the industry, if they view themselves as artists then that's what they will be.... I do think it is definitely shifting.

Despite these changes, Marich points out that, in Australia at least, many stage managers do not value stage management as an artform but regard it as a stepping stone to further management positions – positions which involve the hiring of stage managers.

> Michael: Did they go into production management?
> Marich: Yes and to middle and upper management. What I find sad is that they don't value the role. So when they move up the ladder, they continue to perpetuate that lack of value to the role. That to me is almost criminal ... It's indicative of a lack of trust in a stage manager's ability to contribute to the production.

If all theatre-makers understood stage management's role in designing the communication to enhance the audience's experience it would enhance their collaboration. Effective collaboration relies on trust and respect. If theatre-makers expect stage managers to perform only as administrators then a stage manager's concern over the scenographic aspects of a production may be interpreted as a lack of respect manifesting in criticism or trying to do someone else's job for them. In the other direction, the way another collaborator treats stage managers who they expect to only perform administrative functions may inadvertently be disrespectful by being patronizing with regards to the stage manager's artistic contribution or through the mistaken belief that stage management is in service to the creative individuals, not in service to the production in concert with the other creative individuals.

Marich points out that this lack of respect for stage management, ultimately, is a disservice to the production.

> Marich: I have encountered a lot of theatre technicians who will behave rather obstructively and hold onto vital information and purposefully not share it, because it gives them power. For example, I've had a mechanist suggest it was not any of my business to be looking at the drafts of a floor plan for the next three venues they were working on. I don't understand why they don't want to consult the team and share the information and simply focus on presenting the best show we can at each venue? It's not only totally disrespectful to the stage manager, but ultimately disrespectful of the cast, and the venues' crews, and the audiences.

Here, Marich returns the focus to the audience. Anything which centres the audience's experience as the common ground for all in the performing arts industry has the potential to enhance their collaboration. Enhancing the understanding of the scenographic functions of stage management amongst theatre-makers furthers this aim.

Including a scenographic perspective has implications for stage management practice itself. In the end what an administrative, managerial, scenographic or holistic stage manager does in their day-to-day practice will look very similar. As Abel points out, not every decision that a stage manager makes has a profound impact on the scenography of a performance, and a stage manager learns more about the scenography of a production as rehearsals progress. Especially early during rehearsals, the stage manager should be concentrating much more on meeting the objectives of stage management and trusting that this is contributing to the scenography of a production rather than worrying about the patterns of concordance, dissonance and topology that the audience will use to ascribe meaning during the performance. The closer you get to the interaction with the audience as a stage manager the more your focus will shift to directly attending to the scenography.

> Abel: It's interesting, because I don't know if you really have time to [implement all of the coordinates model of scenography] in a short run. But I would say definitely, in something that lasts longer than a year, that you can definitely see that happening almost naturally.
>
> I think that you handle this in such a different way when you're just starting a show. Because the bottom line is what you want to make sure of, is that you've got communication. That you're the hub of communication, and that you're dealing with all of that stuff.
>
> So, you're not really concentrating so much on the style of the show. You're relying on the designers to do that. So then, as a stage manager, I always say those first weeks are all about sending information out correctly. Not whether or not the dissonance or the concordance is being achieved.
>
> Michael: Sure. And that's why I think there's a hierarchy of objectives, which is why we started this conversation with step one: make sure the information is –
>
> Abel: Is getting out. Exactly. Start there and then you can develop those. Yeah, I think so.
>
> Michael: And then if you've got the time, or the resources or whatever, make sure the right bits of the right information are getting to the right people at the right time.
>
> Abel: Because we all know that during pre-production, 90% of the time you miss somebody. Daily. And then you're like, out of bed with the list, 'Oh my God, how did your name drop off that?' That kind of thing. So you're more involved in the actual technical aspect of trying to get the information out. Rather than moulding it into scenography.
>
> Michael: Which is where our training starts from. And why it concentrates on the administrative. But the interesting thing for me, is that audiences come at it from a scenographic perspective.
>
> Abel: Right.

Michael: They're at the other end of the process because they can't not be. Even if it's a two-week off, off, off-Broadway, show . . .
Abel: . . . there has to be that. That's how they're perceiving it. They're getting all three of those elements. Absolutely. Without anybody consciously working towards it.
Michael: And, you know, that's why it's important to me, is because that's what our audiences experience. They don't know the terminology.
Abel: Exactly.
Michael: And most of the time, let's be honest, we don't use this terminology. I created it because I have to teach this stuff and I couldn't find the right words. But in my practice, I don't go to the director and have meaningful discussions about topology with them using that terminology. Because that's not their language and then it would just get in the way of doing a good show, right?
Abel: Of course, yeah.
Michael: But now that I have that language, I see how I can support a show to enable a better audience experience.
Abel: Yeah. I think you're right.
Michael: And a lot of the time, it's done on instinct. Because if everyone's doing a good job, and you help everyone communicate, the scenography kind of falls into place.
Abel: It does that without us having to work at it. Right. You don't have to do that consciously. You're right. It does.
Michael: It's been most useful to me when our collective instincts fall down, and there's a problem, 'Okay, why isn't this reading?' I consciously stop and kind of put my audience . . .
Abel: . . . audience hat on, yeah. 'What is it that they're not getting?'
Michael: Exactly. So *we* start at the nuts and bolts of the communication. But the *audience* starts with the experience, and scenography is about . . .
Abel: How we bridge that gap. Exactly.

While I whole-heartedly agree with Abel that during the earlier stages of a project the stage manager is less overtly concerned with scenography, it should be noted that what she calls 'the technical aspects of communication' rely on a stage manager's scenographic knowledge of a production as was outlined in Chapter 8. How this is all put together and the implications for the production process are considered in the conclusions section (especially in Figure 4).

Three hypothetical stage managers who were only concerned with only one perspective each would all still produce rehearsal reports on a daily basis. The difference would lie in what they chose to report from the rehearsal, how they reported it and, most significantly, why they thought it must be included. The scenographic stage manager's report would be too long, and be distributed too late to be of use, but would be replete with notes about the relationships created between every decision made in the rehearsal room and those already made in terms of how the audience should experience them.

The administrative stage manager's report would be very short, be distributed within five minutes of the rehearsal's completion and would report only decisions which changed the existing lists, systems and processes in as few words as possible. The managerial stage manager would be concerned with the time needed to implement each note, any budgetary considerations and any implications for teamwork that the decisions may have. By now I hope that it is obvious that these extremes are neither achievable nor desirable. Even in the most administrative of tasks, stage managers should be mindful of the audience's experiences; in the most artistic of tasks, stage managers should be mindful of their efficient recording, reporting and replication; and at all times stage managers must be aware of the time, technical, budgetary and human resources available, especially with regards to any impact decisions made will have on the team's ability to collaborate effectively.

Including all of these perspectives and getting the balance right, with the understanding that the balance is not predetermined but is itself a product of the project's changing circumstances, is the challenge of stage management. For me, understanding the role stage management has in communicating an experience to an audience is why it is endlessly fascinating. As I discussed with Marich those whose view of stage management is out of balance tend not to have long stage management careers. Those who are overly administrative tend to get burnt out trying to force an artistic production to comply. Those who are overly management focused tend to use stage management as a stepping stone.

> Michael: I graduated with a bunch of other stage managers, some of whom were far more diligent and got better marks than me and whatever, but they burnt out really, really quickly because they didn't understand the scope of the role, the depth of the role, and really that the role is flexible because of the needs of the audience.
>
> Marich: I've never met those stage managers. I've only met the ones who have been really ambitious and never intended to remain in the industry as a stage manager. They're the stage managers I have encountered in the past and I would say most of them are puzzled at my choice for having remained a stage manager.
>
> Whereas I've never seen it as anything other than a vocation – not a job but a vocation. Very different. Very different approaches to how one views the role. I'm not saying that they're wrong and I'm right. It's just I think there is far more [artistic] scope in the role than what is taught.

It is tempting to conclude by its absence in the above conversation that being too scenographic in one's approach as a stage manager does not tend to lead to a similar problem. I suspect, though, the truth is that the discussion of stage management so rarely acknowledges the scenographic perspective that it is just harder to generalize the issues that befall them. Perhaps, and it is only wild supposition, they are the stage managers who become resident directors or directors. Or are they the stage managers like Marich and Simpson (and I suspect many others I interviewed) who see it as a vocation and become so enamoured with how their role contributes to the audience's experience that they have long careers?

Conclusions

This book attempts to start conversations by proposing answers to three questions about contemporary stage management practice: Why do stage managers do what they do? Who are stage managers? Why does it matter? First, the short answers. Stage management is concerned with the coordination of a performance's elements. A stage manager is an administrator, manager *and* a scenographer. Understanding stage management more fully could be of benefit to stage managers, other theatre-makers and researchers in such diverse fields as scenography, performance studies, cognitive theory, management, pedagogy and phenomenology to name a few. Slightly longer answers follow.

Stage management is a diverse set of practices that responds to the needs of each production. Despite this specificity, there is a core practice which involves the supervision, coordination and delegation required for a performance to be realized according to the experience planned for the audience. As outlined in Chapter 1 this core has remained stable, even if the job titles haven't, since at least the time of the Ordinary, 'an overseer who keeps order'[3] of the sixteenth century. This sense of keeping order, in combination with other factors, has led to the widely held conception of stage management as being an administrative position. These other factors include a suspicion of the artistry involved with the technical effects of theatre which has persisted since Aristotle and the eventual separation of stage management from direction. This conception, which focuses on the enforcement of correct procedures, is widely held within the field of stage management, and even in the general public, when they speak of an event being stage managed. Included in this conception is the notion that such control is being exercised by an invisible figure. This notion of the invisible stage manager has been 'seen' and interrogated repeatedly throughout the book.

While this core practice persists, the need to respond to the specifics of each production's needs leads to a diverse set of approaches to this task. Thus, the paradox that stage managing any production is exactly the same and precisely different from stage managing any other arises. That said, some productions' needs are shared with enough other productions that understanding these needs has led to the different approaches to stage management outlined in Part 1.

These needs include understanding the culture or cultures involved and implicated by the production and the consequent needs and expectations of the people involved as outlined in Chapter 2. Similarly, understanding the typical needs required for a production with a similar genre and scale as their current one, and seeing if those needs apply to it, can shape a stage manager's approach to their work as considered in Chapter 3. Stage managers also need to adapt their approach as stage management evolves – as it always has – in line with changes to the aesthetics of performance, the technical apparatus used to realize the productions, the technological and other changes of the broader society and the interplay between these factors as explored in Chapter 4. Through analysing the interview responses from the stage managers who discussed these variations, a number of common themes emerged. Many of these themes fit the administrative conception of stage management, but some did not.

These themes coalesced into the three conceptions of stage management presented in Chapter 5. Firstly, the administrative model which seeks to regulate the process of mounting a production so that it can be as efficient as possible. This has many strengths especially for routine tasks or those where there is only one correct procedure. Time is always short when working on a production, so efficiency is imperative. The managerial model concentrates on the effective management of the resources of a production, especially the people involved. This model seeks to ensure that the team is as productive as possible. An appropriate management style for a creative endeavour must be adopted but one which balances the needs of the audience as well as the needs of the practitioners. The third model considered the audience's experience as fundamental. This is the artistic model which conceptualizes a stage manager as the communication designer for the production. This model was shown in Part 2 to be synonymous with scenographic stage management.

Chapter 6 outlined the history and frameworks by which other technical theatre disciplines came to be known as artistic and scenographic. It suggests that a stage manager is a scenographer because of their 'manipulation and orchestration of the performance environment'.[4] As such a stage manager should be aware of how space, semiotics, phenomenology and scenography inform the audience's experience of a production. These can be combined into the coordinates model which uses relational semiotics to suggest that audiences recognize the patterns of concordance, dissonance and topology as they experience the performance. This focus on the audience's experience is the common ground amongst all the scenographic contributors to a production. Stage managers are concerned with coordinating these patterns in the performance environment with the desired audience experience in mind. This coordination involves achieving the objectives of stage management.

These objectives are outlined in Chapter 7. They form a hierarchy because achieving them in order usually results in the later objectives being achieved with much less effort. The objectives are selective information flow, targeted information flow, distributed cognition, controlling the mood and atmosphere and translation. The stage manager uses their understanding of the scenography of a production to determine how these objectives need to be met for that production. This means that the patterns of concordance, dissonance and topology that are being created for the audience to experience are used to inform the specific selection, targeting, distribution, mood of their communication and which aspects need to be translated. At the moment of the performance, the stage management team is translating all of the information that they have gained about the performance into an embodied experience for the audience. Achieving these objectives relies on manipulating the various properties of communication which is the medium of the stage manager's art.

Rationales, Implications and Conclusions

The properties of communication which a stage manager manipulates also form a hierarchy. This time the hierarchy is one of perception for the recipient of the communication. That means that the recipient needs to perceive an earlier property before they can discern a later one. The properties of communication which stage managers control are the message, mode, distribution and updates.

All of this comes together in the production process as outlined in Figure 4. From an administrative perspective of stage management, the production process is linear. This emphasizes what stage managers must accomplish before rehearsals start, and then during rehearsals, then technical rehearsals, then performances and then after the performances have finished. This view of the production process is very important and it reminds stage managers, and encourages them to remind everyone else, of important deadlines and milestones. As the discussion with Abel earlier in the chapter suggests, this linearity is influential even from a scenographic perspective. If the production process was solely linear, making a diagram of it would be a simple timeline. While Figure 4 is obviously more complicated than that, this linear process is represented by the movement from the outer parts to the centre – that is, from the practitioner to the audience.

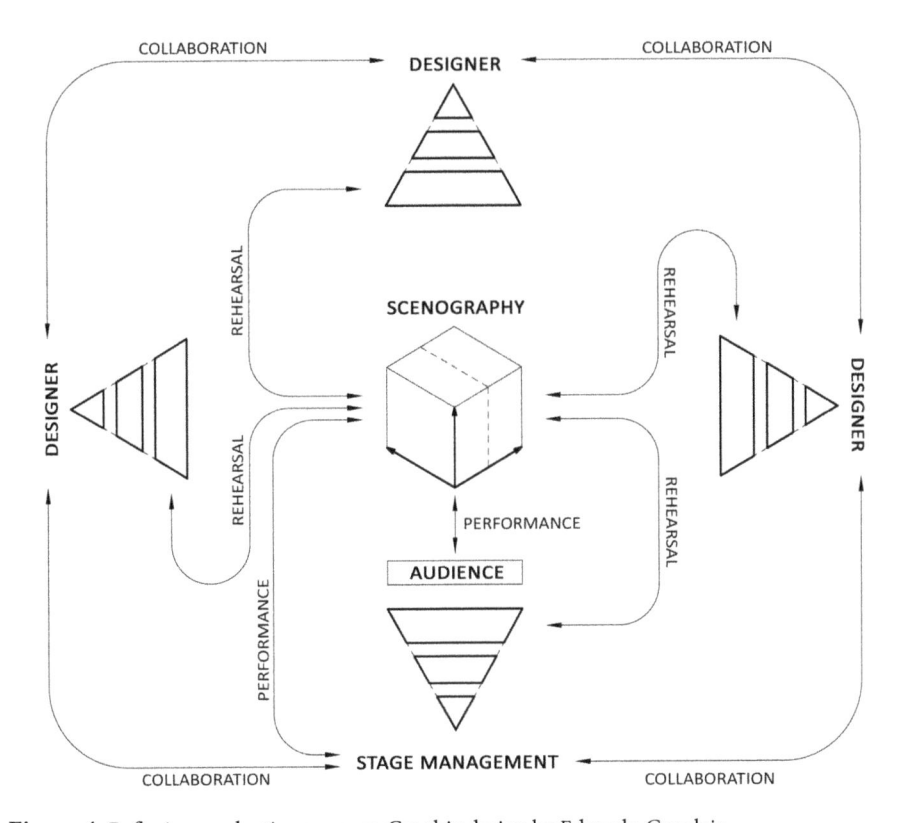

Figure 4 Reflexive production process. Graphic design by Eduardo Canalejo.

This suggests that the further away in time from the performance the more time and focus there is for a scenographer to further develop their understanding of the medium of their artform, its properties and the earlier objectives. For example, a lot of the stage manager's 'prep week' tasks (before rehearsals start) involve establishing the specifics of the properties of the communication required for this production. For example, collating contact information, extracting information from the text if one exists and having initial conversations with the rest of the creative team so that they can determine which processes, tools and templates may be required for this production, and establishing the appropriate infrastructure for information to flow.

Even though the focus is on this part of the process, the latter parts are implied. This is because completing these initial tasks effectively results in the distribution of cognition across the team, establishes a trust and rapport and involves translation, for example, of a floor plan into a rehearsal room markup of the set design. There is even consideration of the audience's experience in these earliest moments. For example, in deciding which bits of the markup to compromise if there is not enough space in the rehearsal room, stage managers usually instinctively predict and assess the topological relationships which are going to be most potent for an audience and privilege this use of space.

Conversely, the closer in time to the performance the more direct attention is placed on the later objectives. This is not because the earlier ones are suddenly less important but, having established the appropriate systems for selecting and targeting the information flow, these objectives are easier to maintain and the problems which are likely to occur at this stage will have more of an impact on the morale of the company and require correcting a misunderstanding where something has got lost in translation. During the moment of performance itself, stage management is nearly wholly concerned with the translation into an embodied experience for the audience; monitoring that the patterns of concordance, dissonance and topology are being orchestrated so that the experience is 'landing' in the desired way; and maintaining the appropriate mood for this to happen. Of course, the way they achieve this is by, as ever, using the properties of communication to select information to pass on, in a targeted way, so that everyone else only has to think about their part in terms of this interaction with the audience as much as possible.

Notions of reflexivity have been constant throughout this book. It can be seen most directly in Figure 4 by the double-headed arrows which further problematize the notion of the linearity of the production process. During rehearsals there is a feedback loop between the experience being designed for the audience and all the practitioners which may necessitate them to start again. From a stage management perspective, a discovery in the rehearsal room may necessitate them developing a whole new system, process or communication tool than what had been administered or may even cause them to contemplate how or whether communication itself can contribute to realizing this discovery. Reciprocally, the way they communicate has an influence on the discoveries being made in rehearsals. Similarly, their collaboration with the other members of the production team may cause either party to change their contribution to the production.

During the performances, the scenography is both experienced and shaped by the audience. This shaping happens because their responses are fed back to the scenographers present. In the diagram, this feedback loop generated by the performance only points to the stage management team because often they are the only scenographers able to make changes during the performance itself by, for example, delaying the calling of a cue. Of course, if the feedback from an audience or another aspect of a performance creates the need for subsequent performances to be adapted, the stage management team will communicate this to their relevant colleagues who will contribute to the necessary adaptation between performances. In these ways, while there may be a change of emphasis or focus during the timeline of a production, all those involved in creating the performance environment are reflexively determining and adapting to the needs of that environment throughout the process.

While viewing the production process in a reflexive manner is harder to describe and creates messier diagrams than viewing it linearly, it does have the advantage of explaining to all involved, especially administratively focused stage managers, that continual adaptation in light of the desired and actual audience's experience is fundamental and is at the heart of the system. That is, despite the need for deadlines and working within the constraints of finite resources, the system is designed to be dynamic, and changes are to be celebrated, rather than seen as the result of some failure of process. As ever, both views must be held in balance: missed deadlines and wasted resources can cause problems for the audience experience, so too can the view that change is unwelcome and should only be tolerated in certain respects and at certain times in the process.

Stage management, then, is the administration, management *and* artistry of the communication required to coordinate the elements of a performance. This chapter considered some of the rationales and implications of this conclusion. The implications for broadening our conception of stage management are really my thinly disguised hopes for where this conversation may go to next. I hope that the pedagogy of stage managers and, by extension, of the performing arts will be developed. I hope that a deeper and broader understanding of stage management will lead to richer collaboration by performing artists and consequently more engaging experiences for audiences. I hope that by rendering stage management more visible humanities researchers from diverse fields will find the practice of stage management as a site worthy of their study and that both reflexively benefit.

The rationales of stage managers both in terms of their personal motivations and their decision-making processes are diverse. However, in terms of personal drives there seems to be a blend of valuing the artistry involved in their work or that of the performing arts; the intense collaborations and relationships that are necessary to mount productions; and the sense of belonging and professional fulfilment that comes from identifying as a stage manager. Their decision-making processes are diverse in terms of the weight given to the various administrative, management and artistic constraints which need to be considered, but, ultimately, the desired outcome shared by all is what is best for the production.

If maintaining this balance of personal motivations and perspectives; administering a process that has extremely limited resources but which serves infinite creativity; and managing a group of widely divergent, passionate people to ensure that they have a shared vision, purpose and work together with a productive but fun atmosphere, while manipulating the properties of communication to meet certain objectives, in a fluid reflexive manner based on the constraints of the production and the desired audience experience sounds impossible, that's because it is. If attempting to do all of this in a way that enhances the collaboration of other theatre-makers and is mindful of the relational semiotics of scenography sounds exhilarating and enjoyable as well, then you may want to consider a career in stage management if you don't have one already. With that in mind, I think this extract from Hawley provides fitting last words.

> Hawley: You can have innate ability, but over time with different experiences, you can get much, much better at it as well, definitely.
> Michael: I can only talk from my perspective really, but if I was still as bad as I was after I graduated, I don't think I would still be in the game now. If you're not getting better at it, then it's probably time to get out.
> Hawley: Yeah, absolutely. I think you only get better at it by enjoying it. I say to the students here, 'There's no point in doing this course if you're not going to love what you do.' And I don't mean grinning like the Cheshire Cat every day, but innately something keeps bringing you back to it. Because there's no money involved, or anything fancy. You're not going to get a fat bonus. You're going to be badly paid for most of your career. You're going to be working incredibly long hours. And you're going to be expected to be able to pull a rabbit out of a hat, or find the holy grail . . .
> Michael: Both, by eight pm tonight.
> Hawley: Yeah, exactly! When they've only told you five minutes before eight! So you need to have this innate love of doing it.

This book is offered to all those who have this 'innate love' of stage management or are about to develop one. It is also for all those who they collaborate with and all who see value in the practice both within and outside the performing arts. I hope that it may help us *all* get better at building experiences for our various audiences.

NOTES

Introductions

1 Doris Schneider, *The Art and Craft of Stage Management* (Orlando: Harcourt Brace & Company, 1997), vii.
2 Joslin McKinney and Philip Butterworth, *The Cambridge Introduction to Scenography*, Cambridge Introductions to Literature (Cambridge: Cambridge University Press, 2009), 4.
3 Charlotte Aull Davies, *Reflexive Ethnography: A Guide to Researching Selves and Others*, Asa Research Methods in Social Anthropology (London: Routledge, 1999).
4 Robert E. Stake, *Multiple Case Study Analysis* (New York: Guilford Publications, 2005).
5 Steinar Kvale and Svend Brinkmann, *Interviews: Learning the Craft of Qualitative Research Interviewing*, 2nd edn (London: SAGE Publications, 2007), 3.
6 Svend Brinkmann and Steinar Kvale, *Doing Interviews*, 2nd edn (London: SAGE Publications, 2018).

Chapter 1

1 Aristotle, *Poetics*, trans. S. H. Butcher (Mineola: Dover Publications, 1951), 29–31.
2 Ibid., 29.
3 Tracey Catherine Cattell, *The Living Language of Stage Management: An Interpretative Study of the History and Development of Professional Stage Management in the United Kingdom, 1567-1968* (Coventry: University of Warwick, 2015).
4 Ibid., 2–3.
5 Ibid., 19–22.
6 Ibid., 60–3.
7 Ibid., 63.
8 Evelyn B. Tribble, *Cognition in the Globe: Attention and Memory in Shakespeare's Theatre*, ed. B McConachie and B Vermeule, Cognitive Studies in Literature and Performance (New York: Palgrave Macmillan, 2011), 45.
9 Ibid.
10 Ibid., 47.
11 Walter Wilson Greg, *Dramatic Documents from the Elizabethan Playhouses: Stage Plots: Actors' Parts: Prompt Books*, vol. 1 (Oxford: Clarendon Press, 1931), 3.
12 David Bradley, *From Text to Performance in the Elizabethan Theatre: Preparing the Play for the Stage* (Cambridge: Cambridge University Press, 1992), 78.

Notes

13 Tiffany Stern, *Documents of Performance in Early Modern England* (Cambridge: Cambridge University Press, 2009), 207–14.
14 Tribble, 50.
15 Ibid.
16 Stern, 212.
17 Tribble, 52.
18 Ibid., 50.
19 Cattell, 182.
20 Ibid., 183.
21 Ibid., 192.
22 Ibid., 235–9 and 48–54.
23 Ibid., 263.
24 Georges Bourdon, 'Staging in the French and English Theatre', *Fortnightly Review* 71, no. 421 (1902): 154–69.
25 Edward Gordon Craig, *On the Art of the Theatre* (New York: Theatre Arts Books, 1980), 147–55.
26 Hal D. Stewart, *Stage Management* (London: Pitman, 1957).
27 P. P. Howe, *The Repertory Theatre: A Record & a Criticism* (London: M. Secker, 1910), 185.
28 Simon Shepherd, *Direction*, ed. Simon Shepherd, Readings in Theatre Practice (London: Palgrave Macmillan, 2012), 12.
29 Cattell, 324–9.
30 Hendrik Baker, *Stage Management and Theatercraft* (London: J. Garnet Miller, 1968).

Chapter 2

1 Lisa Porter and Narda E. Alcorn, *Stage Management Theory as a Guide to Practice: Cultivating a Creative Approach* (New York: Routledge, 2019), 77.
2 J. R. Baldwin et al., *Intercultural Communication for Everyday Life* (Chichester: Wiley Blackwell, 2014).
3 Larry A. Samovar and Richard E. Porter, 'Understanding Intercultural Communication: An Introduction and Overview', in *Intercultural Communication: A Reader*, ed. Larry A. Samovar and Richard E. Porter (Belmont: Wadsworth, 2003), 8.
4 Maccoy, *Essentials of Stage Management* (London: A & C Black, 2004), 21–3.
5 Ibid., 23.
6 Baldwin et al., 137–99.
7 Ibid., 336.
8 Samovar and Porter, 8.
9 Sue Fenty Studham, *Stage Management: A Question of Approach in Intercultural Theatre* (Perth: Edith Cowan University, 2015).

10 Prue Holmes and Gill O'Neill, 'Developing and Evaluating Intercultural Competence: Ethnographies of Intercultural Encounters', *International Journal of Intercultural Relations* 36, no. 5 (2012): 707–18.

11 Porter and Alcorn, 77.

12 Kirsty Sedgman, *The Reasonable Audience: Theatre Etiquette, Behaviour Policing, and the Live Performance Experience* (Cham: Springer International Publishing AG, 2018), 113. Emphasis in original.

13 Patricia Hill Collins and Sirma Bilge, *Intersectionality*, 2 edn (Cambridge: Polity Press, 2020), 1.

14 Ibid., 2.

15 Sumi Cho, Kimberlé Williams Crenshaw, and Leslie McCall, 'Toward a Field of Intersectionality Studies: Theory, Applications, and Praxis', *Signs: Journal of Women in Culture and Society* 38, no. 4 (2013): 795.

16 Porter and Alcorn, 79.

17 Ibid., 74–88.

18 Ibid., 74.

19 Ibid., 75.

Chapter 3

1 Michael Vitale, *Introduction to the Art of Stage Management*, ed. Volz, Introductions to Theatre (London: Methuen Drama, 2019).

2 Porter and Alcorn, 78–9.

3 Ibid., 76.

4 Lawrence Stern and Jill Gold, *Stage Management*, 11 edn (New York: Routledge, 2016), 222.

5 Ibid., 222–38.

6 Ibid., 235.

7 Peter Lawrence, *Production Stage Management for Broadway: From Idea to Opening Night & Beyond* (West Hollywood: Quite Specific Media Limited, 2015).

Chapter 4

1 Gail Pallin, *Stage Management: The Essential Handbook*, 4th edn (London: Nick Hern Books, 2017), 108.

2 Laurie Kincman, *The Stage Manager's Toolkit: Templates and Communication Techniques to Guide Your Theatre Production from First Meeting to Final Performance*, 3rd edn (New York: Focal Press, 2020), 162.

3 Porter and Alcorn, 95.

4 Kincman, 160–4.

Notes

Chapter 5

1. Schneider, vii.
2. Winston Morgan, *Stage Managing the Arts in Canada* (Toronto: S.M.Arts, 2000).
3. Ibid., 78–84.
4. Stern and Gold, 1.
5. Daniel A. Ionazzi, *The Stage Management Handbook* (Cincinnati: Betterway Books, 1992).
6. Pauline Menear and Terry Hawkins, *Stage Management and Theatre Administration*, Phaidon Theatre Manuals (Oxford: Phaidon, 1988), 7.
7. Stern and Gold, v–vii.
8. Menear and Hawkins, 7.
9. Larry Fazio, *Stage Manager: The Professional Experience* (Boston: Focal Press, 2000), 13.
10. Menear and Hawkins, 7.
11. Stern and Gold, 141.
12. Ibid.
13. David McGraw, '2009 Stage Management Survey – United States', http://www.smsurvey.info/uploads/6/4/6/6/6466686/2009smsurvey.pdf.
14. Ibid., 12.
15. Fazio, 21.
16. Stern and Gold, 3–8.
17. Maccoy, 5.
18. Ibid. See especially Chapter 2 (24–56).
19. Stern and Gold, 9–14.
20. Pallin, 66–75.
21. Maccoy, 56.
22. Porter and Alcorn, 91.
23. Virginia Held, *The Ethics of Care: Personal, Political, and Global* (New York: Oxford University Press, 2005).
24. Robert K. Greenleaf, *Servant Leadership: A Journey into the Nature of Legitimate Power and Greatness* (Mahwah: Paulist Press, 2002).
25. Menear and Hawkins, 7.
26. John Dewey, *Art as Experience*, A Putnam Capricorn Book, Cap 1 (New York: Capricorn Books, 1959), 51.
27. Susanne Katherina Knauth Langer, *Feeling and Form: A Theory of Art* (New York: Charles Scribner's Sons, 1953), 31.
28. Pallin, 72.
29. See, for example, ibid., 17–18. and Maccoy, 39.
30. Pallin, 100.
31. Vitale, 97.
32. Larry Fazio, *Stage Manager: The Professional Experience – Refreshed*, 2nd edn (New York: Routledge, 2017), 22.

Notes

Part Two

1. Richard Pilbrow, *Stage Lighting Design: The Art, the Craft, the Life* (London: Nick Hern Books, 1997), 4–10.

Chapter 6

1. Ibid.
2. Christopher Baugh, *Theatre, Performance and Technology: The Development of Scenography in the Twentieth Century*, Theatre and Performance Practices (New York: Palgrave Macmillan, 2005).
3. Ibid., 214.
4. As examples, I offer those that I have found most helpful to me as a stage manager seeking to understand the artistry of my colleagues: Deena Kaye and James LeBrecht, *Sound and Music for the Theatre: The Art and Technique of Design*, 3rd edn (Burlington: Focal Press, 2009); Ali Maclaurin and Aoife Monks, *Costume*, ed. Simon Shepherd, Readings in Theatre Practice (London: Palgrave, 2015); Darwin Reid Payne, *Scenographic Imagination*, 3rd edn (Carbondale: Southern Illinois University Press, 1993).
5. Pilbrow.
6. Ibid., 78.
7. In Jarka Burian, *The Scenography of Josef Svoboda* (Middletown: Wesleyan University Press, 1971), 15.
8. Arnold Aronson, *The Routledge Companion to Scenography* (London: Routledge, 2018), 1–13.
9. In Burian, 15.
10. Arnold Aronson, *Looking into the Abyss: Essays on Scenography* (Ann Arbor: The University of Michigan Press, 2005), 7.
11. Baugh.
12. Ibid., 84.
13. McKinney and Butterworth, 4.
14. Rachel Hann, *Beyond Scenography* (London: Routledge, 2018), 39–52.
15. Elaine Aston and George Savona, *Theatre as Sign System: A Semiotics of Text and Performance* (London: Routledge, 1991).
16. Keir Elam, *The Semiotics of Theatre and Drama*, 2nd edn (London: Routledge, 2002).
17. Martin Esslin, *The Field of Drama: How the Signs of Drama Create Meaning on Stage and Screen* (London: Methuen, 1987).
18. Patrice Pavis, *Analyzing Performance: Theater, Dance, and Film*, trans. David Williams (Ann Arbor: University of Michigan Press, 2003).
19. Lois Tyson, *Critical Theory Today: A User-Friendly Guide*, 3rd edn (London: Routledge, 2015), 205–7.
20. Ibid., 206.
21. McKinney and Butterworth, 161.

Notes

22 Maurice Merleau-Ponty, *Phenomenology of Perception*, trans. Donald A. Landes (Abingdon: Routledge, 2012), 238.
23 McKinney and Butterworth, 169.
24 Bert O. States, *Great Reckonings in Little Rooms: On the Phenomenology of Theater* (Berkeley: University of California Press, 1985), 8.
25 Elam, 51.
26 Merleau-Ponty, 150.
27 Jane Collins and Andrew Nisbet, *Theatre and Performance Design: A Reader in Scenography* (London: Routledge, 2010), 65.
28 Gay McAuley, *Space in Performance: Making Meaning in the Theatre*, Theater--Theory/Text/Performance (Ann Arbor: University of Michigan Press, 2000).
29 Ibid., 24–35.
30 Ibid., 5.
31 Ibid., 17.
32 Aronson, *Looking into the Abyss: Essays on Scenography*, 7–8.
33 Marvin Carlson, *Performance: A Critical Introduction*, 2nd edn (New York: Routledge, 2004), 205.
34 Joslin McKinney and Scott Palmer, eds., *Scenography Expanded: An Introduction to Contemporary Performance Design*, Performance + Design (London: Bloomsbury, 2017).
35 Hann.
36 Hans-Thies Lehmann, *Postdramatic Theatre* (London: Routledge, 2006), 157.
37 McKinney and Butterworth.
38 Collins and Nisbet.
39 Carlson, 11.
40 McAuley, 7.
41 Ibid., 35.
42 Scott Taylor, 'The Field: Multilateral and Holistic Perspectives in Contemporary Performance Theory: Understanding Patrice Pavis's Integrated Semiotics', *Journal of Dramatic Theory and Criticism* 19, no. 2 (2005): 105.
43 In Payne, 69.
44 Ibid.
45 Josef Svoboda, *The Secret of Theatrical Space: The Memoirs of Josef Svoboda*, trans. Jarka Burian (New York: Applause Theatre Books, 1993), 23.
46 McAuley, 35.
47 Ibid.

Chapter 7

1 Pilbrow, 6–10.
2 Pallin, 72.

Notes

3 Kincman, 2.
4 Evelyn Tribble, 'Distributing Cognition in the Globe', *Shakespeare Quarterly* 56, no. 2 (2005): 139.
5 Ibid.
6 Ibid., 135.
7 Ibid., 142.
8 Donald A. Norman, *Things That Make Us Smart: Defending Human Attributes in the Age of the Machine* (New York: Addison-Wesley, 1993), 142.
9 Katherine Graham, 'The Play of Light: Rethinking Mood Lighting in Performance', *Studies in Theatre and Performance* 42, no. 2 (2022): 139–40.
10 McAuley, 24–35.
11 Fazio, *Stage Manager: The Professional Experience*, 21, 103.
12 Maccoy, 10.

Chapter 8

1 S. W. Littlejohn, K. A. Foss, and J. G. Oetzel, *Theories of Human Communication: Twelfth Edition* (Long Grove: Waveland Press, 2021).
2 Pilbrow, 4–6.

Chapter 9

1 Lee S. Shulman, 'Signature Pedagogies in the Professions', *Daedalus* 3, no. 134 (2005): 52–9.
2 Clar Doyle, *Raising Curtains on Education: Drama as a Site for Critical Pedagogy*, Critical Studies in Education and Culture Series (Westport: Bergin & Garvey, 1993).
3 Cattell, 20.
4 McKinney and Butterworth, 4.

BIBLIOGRAPHY

Aristotle. *Poetics*. Translated by S. H. Butcher. Mineola: Dover Publications, 1951.
Aronson, Arnold. *Looking into the Abyss: Essays on Scenography*. Ann Arbor: The University of Michigan Press, 2005.
Aronson, Arnold. *The Routledge Companion to Scenography*. London: Routledge, 2018.
Aston, Elaine and George Savona. *Theatre as Sign System: A Semiotics of Text and Performance*. London: Routledge, 1991.
Baker, Hendrik. *Stage Management and Theatercraft*. London: J. Garnet Miller, 1968.
Baldwin, J. R., R. R. M. Coleman, A. González and S. Shenoy-Packer. *Intercultural Communication for Everyday Life*. Chichester: Wiley Blackwell, 2014.
Baugh, Christopher. *Theatre, Performance and Technology: The Development of Scenography in the Twentieth Century*. Theatre and Performance Practices. New York: Palgrave Macmillan, 2005.
Bourdon, Georges. 'Staging in the French and English Theatre'. [In English]. *Fortnightly Review* 71, no. 421 (January 1902): 154–69.
Bradley, David. *From Text to Performance in the Elizabethan Theatre: Preparing the Play for the Stage*. Cambridge: Cambridge University Press, 1992.
Brinkmann, Svend and Steinar Kvale. *Doing Interviews*. 2 edn. London: SAGE Publications, 2018.
Burian, Jarka. *The Scenography of Josef Svoboda*. Middletown: Wesleyan University Press, 1971.
Carlson, Marvin. *Performance: A Critical Introduction*. 2nd edn. New York: Routledge, 2004.
Cattell, Tracey Catherine. 'The Living Language of Stage Management: An Interpretative Study of the History and Development of Professional Stage Management in the United Kingdom, 1567–1968', University of Warwick, 2015.
Cho, Sumi, Kimberlé Williams Crenshaw and Leslie McCall. 'Toward a Field of Intersectionality Studies: Theory, Applications, and Praxis'. *Signs: Journal of Women in Culture and Society* 38, no. 4 (2013): 785–810.
Collins, Jane and Andrew Nisbet. *Theatre and Performance Design: A Reader in Scenography*. London: Routledge, 2010.
Collins, Patricia Hill and Sirma Bilge. *Intersectionality*. 2 edn. Cambridge: Polity Press, 2020.
Craig, Edward Gordon. *On the Art of the Theatre*. New York: Theatre Arts Books, 1980.
Davies, Charlotte Aull. *Reflexive Ethnography: A Guide to Researching Selves and Others* [in English]. Asa Research Methods in Social Anthropology. London: Routledge, 1999.
Dewey, John. *Art as Experience*. A Putnam Capricorn Book, Cap 1. New York: Capricorn Books, 1959.
Doyle, Clar. *Raising Curtains on Education: Drama as a Site for Critical Pedagogy*. Critical Studies in Education and Culture Series. Westport: Bergin & Garvey, 1993.
Elam, Keir. *The Semiotics of Theatre and Drama*. 2nd edn. London: Routledge, 2002.
Esslin, Martin. *The Field of Drama: How the Signs of Drama Create Meaning on Stage and Screen*. London: Methuen, 1987.
Fazio, Larry. *Stage Manager: The Professional Experience*. Boston: Focal Press, 2000.
Fazio, Larry. *Stage Manager: The Professional Experience - Refreshed*. 2 edn. New York: Routledge, 2017.
Graham, Katherine. 'The Play of Light: Rethinking Mood Lighting in Performance'. *Studies in Theatre and Performance* 42, no. 2 (2022): 139–55.

Bibliography

Greenleaf, Robert K. *Servant Leadership: A Journey into the Nature of Legitimate Power and Greatness*. Mahwah: Paulist Press, 2002.

Greg, Walter Wilson. *Dramatic Documents from the Elizabethan Playhouses: Stage Plots: Actors' Parts: Prompt Books*. Vol. 1. Oxford: Clarendon Press, 1931.

Hann, Rachel. *Beyond Scenography*. London: Routledge, 2018.

Held, Virginia. *The Ethics of Care: Personal, Political, and Global*. New York: Oxford University Press, 2005.

Holmes, Prue and Gill O'Neill. 'Developing and Evaluating Intercultural Competence: Ethnographies of Intercultural Encounters'. *International Journal of Intercultural Relations* 36, no. 5 (2012): 707–18.

Howe, P. P. *The Repertory Theatre: A Record & a Criticism*. London: M. Secker, 1910.

Ionazzi, Daniel A. *The Stage Management Handbook*. Cincinnati: Betterway Books, 1992.

Kaye, Deena and James LeBrecht. *Sound and Music for the Theatre: The Art and Technique of Design*. 3rd edn. Burlington: Focal Press, 2009.

Kincman, Laurie. *The Stage Manager's Toolkit: Templates and Communication Techniques to Guide Your Theatre Production from First Meeting to Final Performance*. 3 edn. New York: Focal Press, 2020.

Kvale, Steinar and Svend Brinkmann. *Interviews: Learning the Craft of Qualitative Research Interviewing* [in English]. 2nd edn, 326. London: SAGE Publications, 2007.

Langer, Susanne Katherina Knauth. *Feeling and Form: A Theory of Art*. New York: Charles Scribner's Sons, 1953.

Lawrence, Peter. *Production Stage Management for Broadway: From Idea to Opening Night & Beyond*. Quite Specific Media Limited, 2015.

Lehmann, Hans-Thies. *Postdramatic Theatre*. London: Routledge, 2006.

Littlejohn, S. W., K. A. Foss and J. G. Oetzel. *Theories of Human Communication: Twelfth Edition*. Long Grove: Waveland Press, 2021.

Maccoy, Peter. *Essentials of Stage Management*. London: A & C Black, 2004.

Maclaurin, Ali and Aoife Monks. *Costume. Readings in Theatre Practice*. Edited by Simon Shepherd. London: Palgrave Macmillan, 2015.

McAuley, Gay. *Space in Performance: Making Meaning in the Theatre*. Theater–Theory/Text/Performance. Ann Arbor: University of Michigan Press, 2000.

McGraw, David. '2009 Stage Management Survey – United States'. http://www.smsurvey.info/uploads/6/4/6/6/6466686/2009smsurvey.pdf.

McKinney, Joslin and Philip Butterworth. *The Cambridge Introduction to Scenography*. Cambridge Introductions to Literature. Cambridge: Cambridge University Press, 2009.

McKinney, Joslin and Scott Palmer, eds. *Scenography Expanded: An Introduction to Contemporary Performance Design, Performance + Design*. London: Bloomsbury, 2017.

Menear, Pauline and Terry Hawkins. *Stage Management and Theatre Administration*. Phaidon Theatre Manuals. Oxford: Phaidon, 1988.

Merleau-Ponty, Maurice. *Phenomenology of Perception*. Translated by Donald A. Landes. Abingdon: Routledge, 2012.

Morgan, Winston. *Stage Managing the Arts in Canada*. Toronto: S.M.Arts, 2000.

Norman, Donald A. *Things That Make Us Smart: Defending Human Attributes in the Age of the Machine*. New York: Addison-Wesley, 1993.

Pallin, Gail. *Stage Management: The Essential Handbook*. 4 edn. London: Nick Hern Books, 2017.

Pavis, Patrice. *Analyzing Performance: Theater, Dance, and Film*. Translated by David Williams. Ann Arbor: University of Michigan Press, 2003.

Payne, Darwin Reid. *Scenographic Imagination*. 3rd edn. Carbondale: Southern Illinois University Press, 1993.

Bibliography

Pilbrow, Richard. *Stage Lighting Design: The Art, the Craft, the Life.* London: Nick Hern Books, 1997.

Porter, Lisa and Narda E. Alcorn. *Stage Management Theory as a Guide to Practice: Cultivating a Creative Approach.* New York: Routledge, 2019.

Samovar, Larry A. and Richard E. Porter. 'Understanding Intercultural Communication: An Introduction and Overview'. In *Intercultural Communication: A Reader*, edited by Larry A. Samovar and Richard E. Porter, 6–17. Wadsworth: Belmont, 2003.

Schneider, Doris. *The Art and Craft of Stage Management.* Orlando: Harcourt Brace & Company, 1997.

Sedgman, Kirsty. *The Reasonable Audience: Theatre Etiquette, Behaviour Policing, and the Live Performance Experience.* Cham, Switzerland: Springer International Publishing AG, 2018.

Shepherd, Simon. *Direction. Readings in Theatre Practice.* Edited by Simon Shepherd. London: Palgrave Macmillan, 2012.

Shulman, Lee S. 'Signature Pedagogies in the Professions'. *Daedalus* 3, no. 134 (2005): 52–9.

Stake, Robert E. *Multiple Case Study Analysis.* New York: Guilford Publications, 2005.

States, Bert O. *Great Reckonings in Little Rooms: On the Phenomenology of Theater.* Berkeley: University of California Press, 1985.

Stern, Lawrence and Jill Gold. *Stage Management.* 11 edn. New York: Routledge, 2016.

Stern, Tiffany. *Documents of Performance in Early Modern England.* Cambridge: Cambridge University Press, 2009. doi: 10.1017/CBO9780511635625.012.

Stewart, Hal D. *Stage Management.* London: Pitman, 1957.

Studham, Sue Fenty. 'Stage Management: A Question of Approach in Intercultural Theatre'. Perth: Edith Cowan University, 2015.

Svoboda, Josef. *The Secret of Theatrical Space: The Memoirs of Josef Svoboda.* Translated by Jarka Burian. New York: Applause Theatre Books, 1993.

Taylor, Scott. 'The Field: Multilateral and Holistic Perspectives in Contemporary Performance Theory: Understanding Patrice Pavis's Integrated Semiotics'. *Journal of dramatic theory and criticism* 19, no. 2 (2005): 87–108.

Tribble, Evelyn. 'Distributing Cognition in the Globe'. *Shakespeare Quarterly* 56, no. 2 (2005): 135–55.

Tribble, Evelyn B. *Cognition in the Globe: Attention and Memory in Shakespeare's Theatre.* Cognitive Studies in Literature and Performance. Edited by B. McConachie and B. Vermeule. New York and Houndmills: Palgrave Macmillan, 2011.

Tyson, Lois. *Critical Theory Today: A User-Friendly Guide.* 3 edn. London: Routledge, 2015.

Vitale, Michael. *Introduction to the Art of Stage Management.* Introductions to Theatre. Edited by Volz. London: Methuen Drama, 2019.

INDEX

Abel, Marybeth   7
   adapting communication   101
   administrative stage management degrees   79
   Associate Directors   70–1, 73
   audience experience   103
   communication as artistic medium   154
   communication channels   67
   coordinates model   125, 130–1
   cue calling   104–5
   differences on Broadway   54
   distributed cognition   141–2
   maintaining open-ended runs   55, 58
   mode of communication   159–60
   mood and atmosphere   148–9
   production process   182–3, 187
   rationale   167
   scenography   118–19, 182–3
   semiotics   120–1, 164
   space   124
   targeted information flow   139–40
   updates   164
administrative stage management   1–2, 77–90, 107, 155, 186
   in Australia   26–7
   blocking notation   150
   clean show   79, 104–5, 122, 129, 151
   health and safety   75
   history of   16–17
   linear production process   78, 80, 187–9
   modern communication techniques   62
   predominance   1, 26, 77–9, 83, 90, 103, 155, 173–4
   rehearsal reports   26–7, 78, 150, 155, 183–4
   selective information flow   135–7
   touring   51
   training   174–9
Alexander, Jo   7
   absence of messages   158
   decision making   172
   distributed cognition   141–5
   fringe theatre   48
   rationale   167
   scenography   118
   unconscious artistry   156
artistic maintenance
   Associate Directors   70–4
   ballet   42

Broadway   53–9
   regional differences   22–7
   touring   52
artistic stage management. *See* scenographic stage management
Associate Directors. *See* artistic maintenance
Athens, Jim   7
   avoiding complacency   57–8
   controlling mood and atmosphere   146
   decision making   172
   need for direct communication   65
   rationale   168
   selective information flow   136
   timing of communication   163
Australian stage management   20–8
   barriers for culturally diverse theatre makers   35–6
   corporate *vs.* independent theatre companies   48–50
   views of artistry of stage management in   98–9, 181

ballet   40–4
Broadway   23–4, 37–8, 53–9, 70–4, 91–2

calling. *See* cue calling
circus   39–43
collaboration. *See also* relationships
   compromise   81
   creative approach   88–90, 95, 99
   distributed cognition   144
   health and safety   74, 151–2
   navigating cultural differences   21, 36
   rationale   166–8, 173
   smaller-scale productions   49
   using scenography to enhance   111, 115, 132–3, 152, 181–4
contemporary dance   37–44
creativity
   artistry   84–6, 96–100, 103–4, 180
   atmosphere   148, 152, 170
   collaboration   88–90, 95, 103–4, 181
   DSM   24–5
   health and safety   74
   intercultural sensitivity   31–2
   lack of   1, 78, 81, 84, 111, 118
   regional differences   21, 23–8

Index

small scale *vs.* large scale   47–50, 59
touring   52, 59
cue calling
  adapting protocols   161–2
  artistry   88, 98–9, 104–5, 151 (*See also* feeling and landing)
  clean show   79, 104–5, 122, 129, 151
  DSM   19, 24
  feeling   104, 122
  history   15, 17–19, 62, 68
  landing   105, 122, 151
  musically   40
  position   53
  regional differences   24–7
  technical *vs.* performance perfection   68–70
  topology   129–30
culture
  corporate   49–50
  cultural diversity   31–6
  cultural studies   20
  definition   20
  disciplinary culture   20, 31, 36
  geographic culture   36
  intercultural communication   20–1, 29–32
  interior culture   36, 45
  production culture   36, 39

Deputy Stage Manager   18–25, 28, 169
devised work   37, 39, 43, 46, 59
director. *See also* artistic maintenance
  different regional relationships with stage management   18, 22–8
  key collaborator   89
  separation from stage management   18
  setting the mood of the room   147–8, 151–2
  visionary within administrative model   81, 95
DSM. *See* Deputy Stage Manager
Dyer, Mel   7
  administrative model's predominance historically   80
  instinct   171–2
  passion   85
  power   93–4
  rationale   168
  recent changes to communication technology   62
  respect for artistry in stage management growing   99
  shifting to a more artistic approach in training   180–1
  theatre not just for the audience   106–7

education. *See* training
Evans, Ian   7
  audience impact   103
  creativity   97
  digital networking   69
  rationale   168
  regional differences   22–3
  scenography   116–17
Fenton, Andy   7
  avoiding complacency   57
  direct communication   65
  information flow   136–7
  mood and atmosphere   146
  rationale   168
  timing of communication   163
Franklin, Jo   7
  administrative training   82, 174–5
  balancing theory and practice in training   176–7
  inaccessible research   123–4
  instinct   171–2
  making cultural assumptions   29
  rationale   168
  respect for creativity in stage management   23–4
  scenography   117
  training shift to include scenography   175–6, 178–80
  unconscious artistry   156
Freeburg, Chris   7
  audience experience   103, 105, 115
  communication design as artistry   101–2
  company tone   51
  dissonance   127–8
  distributed cognition   142
  flexibility and adaptability   84, 89
  mood and atmosphere   147–8
  rationale   168
  scenography   118
  semiotics   121
  storefront theatre   46–8
  topology   129
  translation   152–3
  understanding art   87–8

Hawley, Susan May   7
  character traits required   84
  communication technology   62
  genres   37, 40
  health and safety   74, 76
  maintaining professional distance   86
  making decisions   171
  making tea   143
  passion   190
  rationale   168
  relationships   41–4
  structured communication   64

Index

hierarchy
   Australian corporate theatre companies   48–9
   culture   20
   properties of communication   157, 164, 187
   stage management roles   19, 24–5, 56, 71, 169
   stage management objectives   135, 153, 182, 187
Hobden, Sharon   8
   adapting communication during performances   160–2
   collaborative   88
   DSM   25
   health and safety   74–5
   immediate communication   63–4, 66, 136
   rationale   168
   scenography   119
holistic stage management   13, 77, 173, 178, 180, 182

immediate vs. structured communication   62–7, 137
intersectionality   35
invisibility   15–17, 83–4, 100, 103, 136, 156–8, 166, 186

Lawrence, Peter   8
   accuracy over creativity   81
   Associate Directors   71–3
   cultural differences   30–1
   making decisions   171
   management style   94
   power   93
   rationale   168
   stage management replacements   55–6
Legah, Adam   8
   company tone   47, 50–1
   cultural diversity   33–5
   feeling connected to work   33
   rationale   168
   training   177–8
Livoti, Greg   8
   Associate Directors   72–3
   decision making   170
   management styles   92
   rationale   169
   selective information flow   136
   stage management rotations   56–7
   targeted information flow   138, 140–1
   timing of communication   162–3
   updates   164
Loth, Pip   8
   audience relationship   52–3
   rationale   169
   touring   37, 52

Maccoy, Peter   8
   communication devices as potential distractions   65–6, 158
   decision making   172
   DSM   24–5
   external topology and authenticity   132
   health and safety   74–5
   immediate communication   64, 66
   managerial stage management   91, 94, 95
   rationale   169
   regional differences   23
   translation   151–2
McMillan, Abigail   8
   adaptability   88
   communication as medium   154–5
   distributed cognition   141, 144
   flexibility   84
   professional tone   146–7
   rationale   169
   textbooks   78
   training   82–3, 173–4
management style   92–5, 168, 186
managerial stage management   2, 76–7, 90–5, 101, 107, 166, 173, 184, 186
Marich, Natasha   8
   Australian stage management   26–7
   corporate vs. independent theatre   47–50
   creativity   98–9
   cultural diversity   31, 35–6
   rationale   169
   rehearsal reports   78–9
   technical vs. performance perfection   68–70
   touring   52
   training   82
   understanding and valuing stage management   180–2
   vocation   184–5
Mont, Ira   9
   adaptability   88–9
   administrative stage management   79
   artistic knowledge   86–7
   audience experience   103
   Broadway   54
   consistency over time   61
   human resource management   91
   performance technology   68
   rationale   169
morale   2, 55, 58–9, 90, 94–5, 101, 145, 149, 188
musical   4, 25, 37, 41–3, 46, 52–3, 92, 149, 160

North American stage management   19–28, 54–5. See also Broadway

Oliver, Jillian   9
   avoiding complacency   57–8
   ballet   41–2

Index

decision making   170
mood and atmosphere   146
rationale   169
selective information flow   136
timing of communication   163
opera   4, 37–45, 59–60

Passaro, Michael   9
artistic maintenance   70–1
Associate Directors   71–2
audience experience   133
hamburger   93
immediate communication   65
managerial stage management   91–3
rationale   169
regional differences   22–3
trust   146–7
pedagogy. *See* training
performance studies   123–4, 132, 134, 176, 185
phenomenology   120–6, 129, 132–4, 179, 185–6
plot   16–17, 140
power   21, 31, 35, 56, 90, 93–5, 181
production process   78–81
prompt copy (book)   15, 17, 21, 104–5, 122, 150, 155, 162

Rawlinson, Joanna   9
arts funding   32–3
cultural diversity   31–3
flexibility in opposition to administration   84–5
need for passion   85–6
rationale   169
variations within genre   43
reflexivity   6
artistic model   96
audience reach and resources   46
communication design   101
data analysis   10
in design   114
evolution of stage management   19, 113
future stage management research   111, 189
objectives   153
production process   188–90
properties of communication   162, 164
training   166
translation   150
understanding the artform and its content   86
rehearsal reports
absence of messages   158
administrative approach   26–7, 78, 150, 155, 183–4
artistry   101
managerial   183–4

scenography   121, 150, 155, 179, 183–4
structured communication   63–5
targeted information flow   138
relationships   60, 89. *See also* director
with audiences   52, 59
with the company   41–3, 46, 51, 59
within the team   56
respect   148, 169, 181
in intercultural work   21, 30–1, 36
for stage management creativity   23–4, 26, 59

scenographic stage management   2–3, 5, 107, 109–65, 182–3, 185–6, 188, 190
score   39–40, 43, 46
Scribner, Justin   9
administrative stage management   79
artistic knowledge   86–7
artistry   97
communication design   102, 160
maintaining morale   58
mood and atmosphere   148
rationale   170
rehearsal reports   101
stage management replacements   55–6
training   174–5
translation   150
semiotics   110, 120–5, 127, 132–4, 164, 179, 187, 190
Simpson, Mark   9
accessibility of art   45
building relationships   89–90
creativity   99–100
creativity police   78
different genres   44–6
distributed cognition   142
invisibility   100
power and humility   94–5
rationale   170
training   180
vocation   44, 185
Studham, Sue Fenty   9
artistry or creativity   96–7
decision making   172–3
differences across genres   41–4
health and safety   41–2, 172–3
invisibility   82–3
mood and atmosphere   145–6
phenomenology   122
regional differences   26
respect   30
similarities across genre   38–9, 41–2
technological change   68
training   82
working interculturally   28–31, 36

Index

templates 51, 78–9, 88, 139, 188
touring 32, 37, 46, 51–3, 59
training
   fragmentation of technical theatre training 121
   history 19
   including paradigms other than the administrative 175–82
   predominance of administrative model 77, 82–4, 90, 96, 103, 137, 173–4
   small-scale venues 46–7
Trott, Abbie 10
   administrative stage management 80–1
   circus 39–40
   corporate *vs.* independent theatre 47–9
   cultural diversity 31–2
   decision making 172–3
   differences determined by score 39–40
   health and safety 172–3
   interpretive art 99
   invisibility 83
   rationale 170
   similarities across genre 38–9
   similarities based on production methodologies 37, 43
   textbooks 83
   training 176, 178

UK stage management 18–28, 31, 71, 117, 143

vocation 44, 178–9, 185